Start a Business in California

(+CD-ROM)

Third Edition

John J. Talamo
Mark Warda

Attorneys at Law

SPHINX® PUBLISHING
AN IMPRINT OF SOURCEBOOKS, INC.®
NAPERVILLE, ILLINOIS
www.SphinxLegal.com

Third Edition: 2006

Published by: **Sphinx® Publishing, An Imprint of Sourcebooks, Inc.®**

Naperville Office
P.O. Box 4410
Naperville, Illinois 60567-4410
630-961-3900
Fax: 630-961-2168
www.sourcebooks.com
www.SphinxLegal.com

This publication is designed to provide accurate and authoritative information in regard to the subject matter covered. It is sold with the understanding that the publisher is not engaged in rendering legal, accounting, or other professional service. If legal advice or other expert assistance is required, the services of a competent professional person should be sought.

From a Declaration of Principles Jointly Adopted by a Committee of the American Bar Association and a Committee of Publishers and Associations

This product is not a substitute for legal advice.

Disclaimer required by Texas statutes.

Library of Congress Cataloging-in-Publication Data
Talamo, John.
  Start a business in California : +CD-ROM / by John J. Talamo and Mark Warda. -- 3rd ed.
      p. cm.
  Rev. ed. of: How to start a business in California / John J. Talamo, Mark Warda. 2nd ed. 2003.
  Includes index.
  ISBN-13: 978-1-57248-537-2 (pbk. : alk. paper)
  ISBN-10: 1-57248-537-X (pbk. : alk. paper)
 1. Business enterprises--Law and legislation--California--Popular works.
2. Business enterprises--Law and legislation--California--Forms. 3. Business law--California. I. Warda, Mark. II. Title.

KFC337.Z9T35 2006
346.794'065--dc22   2006014446

Printed and bound in the United States of America.
SB — 10 9 8 7 6 5 4 3

Contents

How to Use the CD-ROM

Thank you for purchasing *Start a Business in California (+CD-ROM)*. In this book, we have worked hard to compile exactly what you need to start a business in California. To make this material even more useful, we have included every document in the book on the CD-ROM in the back of the book.

You can use these forms just as you would the forms in the book. Print them out, fill them in, and use them however you need. You can also fill in the forms directly on your computer. Just identify the form you need, open it, click on the space where the information should go, and input your information. Customize each form for your particular needs. Use them over and over again.

The CD-ROM is compatible with both PC and Mac operating systems. (While it should work with either operating system, we cannot guarantee that it will work with your particular system and we cannot provide technical assistance.) To use the forms on your computer, you will need to use Adobe Reader. The CD-ROM does not contain this program. You can download this program from Adobe's website at **www.adobe.com**. Click on the "Get Adobe Reader" icon to begin the download process and follow the instructions.

Once you have Adobe Reader installed, insert the CD-ROM into your computer. Double click on the icon representing the disc on your desktop or go through your hard drive to identify the drive that contains the disc and click on it.

Once opened, you will see the files contained on the CD-ROM listed as "Form #: [Form Title]." Open the file you need through Adobe Reader. You may print the form to fill it out manually at this point, or your can use the "Hand Tool" and click on the appropriate line to fill it in using your computer.

Any time you see bracketed information [ ] on the form, you can click on it and delete the bracketed information from your final form. This information is only a reference guide to assist you in filling in the forms and should be removed from your final version. Once all your information is filled in, you can print your filled-in form.

NOTE: *Adobe Reader does not allow you to save the PDF with the boxes filled in.*

*   *   *   *   *

Purchasers of this book are granted a license to use the forms contained in it for their own personal use. By purchasing this book, you have also purchased a limited license to use all forms on the accompanying CD-ROM. The license limits you to personal use only and all other copyright laws must be adhered to. No claim of copyright is made in any government form reproduced in the book or on the CD-ROM. You are free to modify the forms and tailor them to your specific situation.

The author and publisher have attempted to provide the most current and up-to-date information available. However, the courts, Congress, and your state's legislatures review, modify, and change laws on an ongoing basis, as well as create new laws from time to time. Due to the very nature of the information and the continual changes in our legal system, to be sure that you have the current and best information for your situation, you should consult a local attorney or research the current laws yourself.

This publication is designed to provide accurate and authoritative information in regard to the subject matter covered. It is sold with the understanding that the publisher is not engaged in rendering legal, accounting, or other professional service. If legal advice or other expert assistance is required, the services of a competent professional person should be sought.

—From a Declaration of Principles Jointly Adopted by a Committee of the American Bar Association and a Committee of Publishers and Associations

This product is not a substitute for legal advice.

—Disclaimer required by Texas statutes

Using Self-Help Law Books

Before using a self-help law book, you should realize the advantages and disadvantages of doing your own legal work and understand the challenges and diligence that this requires.

The Growing Trend

Rest assured that you will not be the first or only person handling your own legal matter. For example, in some states, more than 75% of the people in divorces and other cases represent themselves. Because of the high cost of legal services, this is a major trend, and many courts are struggling to make it easier for people to represent themselves. However, some courts are not happy with people who do not use attorneys and refuse to help them in any way. For some, the attitude is, "Go to the law library and figure it out for yourself."

We write and publish self-help law books to give people an alternative to the often complicated and confusing legal books found in most law libraries. We have made the explanations of the law as simple and easy to understand as possible. Of course, unlike an attorney advising an individual client, we cannot cover every conceivable possibility.

Cost/Value Analysis

Whenever you shop for a product or service, you are faced with various levels of quality and price. In deciding what product or service to buy, you make a cost/value analysis on the basis of your willingness to pay and the quality you desire.

When buying a car, you decide whether you want transportation, comfort, status, or sex appeal. Accordingly, you decide among choices such as a Neon, a Lincoln, a Rolls Royce, or a Porsche. Before making a decision, you usually weigh the merits of each option against the cost.

When you get a headache, you can take a pain reliever (such as aspirin) or visit a medical specialist for a neurological examination. Given this choice, most people, of course, take a pain reliever, since it costs only pennies; whereas a medical examination costs hundreds of dollars and takes a lot of time. This is usually a logical choice because it is rare to need anything more than a pain reliever for a headache. But in some cases, a headache may indicate a brain tumor, and failing to see a specialist right away can result in complications. Should everyone with a headache go to a specialist? Of course not, but people treating their own illnesses must realize that they are betting, on the basis of their cost/value analysis of the situation, that they are taking the most logical option.

The same cost/value analysis must be made when deciding to do one's own legal work. Many legal situations are very straightforward, requiring a simple form and no complicated analysis. Anyone with a little intelligence and a book of instructions can handle the matter without outside help.

But there is always the chance that complications are involved that only an attorney would notice. To simplify the law into a book like this, several legal cases often must be condensed into a single sentence or paragraph. Otherwise, the book would be several hundred pages long and too complicated for most people. However, this simplification necessarily leaves out many details and nuances that would apply to special or unusual situations. Also, there are many ways to interpret most legal questions. Your case may come before a judge who disagrees with the analysis of our authors.

Therefore, in deciding to use a self-help law book and to do your own legal work, you must realize that you are making a cost/value analysis. You have decided that the money you will save in doing it yourself outweighs the chance that your case will not turn out to your satisfaction. Most people handling their own simple legal matters never have a problem, but occasionally people find that it ended up costing them more to have an attorney straighten out the situation than it would have if they had hired an attorney in the beginning. Keep this in mind while handling your case, and be sure to consult an attorney if you feel you might need further guidance.

Local Rules   The next thing to remember is that a book which covers the law for the entire nation, or even for an entire state, cannot possibly include every procedural difference of every jurisdiction. Whenever possible, we provide the exact form needed; however, in some areas, each county, or even each judge, may require unique forms and procedures. In our state books, our forms usually cover the majority of counties in the state or provide examples of the type of form that will be required. In our national books, our forms are sometimes even more general in nature but are designed to give a good idea of the type of form that will be needed in most locations. Nonetheless, keep in mind that your state, county, or judge may have a requirement, or use a form, that is not included in this book.

You should not necessarily expect to be able to get all of the information and resources you need solely from within the pages of this book. This book will serve as your guide, giving you specific information whenever possible and helping you to find out what else you will need to know. This is just like if you decided to build your own backyard deck. You might purchase a book on how to build decks. However, such a book would not include the building codes and permit requirements of every city, town, county, and township in the nation; nor would it include the lumber, nails, saws, hammers, and other materials and tools you would need to actually build the deck. You would use the book as your guide, and then do some work and research involving such matters as whether you need a permit of some kind, what type and grade of wood is available in your area, whether to use hand tools or power tools, and how to use those tools.

Before using the forms in a book like this, you should check with your court clerk to see if there are any local rules of which you should be aware or local forms you will need to use. Often, such forms will require the same information as the forms in the book but are merely laid out differently or use slightly different language. They will sometimes require additional information.

Changes in the Law

Besides being subject to local rules and practices, the law is subject to change at any time. The courts and the legislatures of all fifty states are constantly revising the laws. It is possible that while you are reading this book, some aspect of the law is being changed.

In most cases, the change will be of minimal significance. A form will be redesigned, additional information will be required, or a waiting period will be extended. As a result, you might need to revise a form, file an extra form, or wait out a longer time period. These types of changes will not usually affect the outcome of your case. On the other hand, sometimes a major part of the law is changed, the entire law in a particular area is rewritten, or a case that was the basis of a central legal point is overruled. In such instances, your entire ability to pursue your case may be impaired.

Introduction

In 2001, when this book was first published, the first paragraph contained the words "California is booming." When it was revised in 2003, the first paragraph contained the words "California is struggling with a deficit of over 35 billion dollars…and unemployment is high." Today, the outlook is uncertain.

Is this a good time to start a business? Of course. There is no bad *time* to start a business—there are only bad *ways* to start one. A good product or service is always in demand. How you go about setting up, producing, marketing, and selling your product or service are the important considerations.

This book is intended to give you the framework for legally opening a business in California. It also includes information on where to find special rules for each type of business. If you have problems that are not covered by this book, you should seek out an attorney who can be available for your ongoing needs.

In order to cover all of the aspects of any business you are thinking of starting, you should read through this entire book, rather than skipping to the parts that look most interesting. There are many laws that may not sound like they apply to you, but that do have provisions that will affect your business.

In recent years, the government bureaucracies have been amending and lengthening their forms regularly. The forms included in this book are the most recent available at the time of publication. It is possible that some may be revised at the time you read this book, but in most cases, previous versions of the forms will still be accepted.

Deciding to Start a Business

If you are reading this book, then you have probably made a serious decision to take the plunge and start your own business. Hundreds of thousands of people make the same decision each year, and many of them become very successful. Unfortunately, a lot of them also fail. Knowledge can only help your chances of success. You need to know why some businesses succeed while others fail. Some of what follows may seem obvious, but to someone wrapped up in a new business idea, some of this information is occasionally overlooked.

KNOW YOUR STRENGTHS

The last thing a budding entrepreneur wants to hear is that he or she is not cut out for running a business. You might avoid those "do you have what it takes" quizzes because you are not sure you want to hear the answer. However, you can be successful if you know where to get the skills you lack.

You should consider all of the skills and knowledge that running a successful business requires, and decide whether you have what it takes. If you do not, it does not necessarily mean you are doomed to be an employee all your life. Perhaps you just need a partner who has the skills you lack. Perhaps you can hire someone with the skills you need. You can structure your business to avoid areas where you are weak. If those tactics do not work, maybe you can learn the skills.

For example, if managing employees is not your strong suit, you can:

- handle product development yourself, and have a partner or manager deal with employees;

- take seminars in employee management; or,

- structure your business so that you do not need employees (use independent contractors or set yourself up as an independent contractor).

When planning your business, consider the following factors.

- *If it takes months or years before your business turns a profit, do you have the resources to hold out?* Businesses have gone under or have been sold just before they were about to take off. Staying power is an important ingredient to success.

- *Are you willing to put in a lot of overtime to make your business a success?* Owners of businesses do not set their own hours—the business sets hours for the owner. Many business owners work long hours seven days a week. You have to enjoy running your business and be willing to make some personal time sacrifices.

- *Are you willing to do the dirtiest or most unpleasant work of the business?* Emergencies come up and employees are not always dependable. You might need to mop a flooded room, spend a weekend stuffing 10,000 envelopes, or work Christmas if someone calls in sick.

- *Do you know enough about the product or service?* Are you aware of the trends in the industry and what changes new technology might bring? Think of the people who started typesetting or printing businesses just before type was replaced by laser printers.

✪ *Do you know enough about accounting and inventory to manage the business?* Do you have a good head for business? Some people naturally know how to save money and do things profitably. Others are in the habit of buying the best and the most expensive of everything. The latter can be fatal to a struggling new business.

✪ *Are you good at managing employees?* If your business has employees (or will have in the future), managing them is an unavoidable part of running the business.

✪ *Do you know how to sell your product or service?* You can have the best product on the market, but people will not know about it unless you tell them about it. If you are a wholesaler, shelf space in major stores is hard to get—especially for a new company without a record, a large line of products, or a large advertising budget.

✪ *Do you know enough about getting publicity?* The media receive thousands of press releases and announcements each day, and most are thrown away. Do not count on free publicity to put your name in front of the public.

KNOW YOUR BUSINESS

Not only do you need to know the concept of a business, but you need the experience of working in a business. Maybe you always dreamed of running a bed and breakfast or having your own pizza place. Have you ever worked in such a business? If not, you may have no idea of the day-to-day headaches and problems of the business. For example, do you really know how much to allow for theft, spoilage, and unhappy customers?

You might feel silly taking an entry-level job at a pizza place when you would rather start your own, but it might be the most valuable preparation you could have. A few weeks of seeing how a business operates could mean the difference between success and failure. Working in a business as an employee is one of the best ways to be a success at running such a business. New people with new ideas revolutionize established industries with obvious improvements that no one before dared to try.

SOURCES FOR FURTHER GUIDANCE

There are many things to consider as you prepare to start your own business. Most likely, you will have numerous questions that need to be answered before opening your doors for the first time. Luckily, there are many resources available for help. The sources discussed in this section offer free or low-cost guidance for new businesses.

SCORE California is a haven for retired people, and many of them are glad to give free guidance to new businesses. To facilitate this, the *Small Business Administration* (SBA) has developed a group, known as the *Service Corps of Retired Executives* (SCORE), that provides invaluable assistance to new business ventures. The SCORE website is **www.score.org**. You have the option of asking a question by email or in a face-to-face meeting. If you want to visit a SCORE office, type in the zip code of your area and the address and phone number for a local office will appear. Call for a meeting with someone familiar with your situation. Following is the current list of offices.

Antelope Valley SCORE, Chapter 593
1212 East Avenue S
Suite A-2
Palmdale, CA 93550
661-947-7679
Fax: 661-947-7747

Central California SCORE, Chapter 380
2719 North Air Fresno Drive
Suite 200
Fresno, CA 93727
209-487-5605
Fax: 209-487-5636

Central Coast SCORE, Chapter 491
509 West Morrison Avenue
Santa Maria, CA 93454
805-347-7755
Fax: 805-739-8928

Coachella Valley SCORE, Chapter 367
901 East Tahquitz Canyon Way
Suite A103
Palm Springs, CA 92262
760-320-6682
Fax: 760-323-9426

East Bay SCORE, Chapter 506
519 17th Street
Suite 240
Oakland, CA 94612
510-273-6611
Fax: 510-273-6015

Golden Empire SCORE, Chapter 563
2100 Chester Avenue
1st Floor
Bakersfield, CA 93301
661-861-9249
Fax: 661-395-4134

Greater Chico Area SCORE, Chapter 581
1324 Mangrove Street
Suite 114
Chico, CA 95926
530-342-8932
Fax: 530-342-8932

Inland Empire SCORE, Chapter 503
1700 East Florida Avenue
Hemet, CA 92544
805-652-4390
Fax: 909-929-8543

Los Angeles SCORE, Chapter 9
330 North Brand Boulevard
Suite 190
Glendale, CA 91203
818-552-3206
Fax: 818-547-1220

Monterey Bay SCORE, Chapter 40
Monterey Peninsula
    Chamber of Commerce
380 Alvarado Street
Monterey, CA 93940
831-648-5360

North Coast SCORE, Chapter 450
777 Sonoma Avenue
Room 115 B
Santa Rosa, CA 95404
707-571-8342
707-541-0331

**Orange County SCORE,
    Chapter 114**
200 West Santa Ana Boulevard
Suite 700
Santa Ana, CA 92701
714-550-7369
Fax: 714-550-0191

Sacramento SCORE, Chapter 417
10661 Coloma Road
Rancho Cordova, CA 95670
916-635-9085
Fax: 916-635-9089

Santa Barbara SCORE, Chapter 166
402 East Gutierres Street
Santa Barbara, CA 93130
805-563-0084

San Diego SCORE, Chapter 410
550 West C Street
Suite 550
San Diego, CA 92101
619-557-7272
Fax: 619-557-5894

San Francisco SCORE, Chapter
455 Market Street
Suite 600
San Francisco, CA 94105
415-744-6827
Fax: 415-744-6750

**San Luis Obispo SCORE,
    Chapter 597**
4111 Broad Street
Suite A
San Luis Obispo, CA 93401
805-547-0779

Silicon Valley SCORE, Chapter
84 West Santa Clara Street
Suite 100
San Jose, CA 95113
408-288-8479
Fax: 408-494-0214

Stockton SCORE, Chapter 463
401 North San Joaquin Street
Room 114
Stockton, CA 95202
209-946-6293
Fax: 209-946-6294

**Tuolumne County SCORE,
    Chapter 596**
c/o Tuolumme Chamber of Commerce
222 South Shephard Street
Sonora, CA 95370
209-588-0128
Fax: 209-588-0673

Ventura SCORE, Chapter 255
400 East Esplanade Drive
Suite 300
Oxnard, CA 93035
805-676-7500
Fax: 805-650-1414

Yosemite SCORE, Chapter 556
c/o Modesto Chamber of Commerce
1114 J Street
Modesto, CA 95354
209-577-5757
Fax: 209-577-2673

NOTE: *Many offices no longer list addresses and counseling is available only by email. You can find these offices at www.score.org.*

Small Business Development Centers

Educational programs for small businesses are offered through the *Small Business Development Centers* at many California colleges and universities. You should see if they have any that could help you in any areas in which you are weak.

The Alliance SBDC
1013 11ᵗʰ Street
Modesto, CA 95354
209-567-4910
Fax: 209-567-4955

The Alliance SBDC
    Merced Satellite
P.O. Box 1029
Merced, CA 95341
209-381-6557
Fax: 209-381-6552

Butte College SBDC
19 Williamsburg Lane
Chico, CA 95926
530-895-9017
Fax: 530-566-9851

Cascade SBDC
2400 Washington Avenue
Suite 301
Redding, CA 96001
530-225-2770
Fax: 225-2769

Central California SBDC
1901 East Shields
Suite 202
Fresno, CA 93726
559-230-4056
Fax: 559-230-4045

Central Coast SBDC
6500 Soquel Drive
Aptos, CA 95003
831-479-6136
Fax: 831-479-6166

Central Los Angeles County SBDC
3375 South Hoover Street
Suite H201
Los Angeles, CA 90007
213-821-2100
Fax: 213-746-4587

Contra Costa SBDC
2425 Bisso Lane
Suite 200
Concord, CA 94520
925-646-5377
Fax: 925-646-5299

Cuesta College SBDC
3566 South Higuera Street
Suite 100
San Luis Obispo, CA 94301
805-549-0401
Fax: 805-543-5198

Eastern Los Angeles County SBDC
363 South Park Avenue
Suite 101
Pomona, CA 91766
909-629-2247
Fax: 909-629-8310

East Bay SBDC
519 17ᵗʰ Street
Suite 210
Oakland, CA 94612
510-893-4114
Fax: 510-893-5532

Gavilan College SBDC
8351 Church Street
Building E
Gilroy, CA 95020
408-847-0373
Fax: 408-847-0393

Greater Sacramento SBDC
1410 Ethan Way
Sacramento, CA 95825
916-563-3210
Fax: 916-563-3266

Inland Empire SBDC
1201 Research Park Drive
Suite 100
Riverside, CA 92507
909-781-2345
800-750-2353
Fax: 909-781-2353

Napa Valley College SBDC
1556 First Street
Suite 103
Napa, CA 94559
707-253-3210
Fax: 707-253-3068

North Coast SBDC
520 E Street
Eureka, CA 95501
707-445-9720
Fax: 707-445-9652

North Los Angeles County SBDC
5121 Van Nuys Boulevard
3rd Floor
Van Nuys, CA 91403
818-907-9922
Fax: 818-907-9720

North San Diego County SBDC
1823 Mission Street
Oceanside, CA 92054
760-754-6575
Fax: 760-754-0664

Orange County SBDC
901 East Santa Ana Boulevard
Suite 101
Santa Ana, CA 92701-3455
714-564-5202
Fax: 714-647-1168

Redwood Empire SBDC
606 Healdsburg Avenue
Santa Rosa, CA 95401
707-524-1770
Fax: 707-524-1772

San Francisco SBDC
455 Market Street
6th Floor
San Francisco, CA 94105
415-908-7501
Fax: 415-974-6035

San Joaquin Delta College SBDC
56 South Lincoln Street
Stockton, CA 95203
209-939-0385
Fax: 209-954-5089

Sierra College SBDC
11930 Heritage Oak Place
Suite 1
Auburn, CA 95603
530-885-5488
Fax: 530-823-2831

Silicon Valley SBDC
84 West Santa Clara Street
Suite 100
San Jose, CA 95113
408-494-0240
Fax: 408-494-0245

Solano County SBDC
424 Executive Court North
Suite C
Fairfield, CA 94534
707-864-3382
Fax: 707-864-8025

Southeast Los Angeles County SBDC
5675 Telegraph Road
Suite 250
Commerce, CA 90040
323-887-9627
Fax: 323-887-9670

Southwest Los Angeles County SBDC
13430 Hawthorne Boulevard
Hawthorne, CA 90250
310-973-3177
Fax: 310-973-3132

Southwestern College SBDC
900 Otey Lakes Road
Chula Vista, CA 91910
619-482-6388
Fax: 619-482-6402

Tech Coast SBDC
2 Park Plaza
Suite 100
Irvine, CA 92614
949-794-7244
Fax: 949-476-0763

Weill Institute SBDC
2000 K Street
Suite 320
Bakersfield, CA 93301
661-631-1475
Fax: 661-631-1323

Yuba College SBDC
330 9th Street
Marysville, CA 95901
530-749-0153
Fax: 530-749-0155

California Business Information Centers

The following business information centers are available in the San Francisco, Los Angeles, and San Diego areas. Visit **www.sba.gov/ca** for more information.

U.S. Small Business Administration
San Diego District Office
550 West C Street
Suite 550
San Diego, CA 92101
619-557-7250
Fax: 619-557-5894

Business Information Center
Southwestern College
900 Otey Lakes Road
Chula Vista, CA 91910
619-482-6388
Fax: 619-482-6402

The Entrepreneur Center
U.S. Small Business Administration
455 Market Street
6th floor
San Francisco, CA 94105
415-744-6820
Fax: 415-744-6812

The Entrepreneur Center
U.S. Small Business Administration
84 West Santa Clara Street
Suite 100
San Jose, CA 95113
408-494-0210
Fax: 408-494-0214

Los Angeles District Office
330 North Brand Boulevard
Suite 1200
Glendale, CA 91203
818-552-3215
818-552-3260

The Small Business Administration, **www.sba.gov**, offers both online and live training classes, as well as sample business plans. Small Business Development Centers are located in the cities of Sacramento, San Francisco, Fresno, Los Angeles, Santa Ana, and San Diego. The site also links to courses being offered in less populated areas. Check by zip code. Some are free.

The site also offers advice for those starting a small business and those already in business. If you click on "starting" at the top of the home page, you will find information to help you decide whether you want to start a business, as well as how to start one.

There are also special programs. For example, if you type "women" in the upper right-hand corner on the home page where it says "search this site," you will find information and resources specifically to help women get started in a small business.

The following is a list of SBA specialized programs and their websites.

8(a) Business Development	www.sba.gov/8abd
Disaster Assistance	www.sba.gov/disaster_recov
Financial Assistance	www.sba.gov/financing
Government Contracting	www.sba.gov/gc
Hub Zone Contracting Program	www.sba.gov/hubzone
Office of Native American Affairs	www.sba.gov/starting_business/special/native.html
Small Business Development Centers	www.sba.gov/sbdc
Small Business Training Network	www.sba.gov/training
Veterans Assistance	www.sba.gov/vets
Women's Business Centers	www.sba.gov/ed/wbo/index.html

One Stop Capital Shop

The One Stop Capital Shop was developed to have offices where people located in *Empowerment Zones* (disadvantaged business areas) could have access to extensive training links. Empowerment Zones are now called *HUB Zones* (Historically Underutilized Business Zones). For further information or to see if you qualify, contact the Business Information Centers listed earlier in this section or visit the SBA website.

In Oakland, contact the Oakland One Stop Capital Shop at:

519 17th Street
Suite 700
Oakland, CA 94612
510-763-4297

Miscellaneous

There are also centers that provide help specifically in the area of exports, as well as help to Native Americans and women.

U.S. Export Assistance Center

Orange County Office
Newport Beach U.S. Export Assistance Center
3300 Irvine Avenue
Suite 305
Newport Beach, CA 92660
949-660-1688
Fax: 949-660-8039

California Tribal Business Information Centers (TBIC)

TBIC: Karuk Tribe of Indians
P.O. Box 1148
Happy Camp, CA 96039
530-493-5135
Fax: 530-493-5378

Women's Business Centers

Renaissance Entrepreneurship Center
275 Fifth Street
San Francisco, CA 94103-4120
415-541-8580
Fax: 415-541-8589
www.rencenter.org/wcenter
(A unique, multicultural marketplace of entrepreneurs. Services include an incubator facility, loan packaging, and links to credit resources, core business planning, introduction to business, and advanced action-planning classes.)

West Company—Fort Bragg Center
760 B Stewart Street
Fort Bragg, CA 95437
707-964-7571
Fax: 707- 964-7576
www.westcompany.org

West Company—Ukiah Office Center
631 South Orchard
Ukiah, CA 95482
707-467-5900
Fax: 707-467-5930
www.westcompany.org
(Serves micro-enterprise owners in rural Northern California, targeting low-income women and minorities. Services include business plan training, individual consulting, access to capital through individual micro-loans, business network formation, and assistance with business applications using technology.)

Women's Initiative for Self-Employment (WI) Oakland Center
519 17ᵗʰ Street
Suite 110
Oakland, CA 94612
510-287-3100
Fax: 510-451-3428
www.womensinitiative.org

Women's Initiative for Self-Employment (WI) San Francisco Center
1938 Valencia Street
San Francisco, CA 94110
415-641-3460
Fax: 415-826-1885
www.womensinitiative.org

Women's Initiative for Self-Employment (WI) Spanish Center
1398 Valencia Street
San Francisco, CA 94110
415-826 5090
Fax: 415-826-1885
www.womensinitiative.org
(Provides business training and technical assistance in English and Spanish to low-income women in the San Francisco Bay Area. Services include one-to-one consultations, peer networking, support groups, and special seminars.)

chapter 2

Choosing the Form of Your Business

Before starting your business, you should choose the form of your business. That is, you should choose whether you will do business in your own name, with a partner, or as a legal entity such as a corporation or limited liability company. Forming and maintaining an artificial entity is inexpensive, so most lawyers advise using one for any type of business to protect yourself against liability.

BASIC FORMS OF DOING BUSINESS

The six most common forms for a business in California are *sole proprietorship, partnership, corporation, limited partnership, limited liability company,* and *limited liability partnership.* The characteristics, advantages, and disadvantages of each business form are discussed in this section.

Sole Proprietorship

A *sole proprietorship* is one person doing business in his or her own name or under a fictitious name.

Advantages. Simplicity is a sole proprietorship's greatest advantage. There is also no organizational expense and no extra tax forms or reports. Since there is only one owner, there is complete control. Taxes are personal rather than corporate, so there is no double taxation.

Disadvantages. The proprietor is personally liable for all debts and obligations. There is also no continuation of the business after death. All taxes are directly taxable, which is certainly a disadvantage for the proprietor, and business affairs are easily mixed with personal affairs.

General Partnership

A *general partnership* involves two or more people carrying on a business together and sharing the profits and losses.

Advantages. Partners can combine expertise and assets. A general partnership allows liability to be spread among more people. Also, the business can be continued after the death of a partner if bought out by a surviving partner.

Disadvantages. Each partner is liable for acts of other partners within the scope of the business. This means that if your partner harms a customer or signs a million-dollar credit line in the partnership name, you can be personally liable. Even if you leave all profits in the business, those profits are taxable. All parties share control, and the death of a partner may result in liquidation. In a general partnership, it is often hard to get rid of a bad partner.

Limited Partnership

A *limited partnership* has characteristics similar to both a corporation and a partnership. There are *general partners*, who have the control and personal liability, and there are *limited partners*, who only put up money and whose liability is limited to what they paid for their share of the partnership (like corporate stock).

Advantages. Capital can be contributed by limited partners who have no control of the business or liability for its debts.

Disadvantages. A great disadvantage is high start-up costs. Also, an extensive partnership agreement is required because general partners are personally liable for partnership debts and for the acts of each other. (One solution to this problem is to use a corporation as the general partner.) Limited partnerships may be found in the Corporate Code under the *Uniform Limited Partnership Act,* beginning with Section 15501, and in the *California Revised Limited Partnership Act*, beginning with Section 15611.

NOTE: *A limited partnership is not a good way to structure your new business if you want to avoid personal liability and plan to be the limited partner to do so. The reason is that the limited liability protection is lost if you take an active role in managing the business. You probably do not want to start your business by turning over control to someone else.*

Corporation A *corporation* is an artificial legal "person" that carries on business through its directors and officers for its shareholders. This "legal person" carries on business in its own name, and shareholders are not personally liable for its acts. The California Corporations Code (Cal. Corp. Code) contains the law necessary to form and operate a corporation in California.

An *S corporation* is a corporation that has filed Internal Revenue Service (IRS) Form 2553, thus choosing to have all profits taxed to the shareholders, rather than to the corporation. An S corporation files a tax return, but pays no federal or state tax. The profit shown on the S corporation tax return is reported on the owners' tax returns.

A *C corporation* is any corporation that has not elected to be taxed as an S corporation. A C corporation pays income tax on its profits. The effect of this is that when dividends are paid to shareholders, they are taxed twice—once as corporate tax and once as a tax on shareholders.

A *professional corporation* is a corporation formed by a professional such as a doctor or accountant. California has special rules for professional corporations that differ slightly from those of other corporations. These rules are included in California Corporations Code, Sections 13400–13410. There are also special tax rules for professional corporations.

A *nonprofit corporation* is usually used for organizations such as churches and condominium associations. However, with careful planning, some types of businesses can be set up as nonprofit corporations to save in taxes. While a nonprofit corporation cannot pay dividends, it can pay its officers and employees fair salaries. Some of the major American nonprofit organizations pay their officers well over $100,000 a year. California's special rules for nonprofit corporations are included in several different sections of the Corporations Code, organized by the type of corporation, such as religious, charitable, medical, or legal.

Advantages. If a corporation is properly organized, shareholders have no personal liability for corporate debts and lawsuits, and officers usually have no personal liability for their corporate acts. The existence of a corporation may be perpetual. There are tax advantages allowed only to corporations. There is prestige in owning a corporation. Two of the most important advantages to doing business as a corporation are the ability to raise capital by issuing stock, and the ease of transferring ownership upon death. A small corporation can be set up as an S corporation to avoid corporate taxes and still retain corporate advantages. Some types of businesses can be set up as nonprofit corporations, which provide significant tax savings.

NOTE: *A corporation theoretically allows shareholders to avoid personal liability for borrowed money. As a practical matter, you may be asked to personally guarantee (make yourself liable for) loans, leases, inventory, and equipment purchased on credit, or other obligations of the corporation. Only when your corporation has sufficient assets to satisfy creditors will you be able to use only your corporate identity.*

Disadvantages. The start-up costs for forming a corporation are certainly a disadvantage. Plus, there are certain formalities to comply with, such as annual meetings, separate bank accounts, and more complicated tax forms. Unless a corporation registers as an S corporation, it must pay federal income tax separate from the tax paid by the owners, and it must pay California income tax as set forth in the California Revenue and Taxation Code (Cal. Rev. and Tax. Code), Sections 23151–23155. Over the years, there have occasionally been proposals to tax S corporations with an exemption for small operations, but none have passed the legislature.

Limited Liability Company

A *limited liability company* (LLC) is like a limited partnership without general partners. The owners are called *members*. An LLC has characteristics of both a corporation and a partnership—none of the partners have liability and all can have some control. An

LLC may be treated as either a partnership or a corporation for both federal and California tax purposes. For California tax purposes, it will be treated as a partnership if it lacks two or more of the following corporate characteristics:

❂ limited liability of members;

❂ continuity of life (it continues after a change in owners);

❂ free transferability of interests; and,

❂ centralized management.

It may be taxed as a corporation if it possesses more than two of these corporate characteristics.

Certain professions are prohibited from forming limited liability companies. For forms and more information, contact the secretary of state's department on limited liability companies at 916-653-3794. General provisions governing LLCs are found in California Corporations Code, commencing with Section 17000. For information about taxation of LLCs, see California Revenue and Taxation Code, Sections 17941–17946.

Advantages. The LLC offers members the limited liability of corporate shareholders and the tax advantages of a partnership. It offers more tax benefits than an S corporation, because it may pass through more depreciation and deductions. It also has more flexibility because it may have different classes of ownership and an unlimited number of members. If it owns appreciated property, it has more favorable tax treatment upon dissolution than an S corporation. The LLC is also extremely flexible in structure and operational aspects.

Disadvantages. There are higher start-up costs for an LLC than for a corporation. Because of the flexibility in structural and operational aspects, the governing documents are more complex. The LLC is a relatively new type of business entity. Therefore, the laws governing LLCs are not as well established as for partnerships and corporations.

Limited Liability Partnership

The *limited liability partnership* (LLP) is a specialized type of partnership for accountants, attorneys, and architects. It is like a general partnership, but with limited liability. The LLP was devised to allow partnerships of these professionals to limit their personal liability without losing the tax advantages of the partnership structure. However, the law does not allow these professionals to limit their liability for negligence in their professional function (i.e., for malpractice).

Advantages. The LLP offers the flexibility and tax benefits of a partnership, with the protection from liability of a corporation.

Disadvantages. Start-up and annual fees are higher than for a corporation. Other disadvantages are the same as for the LLC.

START-UP PROCEDURES

Except for a sole proprietorship, you must prepare some paperwork to start your business, and for some types, you must file the paperwork and pay a registration fee.

Sole Proprietorship

In a sole proprietorship, all accounts, property, and licenses are taken in the name of the owner. (See Chapter 3 for a discussion of fictitious names.)

Partnership

To form a partnership, a written agreement should be prepared to spell out the rights and obligations of the parties. It may be registered with the secretary of state, but this is not required. If you do register, the filing fee is $70.

Limited Partnership

A written *limited partnership agreement* must be registered with the secretary of state in Sacramento in order to form a limited partnership. The form used is relatively simple to fill out (instructions come with it), but the law governing the duties of the partnership and the rights of the limited partners is complex. If you wish to use this form of business, start with a lawyer and accountant.

Corporation

To form a corporation, file *articles of incorporation* with the secretary of state in Sacramento, along with $100 in filing fees and $300–$800 in prepaid taxes. An organizational meeting is then held. At the meeting, officers are elected, stock is issued, and other formalities are complied with in order to avoid the corporate entity being set aside later. Licenses and accounts are titled in the name of the corporation.

For further instructions, you may contact the main office at:

Secretary of State
1500 11th Street
Sacramento, CA 95814
916-657-5448
www.ss.ca.gov

Limited Liability Company

One or more persons or business entities may form a limited liability company by filing *articles of organization* with the secretary of state in Sacramento and paying the $70 filing fee. Licenses and accounts are in the name of the company, and the members must enter into an operating agreement after filing the articles of organization. (Corp. Code, Section 17050.) You would be wise to contact an attorney or accountant to assist you with this form of business.

Limited Liability Partnership

Two or more persons may form a *limited liability partnership* by filing a registration with the secretary of state in Sacramento and paying the $70 filing fee. A registration contains the following: 1) the name of the partnership; 2) the address of its principal office; 3) the name and address of the agent for service of process on the limited liability partnership in California; 4) a brief statement of the business in which the partnership engages; 5) any other matters that the partnership determines to include; and, 6) a statement that the partnership is registering as a registered limited liability partnership. Licenses and accounts are in the name of the company. (Cal. Corp. Code, beginning with Section 16951.) (As stated earlier, this form of business is limited to accountants, attorneys, and architects in California. (Cal. Corp. Code, beginning with Section 16951.))

Fees, forms, and other valuable information, including new legislation, can be found at the website of the California secretary of state. Type "California secretary of state" into your favorite search engine or go directly to the website at **www.ss.ca.gov**. At the bottom of the page, you will find the "California Business Portal." Click on it and you will find business entities, fees, advice, and links to other helpful sites, such as the Small Business Administration.

BUSINESS START-UP CHECKLIST

❏ Make your plan
    ❏ Obtain and read all relevant publications on your type of business
    ❏ Obtain and read all laws and regulations affecting your business
    ❏ Calculate whether your plan will produce a profit
    ❏ Plan your sources of capital
    ❏ Plan your sources of goods or services
    ❏ Plan your marketing efforts
❏ Choose your business name
    ❏ Check other business names and trademarks
    ❏ Register your name, trademark, etc.
❏ Choose the business form
    ❏ Prepare and file organizational papers
    ❏ Prepare and file fictitious name if necessary
❏ Choose the location
    ❏ Check competitors
    ❏ Check zoning
❏ Obtain necessary licenses
    ❏ City   ❏ State
    ❏ County   ❏ Federal
❏ Choose a bank
    ❏ Checking
    ❏ Credit card processing
    ❏ Loans
❏ Obtain necessary insurance
    ❏ Workers' Comp   ❏ Automobile
    ❏ Liability   ❏ Health
    ❏ Hazard   ❏ Life/disability
❏ File necessary federal tax registrations
❏ File necessary state tax registrations
❏ Set up a bookkeeping system
❏ Plan your hiring
    ❏ Obtain required posters
    ❏ Obtain or prepare employment application
    ❏ Obtain new hire tax forms
    ❏ Prepare employment policies
    ❏ Determine compliance with health and safety laws
❏ Plan your opening
    ❏ Obtain all necessary equipment and supplies
    ❏ Obtain all necessary inventory
    ❏ Do all necessary marketing and publicity
    ❏ Obtain all necessary forms and agreements
    ❏ Prepare your company policies on refunds, exchanges, returns

BUSINESS COMPARISON CHART

	Sole Proprietorship	General Partnership	Limited Partnership	Limited Liability Co.	Corporation C or S	Nonprofit Corporation
Liability protection	No	No	For limited partners	For all members	For all shareholders	For all members
Taxes	Pass through	Pass through	Pass through	Pass through or corporate	S corps. pass through, C corps. pay tax	None on income charities, Employees pay on wages
Minimum # of members	1	2	2	1	1	3
Start-up fee	None	$100	$125	$285	$145	$75
Annual fee	None	None	None	None	None	None
Different classes of ownership	No	Yes	Yes	Yes	S corps. no, C corps. yes	No ownership, Diff. classes of membership
Survives after death	No	No	Yes	Yes	Yes	Yes
Best for	One person, low-risk business or no assets	Low-risk business	Low-risk business with silent partners	All types of business	All types of business	Educational

Your Business Name

Before deciding upon a name for your business, be sure that it is not already being used by someone else. Many business owners have spent thousands of dollars on publicity and printing, only to throw it all away because another company owned the name. A company that owns a name can take you to court and force you to stop using that name. It can also sue you for damages if it thinks your use of the name caused it a financial loss.

Even if you will be running a small local shop with no plans for expansion, you should at least check out whether the name has been trademarked. If someone else is using the same name anywhere in the country and has registered it as a federal trademark, they can sue you. If you plan to expand or to deal nationally, then you should do a thorough search of the name.

The first places to look are the local phone books and official records of your county. Next, you should check with the secretary of state's office in Sacramento to see if someone has registered a corporate name the same as, or confusingly similar to, the one you have chosen. This can be done at the California secretary of state's website (**www.ss.ca.gov**). Simply click on "California Business Portal" and follow the directions.

To do a national search, you should check trade directories and phone books of major cities. These can be found at many libraries and are usually reference books that cannot be checked out. The *Trade Names Directory* is a two-volume set of names compiled from many sources, published by Gale Research Company.

With Internet access, you can search all of the Yellow Page listings in the U.S. at a number of sites at no charge. One website, **www.superpages.com**, offers free searches of Yellow Pages for all states at once. You can also use **www.google.com** to see if your company name is used anywhere on the Internet.

To be sure that your use of the name does not violate someone else's trademark rights, you should have a trademark search done of the mark in the *United States Patent and Trademark Office* (PTO). In the past, this required a visit to their offices or the hiring of a search firm for over a hundred dollars. However, in 1999, the PTO put its trademark records online, so you can now search them at **www.uspto.gov**.

Even if you do not have access to the Internet, you might be able to search at a public library or have one of their employees order an online search for you for a small fee. If this is not available to you, you can have the search done through a firm. One such firm, Government Liaison Services, Inc., offers searches of one hundred trade directories and 4800 phone books.

Government Liaison Services, Inc.
200 North Glebe Road
Suite 321
Arlington, VA 22203
800-642-6564
www.trademarkinfo.com

No matter how thorough your search is, there is no guarantee that there is not a local user somewhere with rights to the mark. If, for example, you register a name for a new chain of restaurants and later find out that someone in Tucumcari, New Mexico has been using the name longer than you, that person will still have the right to use the name, but just in his or her local area. If you do not want that restaurant to cause confusion with your chain, you can try to buy him or her out. Similarly, if you are operating a small business under a unique name, and a law firm in New York writes and offers to buy the right to your name, you can assume that some large corporation wants to start a major expansion under that name.

The best way to make sure a name you are using is not already owned by someone else is to make one up. Names such as Xerox and Exxon were made up and did not have any meaning prior to their use. Remember that there are millions of businesses, and even something you make up may already be in use. Do a search just to be sure.

FICTITIOUS NAMES

In California, as in most states, unless you do business in your own legal name, you must register the name you are using as a *fictitious name*. You must also register if you are using your own name, but in some manner that implies others may also be involved in your business. For example, if your name is *John Doe* and you are operating your own plumbing business, you may operate your business as *John Doe, Plumber*, without registering. However, any other name should be registered, such as:

Doe Plumbing	*John Doe Plumbing*
John Doe and Associates	*West Coast Plumbing*
John the Plumber	*Plumber John*

Even if your business is a corporation, you must register if you are using a name that is different from your corporate name. For example, if your corporation is *XYZ, Inc.*, but is conducting business under the name *California Pizza Station*, registration would be required.

There are also certain words and abbreviations that you may not use. Unless your business is incorporated, you cannot use the words "corporation" or "incorporated," or the abbreviations "corp." or "inc." Similarly, unless your business is a limited liability company, you cannot use the words "limited liability company," or the abbreviations "LLC" or "LC." (California Business and Professional Code (Cal. Bus. and Prof. Code), Section 17910.5.)

The words "limited" or "company," or their abbreviations (Ltd. and Co.) may be used if it does not imply that the business is a limited liability company. For example, John Smith Company, Limited could not be used. The John Smith Company for the Limited use of Fertilizer could be used.

The California Business and Professional Code contains the requirements for registering a fictitious name. It is done by obtaining and filing a **FICTITIOUS BUSINESS NAME STATEMENT** with the clerk of the county in which you have your principal place of business. This must be done within forty days after you begin doing business. A registration is good for five years, and must be renewed by filing a new **FICTITIOUS BUSINESS NAME STATEMENT** before the current one expires.

Within thirty days of filing, you must publish your **FICTITIOUS BUSINESS NAME STATEMENT** for four weeks in a row in a local newspaper. Each of the four publications must be at least five days apart, not counting the day of publication. A sample completed **FICTITIOUS BUSINESS NAME STATEMENT** may be found in Appendix A. A blank form with instructions may be found in Appendix B. (see form 2, p.245.) Be sure to check with your county court clerk before filing to ensure you have the proper form.

CORPORATE NAMES

A corporation does not have to register a fictitious name because it already has a legal name. The name of a corporation must contain one of the following words.

Incorporated	Inc.
Corporation	Corp.

If the name of the corporation does not contain one of the above words or abbreviations, it will be rejected by the secretary of state. It will also be rejected if the name is already taken or is similar to the name of another corporation, or if it uses a forbidden word such as "Bank" or "Trust." To check on a name, you may call the corporate name information number in Sacramento at 916-657-5448. You can also check their website at **www.ss.ca.gov**.

If a name you pick is taken by another company, you may be able to change it slightly and have it accepted. For example, if there is already a Tri-City Upholstery, Inc., and it is in a different county, you may be allowed to use Tri-City Upholstery of Kern County, Inc. However, even if this is approved by the secretary of state, you might still get sued by the other company if your business is close to theirs or there is a likelihood of confusion.

Do not have anything printed until your corporate papers are returned to you. Sometimes a name is approved over the phone, but rejected when submitted. Once you have chosen a corporate name and know it is available, you should immediately register the name.

Professional Corporations

Professionals, such as doctors, can form a corporation in which to practice. The law covering these corporations is found in the California Corporations Code, Section 13400, as well as Sections 200 through 202, which cover the minimum requirements for stock operations.

TRADEMARKS

As your business builds goodwill, its name will become more valuable and you will want to protect it from others who may wish to copy it. To protect a name used to describe your goods or services, you can register it as a *trademark* (for goods) or a *service mark* (for services) with either the secretary of state in California or with the United States Patent and Trademark Office (PTO).

You cannot obtain a trademark for the name of your business, but you can trademark the name you use on your goods and services. In most cases, you use your company name on your goods as your trademark. In effect, it protects your company name. Another way to protect your company name is to incorporate. A particular corporate name can only be registered by one company in California.

State registration would be useful if you only expect to use your trademark within the state of California. Federal registration would protect your mark anywhere in the country. The registration of a mark gives you exclusive use of the mark for the types of goods for which it is registered. The only exception is people who have already been using the mark. You cannot stop people who have been using the mark prior to your registration.

State Registration

The procedure for state registration is simple and the filing fee is $70. Before a mark can be registered, it must be used in California. For goods, this means it must be used on the goods themselves, or on containers, tags, labels, or displays of the goods. For services, it must be used in the sale or advertising of the services. The use must be in an actual transaction with a customer. A sample mailed to a friend is not an acceptable use.

The $70 fee will register the mark in only one class of goods. If the mark is used on more than one class of goods, a separate registration must be filed. The registration is good for ten years. Six months prior to its expiration, it must be renewed. The renewal fee is $30 for each class of goods. The secretary of state provides the registration form with instructions.

Federal Registration

For federal registration, the procedure is a little more complicated. There are two types of applications depending upon whether you have already made actual use of the mark or whether you merely have an intention to use the mark in the future. For a trademark that has been in use, you must file an application form along with specimens showing *actual use*, and a drawing of the mark that complies with all of the rules of the United States Patent and Trademark Office. For an *intent to use* application, you must file two separate forms—one when you make the initial application, and the other after you have made actual use of the mark—as well as the specimens and drawing. Before a mark can be entitled to federal registration, the use of the mark must be in *interstate commerce* or in commerce with another country. The fee for registration is $335, but if you file an *intent to use* application, there is a second fee of $100 for the filing after actual use.

You can register online at the PTO website at **www.uspto.gov**. See the PTO website for more information on fee schedules.

Preparing a Business Plan

Not everyone needs a business plan to start a business, but if you have one it might help you avoid mistakes and make better decisions. For example, if you think it would be a great idea to start a candle shop in a little seaside resort, you might find out after preparing a business plan that considering the number of people who are likely to stop by, you could never sell enough candles to pay the rent.

A business plan lets you look at the costs, expenses, and potential sales of your business, and see whether or not it can be profitable. It also allows you to find alternatives that might be more profitable. In the candle shop example, you might find that if you chose a more populous location or if you sold something else in addition to the candles, you would be more likely to make a profit.

ADVANTAGES AND DISADVANTAGES OF A BUSINESS PLAN

Other than helping you figure out if your business will be profitable, a business plan would also be useful if you hope to borrow money or have investors buy into your business. Lenders and equity investors always require a business plan before they will provide money to a business.

If your idea is truly unusual, a business plan may discourage you from starting your business. A business idea might look like a failure on paper, but if in your gut you know it would work, it might be worth trying without a business plan.

Example:

When Chester Carlson invented the first photocopy machine, he went to IBM. They spent $50,000 to analyze the idea and concluded that nobody needed a photocopy machine because people already had carbon paper—which was cheaper. However, he believed in his machine and started Xerox Corporation, which became one of the biggest and hottest companies of its time.

However, even with a great concept, you need to at least do some basic calculations to see if the business can make a profit.

- ✪ If you want to start a retail shop, figure out how many people are close enough to become customers and how many other stores will be competing for those customers. Visit some of those other shops and see how busy they are. Without giving away your plans to compete, ask some general questions like "how's business?" and maybe they will share their frustrations or successes.

- ✪ Whether you sell a good or a service, do the math to find out how much profit is in it. For example, if you plan to start a house painting company, find out what you will have to pay to hire painters, what it will cost you for all of the insurance, what bonding and licensing you will need, and what the advertising will cost you. Figure out how many jobs you can do per month and what other painters are charging. In some industries, in certain areas of the state there may be a large margin of profit, while in other areas there may be almost no profit.

- ✪ Find out if there is a demand for your product or service. Suppose you have designed a beautiful new kind of candle and your friends all say you should open a shop because "everyone will want them." Before making a hundred of them and renting a store, bring a few to craft shows or flea markets and see what happens.

✪   Figure out what the income and expenses would be for a typical month of your new business. List monthly expenses, such as rent, salaries, utilities, insurance, taxes, supplies, advertising, services, and other overhead. Then, figure out how much profit you will average from each sale. Next, figure out how many sales you will need to cover your overhead and divide by the number of business days in the month. Can you reasonably expect that many sales? How will you get those sales?

Most types of businesses have trade associations, which often have figures on how profitable its members are. Some even have start-up kits for people wanting to start businesses. One good source of information on such organizations is the *Encyclopedia of Associations* published by Gale Research, Inc., available in many library reference sections. Suppliers of products to the trade often give assistance to small companies getting started, in order to win their loyalty. Contact the largest suppliers of the products your business will be using and see if they can be of help.

OUTLINE FOR YOUR BUSINESS PLAN

While you may believe that you do not need a business plan, conventional wisdom says you do and it only makes good business sense to have one. A typical business plan has sections that cover topics such as the following:

✪   executive summary;

✪   product or service;

✪   market;

✪   competition;

✪   marketing plan;

- ✪ production plan;

- ✪ organizational plan;

- ✪ financial projections;

- ✪ management team; and,

- ✪ risks.

The following is an explanation of each.

Executive Summary   The executive summary is an overview of what the business will be and why it is expected to be successful. If the business plan will be used to lure investors, this section is the most important, since many might not read any further if they are not impressed with the summary.

Product or Service   The product or service section is a detailed description of what you will be selling. You should describe what is different about it and why people would need it or want it.

Market   The market section should analyze who the potential buyers of your product or service are. Describe both the physical location of the customers and their demographics. For example, a bodybuilding gym would probably mostly appeal to males in the 18 to 40 age bracket in a ten- to twenty-mile radius, depending on the location.

If you will sell things from a retail shop, you might also want to sell from mail order catalogs or over the Internet if your local customer base would not be large enough to support the business. Describe what you will be doing for those ventures.

If you are manufacturing things, you should find out who the wholesalers and distributors are, and their terms. This information should also be included in this section.

Competition   Before opening your business, you should know who and where your competitors are. If you are opening an antique shop, you might want to be near other antique shops so more customers come by your place, since antiques are unique and do not really compete with other antiques. However, if you open a florist shop, you probably do not want to be near other florist shops, since most florists sell similar products and a new shop would just dilute the customer base.

If you have a truly unique way of selling something, you might want to go near other similar businesses to grab their existing customer base and expand your market share. However, if they could easily copy your idea, you might not take away the business for long and will end up diluting the market for each business. (see Chapter 6.)

Marketing Plan

Many a business has closed just a few months after opening because not enough customers showed up. How do you expect customers to find out about your business? Even if you get a nice write-up in the local paper, not everyone reads the paper, many people do not read every page, and lots of people forget what they read.

Your marketing plan describes how you will advertise your business. List how much the advertising will cost, and describe how you expect people to respond to the advertising.

Production Plan

The production plan needs to address and answer questions like the following.

- If you are manufacturing a product, do you know how you will be able to produce a large quantity of them?

- Do you know all the costs and the possible production problems that could come up?

- If Wal-Mart orders 100,000 units of your product, could you get them made in a reasonable time?

The production plan needs to anticipate the normal schedule you intend to use, as well as how to handle any changes—positive or negative—to that schedule.

If you are selling a service and will need employees to perform those services, your production plan should explain how you will recruit and train those employees.

Organizational Plan

If your business will be more than a mom and pop operation, what will the organizational plan be? How many employees will you need and who will supervise whom? How much of the work will be done by employees and how much will be hired out to other businesses and independent contractors? Will you have a sales force? Will you need manufacturing employees? Will your accounting, website maintenance, and office cleaning and maintenance be contracted out or done by employees?

Financial Projections

Tying all the previously discussed topics together is what your financial plan will discuss. You should know how much rent, utilities, insurance, taxes, marketing, and product costs or wages for labor will cost you for the first year. Besides listing known, expected expenses, you should calculate your financial well-being under a number of different possible scenarios. Some of the questions to think about and answer will be, *how long would you be in business if you have very few customers the first few months?* and *if Wal-Mart does order 100,000 of your products, could you afford to manufacture them, knowing you will not be paid for months?*

Management Team

If you will be seeking outside funding, you will need to list the experience and skills of the management of the business. Investors want to know that the managers have experience and know what they are doing.

Risks

A good business plan weighs all the risks of the new enterprise. Is new technology in the works that will make the business obsolete? Would a rise in the price of a particular needed supply eliminate all your profits? What are the chances of a new competitor entering the market if you show some success, and what are you going to do about it? Part of your analysis should be to look at all of the possible things that could happen in the field you chose and to gauge the likelihood of success.

Gathering Information

Some of the sections of your business plan require a lot of research. People sometimes take years to prepare them. Today, the Internet puts a nearly infinite amount of information at your fingertips, but you might also want to do some personal research.

Sometimes the best way to get the feel for a business is to get a job in a similar business. At a minimum, you should visit similar businesses and perhaps sit outside of one, and see how many customers they have and how much business they do. There are startup guides for many types of businesses, which can be found at Amazon.com, your local bookstores, and the library. Your local chamber of commerce, business development office, or SCORE office might also have materials to help you in your research.

Sample Business Plan

The following plan is one for a simple one-person business that will use its owner's assets to start. Of course, a larger business, or one that needs financing, will need a much longer and more detailed plan.

A website with sixty sample business plans and information on business plan software is **www.bplans.com**.

Executive Summary

This is the plan for a new business, Reardon Computer Repair, LLC by Henry Reardon, to be started locally and then expanded throughout the state and perhaps further if results indicate this is feasible.

The mission of Reardon Computer Repair (RCR) is to offer fast, affordable repairs to office and home computers. The objective is to become profitable within the first three months and to grow at a quick but manageable pace.

In order to offer customers the quickest service, RCR will rely on youthful computer whizzes who are students and have the time and expertise to provide the service. They will also have the flexibility to arrive quickly and the motivation to show off their expertise.

To reach customers, we will use limited advertising, but primarily the Internet and word of mouth from happy customers.

With nearly every business and family having several computers and lack of fast service currently available, it is expected this business could be successful quickly and could grow rapidly.

Product or Service

The company will offer computer repair services both at its shop and at customers' offices and homes. It will sell computer parts as necessary to complete the repairs and it will also carry upgrades, accessories, and peripherals, which will most likely be of value to customers needing repairs.

Market

The market would be nearly every business and family at every address in the city, state, and country, since today nearly everyone has a computer. Figures show nearly 250 million computers in use in America, and that number is expected to grow to over 300 million in five years.

The market for the initial shop would be a fifteen-mile radius, which is a reasonable driving distance for our employees. The population in that area is 300,000 people, which would mean 240,000 potential customers, based on the current level of 800 computers per 1,000 people.

The market would not include new computers, which typically come with a one-year guarantee. It would also not include people who bought extended guarantees.

The growth trend for the industry is 8–10% for the next decade.

Competition

The competition would be the authorized repair shops working with the computer manufacturers. While these have the advantage of being authorized, research and experience has shown that they are slow and do not meet customers' need for an immediate repair.

There is one computer repair shop within a ten-mile radius of the proposed shop and two more within a twenty-five-mile radius. Average wait time for a dropped off repair is one week. The two closest repair services offer no on-site repair. Shipping a computer to a dealer for repair takes one to two weeks. Most customers need their computer fixed within a day or two.

One potential source for competition would be from employees or former employees who are asked to work for customers "on the side" at a reduced rate. To discourage this, the company will have a contract with employees with a noncompete agreement that specifies that they will pay the company three times what they earn. Also, agreements with customers will include a clause that they have the option to hire away one of our employees for a one-time $2,000 fee.

Marketing Plan

The business will be marketed through networking, Internet marketing, advertising, and creative marketing.

Networking will be through the owner's contacts and local computer clubs and software stores. Some local retailers do not offer service and they have already indicated that they would promote a local business that could offer fast repairs.

A website would be linked to local businesses and community groups, and to major computer repair referral sites.

Advertising would include the Yellow Pages and local computer club newsletters. Studies have shown that newspaper and television advertising would be too expensive and not cost effective for this type of business.

Creative advertising would include vinyl lettering on the back window of the owner's vehicle.

Production Plan

The company will be selling the services of computer technicians and computer parts. The owner will supply most of the services in the beginning and then add student technicians as needed.

The parts will all be purchased ready-made from the manufacturers, except for cables, which can be made on an as-needed basis much cheaper than ready-made ones.

Employees

The employees will be students who are extremely knowledgeable about computers. Some would call them computer "geeks"—in a nice way. They have extensive knowledge of the workings of computers, have lots of free time, need money, and would love to show off how knowledgeable they are.

As students, they already have health insurance and do not need full-time work. They would be available as needed. The company would pay them $12 an hour plus mileage, which is more than any other job available to students, but is not cost prohibitive, considering the charge to customers of $50 per hour.

Financial Projections

The minimum charge for a service call will be $75 on-site and $50 in-shop, which will include one hour of service. The parts markup will be the industry standard of 20%. The average customer bill will be estimated to be $100 including labor and markup.

The labor cost is estimated to be $30 per call including time, taxes, insurance, and mileage. The owner will be estimated to handle 75% of the work the first six months and 50% the second six months.

Rent, utilities, insurance, taxes, and other fixed costs is estimated to be $3,000 per month.

Advertising and promotion expenses are expected to be $3,000 per month.

Estimated number of customers will be:

First three months:	10 per week
Second three months:	20 per week
Third three months:	35 per week
Fourth three months:	50 per week

Estimated monthly revenue:

First three months:	$4,000
Second three months:	$8,000
Third three months:	$14,000
Fourth three months:	$20,000

Monthly income and expense projection:

First three months:

Income	$4,000
Labor	$300
Fixed costs	$3,000
Advertising	$3,000
Net	$2,300 loss per month

Second 3 months:

Income	$8,000
Labor	$600
Fixed costs	$3,000
Advertising	$3,000
Net	$1,400 profit per month

Third 3 months:

Income	$14,000
Labor	$2,100
Fixed costs	$3,000
Advertising	$3,000
Net	$5,900 profit per month

Fourth 3 months:

Income	$20,000
Labor	$3,000
Fixed costs	$3,000
Advertising	$3,000
Net	$11,000 profit per month

Organization Plan

The business will start with the owner, Henry Reardon, and three students who are experts at computer repair and available as part-time workers on an as-needed basis.

The owner will manage the business and do as many repairs as are possible with the time remaining in the week.

One of the students, Peter Galt, will work after school in the shop, and the others, Dom Roark and Howard Taggert, are willing to work on an on-call basis, either at the shop or at customers' homes.

As business grows, the company will recruit more student employees through the school job placement offices and at computer clubs.

Management Team

The owner, Henry Reardon, will be the sole manager of the company. He will use the accounting services of his accountant, Dave Burton. The owner anticipates being able to supervise up to ten employees. When there are more than ten, the company will need a manager to take over scheduling and some other management functions.

Risks

Because the business does not require a lot of capital, there will be a low financial risk in the beginning. The biggest reason for failure would be an inability to get the word out that the company exists and can fill a need when it arises. For this reason, the most important task in the beginning will be marketing and promotion.

As the company grows, the risk will be that computers will need fewer repairs, become harder to repair, and become so cheap they are disposable. To guard against this possibility, the company will add computer consulting services as it grows so that it will always have something to offer computer owners.

Financing Your Business

The way to finance your business is determined by how fast you want your business to grow and how much risk of failure you are able to handle. Letting the business grow with its own income is the slowest but safest way to grow. Taking out a personal loan against your house to expand quickly is the fastest but riskiest way to grow.

GROWING WITH PROFITS

Many successful businesses have started out with little money and used the profits to grow bigger and bigger. If you have another source of income to live on (such as a job or a spouse's job), you can plow all the income of your fledgling business into growth.

Some businesses start as hobbies or part-time ventures on the weekend while the entrepreneur holds down a full-time job. Many types of goods or service businesses can start this way. Even some billion-dollar corporations, such as Apple Computer, started out this way.

This allows you to test your idea with little risk. If you find you are not good at running that type of business, or the time or location was not right for your idea, all you are out is the time you spent and your start-up capital.

However, a business can only grow so big from its own income. In many cases, as a business grows, it gets to a point where the orders are so big that money must be borrowed to produce the product so the orders can be filled. With this kind of order, there is the risk that if the customer cannot pay or goes bankrupt, the business will also go under. At such a point, a business owner should investigate the creditworthiness of the customer and weigh the risks. Some businesses have grown rapidly, some have gone under, and others have decided not to take the risk and stayed small. You can worry about that down the road.

Having Too Much Money

It probably does not seem possible to have too much money with which to start a business, but many businesses have failed for that reason. With plenty of start-up capital available, a business owner does not need to watch expenses and can become wasteful. Employees get used to lavish spending. Once the money runs out and the business must run on its own earnings, it fails.

Starting with the bare minimum forces a business to watch its expenses and be frugal. It necessitates finding the least expensive solutions to problems and creative ways to be productive.

Undercapitalization

Undercapitalization is the other side of the coin. Many potentially good businesses go under before they give themselves a chance to succeed. It is a good idea to line up sources for money that you do not believe you will ever have to use—just in case.

USING YOUR SAVINGS

If you have savings you can tap to get your business started, that is the best source. You will not have to pay high interest rates and you will not have to worry about reimbursing someone, such as a relative.

Home Equity

If you have owned your home for several years, it is possible that the equity has grown substantially and you can get a second mortgage to finance your business. If you have been in the home for many years and have a good record of paying your bills, some lenders will make second mortgages that exceed the equity. Just remember, if your business fails, you may lose your house.

Retirement Accounts Be careful about borrowing from your retirement savings. There are tax penalties for borrowing from or against certain types of retirement accounts. Also, your future financial security may be lost if your business does not succeed.

BORROWING MONEY

It is extremely tempting to look to others to get the money to start a business. The risk of failure is less worrisome and the pressure is lower, but that is a problem with borrowing. If it is others' money, you do not have quite the same incentive to succeed as you do if everything you own is on the line.

Actually, you should be even more concerned when using others' money. Your reputation is at risk, and if you do not succeed, you probably will still have to pay back the loan.

Family Depending on how much money your family can spare, it may be the most comfortable or most uncomfortable source of funds for you. If you have been assured a large inheritance and your parents have more funds than they need to live on, you may be able to borrow against your inheritance without worry. It will be your money anyway, and you need it much more now than you will ten or twenty years from now. If you lose it all, it is your own loss.

However, if you are asking your widowed mother to cash in a CD she lives on to finance your get-rich-quick scheme, you should have second thoughts about it. Stop and consider all the real reasons your business might not take off and what your mother would do without the income.

Friends Borrowing from friends is like borrowing from family members. If you know they have the funds available and could survive a loss, you may want to risk it, but if they would be loaning you their only resources, do not chance it.

Financial problems can be the worst thing for a relationship, whether it is a casual friendship or a long-term romantic involvement. Before you borrow from a friend, try to imagine what would happen if you could not pay it back, and how you would feel if it caused the end of your relationship.

The ideal situation is for your friend to be a co-venturer in your business and the burden would not be totally on you to see how the funds were spent. Still, realize that such a venture will put extra strain on the relationship.

Banks   In a way, a bank can be a more comfortable party from which to borrow, because you do not have the personal relationship with it that you do with a friend or family member. If you fail, it will write your loan off rather than disown you. However, a bank can also be the least comfortable party to borrow from, because it will demand realistic projections (your business plan) and will monitor your performance. If you do not meet the bank's expectations, it may call in your loan just when you need it most.

The best thing about a bank loan is that it will require you to do your homework. You must have plans that make sense to a banker. If the bank approves your loan, you know that your plans are at least reasonable.

Bank loans are not cheap or easy. You will be paying a good interest rate, and you will have to put up collateral. If your business does not have equipment or receivables, the bank may require you to put up your house or other property to guarantee the loan.

Banks are a little easier to deal with when you get a Small Business Administration (SBA) loan, because the SBA guarantees that it will pay the bank if you default on the loan. Small Business Administration loans are obtained through local bank branches.

Credit Cards   Borrowing against a credit card is one of the fastest growing ways of financing a business, but it can be one of the most expensive ways. The rates can go higher than 20%, although many cards offer lower rates. Some people are able to get numerous cards. Some successful businesses have used credit cards to get off the ground or to weather through a cash crunch, but if the business does not begin to generate the cash to make the payments, you could soon end up in bankruptcy. A good strategy is only to use credit cards for a long-term asset, like a computer, or for something that will quickly generate cash, like inventory to fill an order. Do not use credit cards to pay expenses that are not generating revenue.

GETTING A RICH PARTNER

One of the best business combinations is a young entrepreneur with ideas and ambition, and a retired investor with business experience and money. Together, they can supply everything the business needs.

How do you find such a partner? Be creative. You should have investigated the business you are starting and know others who have been in such a business. Have any of them had partners retire over the last few years? Are any of them planning to phase out of the business?

SELLING SHARES OF YOUR BUSINESS

Silent investors are the best source of capital for your business. You retain full control of the business, and if it happens to fail, you have no obligation to them. Unfortunately, few silent investors are interested in a new business. It is only after you have proven your concept to be successful and built up a rather large enterprise that you will be able to attract such investors.

The most common way to obtain money from investors is to issue stock to them. For this, the best type of business entity is the corporation. It gives you almost unlimited flexibility in the number and kinds of shares of stock you can issue.

The easiest way to find companies offering *venture capital* (the money at risk for starting a business that replaces or supplements the other business capital) is on the Internet. Type in "California venture capital" in a search engine, and you will find more than you need.

An additional source is **www.vfinance.com**. This will lead you to a list of California law firms and accounting firms handling venture capital, as well as where to find the money, business plans, and lots of other helpful information.

SECURITIES LAWS

There is one major problem with selling stock in your business, and that is all of the federal and state regulations with which you must comply. Both the state and federal governments have long and complicated laws dealing with the sale of securities. There are also hundreds of court cases attempting to explain what these laws mean. A thorough explanation of this area of law is beyond the scope of this book.

Basically, *securities* have been held to exist in any case in which a person provides money to someone with the expectation that he or she will get a profit through the efforts of that person. This can apply to any situation where someone buys stock in, or makes a loan to, your business. What the laws require is disclosure of the risks involved, and in some cases, registration of the securities with the government. There are some exemptions, such as for small amounts of money and for limited numbers of investors.

Penalties for violation of securities laws are severe, including triple damages and prison terms. You should consult a specialist in securities laws before issuing any security. You can often get an introductory consultation at a reasonable rate to learn your options.

chapter 6

Locating Your Business

The right location for your business will be determined by what type of business it is and how fast you expect to grow. For some types of businesses, the location will not be important to your success or failure, but in others, it will be crucial.

WORKING OUT OF YOUR HOME

Many small businesses get started out of the home. Chapter 7 discusses the legalities of home businesses. This section discusses the practicalities.

Starting a business out of your home can save you the rent, electricity, insurance, and other costs of setting up at another location. For some people this is ideal, and they can combine their home and work duties easily and efficiently. For other people it is a disaster. A spouse, children, neighbors, television, and household chores can be so distracting that no other work gets done.

Since residential rates are usually lower than business telephone rates, many people use their residential telephone line or add a second residential line to conduct business. However, if you wish to be listed in the Yellow Pages, you will need to have a business line in your home. If you are running two or more types of businesses, you can probably add their names as additional listings on the original number and avoid paying for another business line.

You should also consider whether the type of business you are starting is compatible with a home office. For example, if your business mostly consists of making phone calls or emailing clients, then the home may be an ideal place to run it. If your clients need to visit you, or you will need daily pickups and deliveries by truck, then the home may not be a good location. This is discussed in more detail in the next chapter.

If you need to do credit checks as part of your business, contact your local credit bureau. It may have extra charges for home businesses to run credit reports.

CHOOSING A RETAIL SITE

For most types of retail stores, the location is of prime importance. Things to consider include how close it is to your potential customers, how visible it is to the public, and how easily accessible it is to both autos and pedestrians. You should also consider the attractiveness and safety of the site.

Location would be less important for a business that was the only one of its kind in the area. For example, if there was only one moped parts dealer or Armenian restaurant in a metropolitan area, people would have to come to wherever you are if they wanted your products or services. However, even with such businesses, keep in mind that there is competition. People who want moped parts can order them on the Internet and restaurant customers can choose another type of cuisine.

You should look up all the businesses similar to the one you plan to run in the phone book and mark them on a map. For some businesses, like a dry cleaner, you would want to be far from the others. However, for other businesses, like antique stores, you would want to be near the others. (Antique stores usually do not carry the same things, they do not compete, and people like to go to an antique district and visit all the shops.)

CHOOSING OFFICE, MANUFACTURING, OR WAREHOUSE SPACE

If your business will be the type where customers will not come to you, then locating it near customers is not as much of a concern and you can probably save money by locating away from the high-traffic central business districts. However, you should consider the convenience for employees, and not locate in an area that would be unattractive to them or too far from where they would likely live.

For manufacturing or warehouse operations, you should consider your proximity to a post office, trucking company, or rail line. When several sites are available, you might consider which one has the earliest or most convenient pickup schedule for the carriers you plan to use.

LEASING A SITE

A lease of space can be one of the biggest expenses of a small business, so you should do a lot of homework before signing one. There are a lot of terms in a commercial lease that can make or break your business. The most critical are discussed in the following pages.

Zoning
Before signing a lease, be sure that everything your business will need to do is allowed by the *zoning* of the property—regulations that control the use of property and buildings.

Regardless of what is allowed in your lease, city or county zoning laws will control what you can do. You may be able to break your lease if the landlord lied to you about the zoning. If you have already moved into the building, the cost of relocating and the time and expense of a lawsuit could end your business career.

Restrictions
In some shopping centers, existing tenants have guarantees that other tenants will not compete with them. For example, if you plan to open a restaurant and bakery, you may be forbidden to sell carryout baked goods if the supermarket has a bakery and a noncompete clause.

Signs
Business signs are regulated by zoning laws, sign laws, and property restrictions. If you rent a hidden location with no possibility for

adequate signage, your chances for success are less than with a more visible site or much larger sign.

ADA Compliance

The *Americans with Disabilities Act* (ADA) requires that *reasonable accommodations* be made to make businesses accessible to people with disabilities. When a business is remodeled, many more changes are required than if no remodeling is done. Be sure that the space you rent complies with the law, or that the landlord will be responsible for compliance. Be aware of the full costs you will bear.

Expansion

As your business grows, you may need to expand your space. The time to find out about your options is before you sign the lease. Perhaps you can take over adjoining units when those leases expire.

Renewal

Location is a key to success for some businesses. If you spend five years building up a clientele, you do not want someone to take over your locale at the end of your lease. Therefore, you should have a *renewal clause* in your lease. This usually calls for a rent increase, based on many possible factors. Just as with *escalator clauses*, discussed on page 51, you may want to have an expert examine the renewal provisions.

Personal Guarantee

Most landlords of commercial space will not rent to a small corporation without a *personal guarantee* of the lease. This is a very risky thing for a new business owner to do. The lifetime rent on a long-term commercial lease can be hundreds of thousands of dollars, and if your business fails, the last thing you want to do is be personally responsible for five years of rent.

California requires the landlord to *mitigate* damages. This means that the landlord must try to rent the space you vacate. If the court decides that the landlord did not try hard enough, you do not owe the rent for that period. However, do not count on this. Always try to avoid personal liability.

Where space is scarce or a location is hot, a landlord can get the guarantees he or she demands, and there is not much you can do about it (except perhaps set up an asset protection plan ahead of time). However, where several units are vacant or the commercial rental market is soft, often you can negotiate out of the personal guarantee. If the lease is five years, maybe you can get away with a guarantee of just the first year.

Also, consider the space you are going to rent. If there is nothing unusual about it, there should be no trouble re-renting it. However, if it is a *single-purpose building*, it may not be so easy to find another tenant. (Also remember that if the new tenant is paying less than you agreed to pay, you may be responsible for the difference.)

Escalator Clauses

If you are going to sign a lease for several years, especially one that requires improvements by the landlord, you may want to have someone examine the lease for you. There are clauses called *escalator clauses* that provide for periodic rent increases. Some of these clauses are based on formulas that are not easily understood. Find a lawyer, accountant, or real estate agent familiar with this type of lease and get some advice. You do not want any unexpected rent increases.

Duty to Open

Some shopping centers have rules requiring all shops to be open certain hours. If you cannot afford to staff your business the entire required time, or if you have religious or other reasons that make this a problem, you should negotiate it out of the lease or find another location.

Sublease

At some point, you may decide to sell your business, and in many cases, the location is the most valuable aspect of it. For this reason, you should be sure that you have the right to either assign your lease or to sublease the property. If this is impossible, one way around a prohibition is to incorporate your business before signing the lease, and then when you sell the business, sell the stock. However, some lease clauses prohibit transfer of *any interest* in the business, so read the lease carefully.

The duty on the landlord to mitigate damages has weakened the *prohibition of assignment*. If you are going to move out before the end of your lease and you supply the landlord with an acceptable tenant, the landlord must accept the tenant or you do not have to pay any more rent. Whether a tenant is acceptable would be a matter for a court to decide if the landlord refuses your tenant. If your business is not doing well or you want to relocate, finding a tenant to take your place could save you from paying rent after you move.

BUYING A SITE

If you are experienced with owning rental property, you will probably be more inclined to buy a site for your business. If you have no experience with real estate, you should probably rent and not take on the extra cost and responsibility of property ownership.

One reason to buy your site is that you can build up equity. Rather than pay rent to a landlord, you can pay off a mortgage and eventually own the property.

Separating the Ownership

One risk in buying a business site is that if the business gets into financial trouble, the creditors may go after the building as well. For this reason, most people who buy a site for their business keep the ownership out of the business. For example, the business will be a corporation and the real estate will be owned personally by the owner or by a trust unrelated to the business.

Expansion

Before buying a site, you should consider the growth potential of your business. If it grows quickly, will you be able to expand at that site or will you have to move? Might the property next door be available for sale in the future if you need it? Can you get an option on it? If the site is a good investment whether or not you have your business there, then by all means, buy it. But if its main value is for your business, think twice.

Zoning

Some of the concerns when buying a site are the same as when renting. You want to make sure that the zoning permits the type of business you wish to start, or that you can get a variance without a large expense or delay. Be aware that just because your business is now using the site does not mean that you can expand or remodel the business at that site. Check with the zoning department and find out exactly what is allowed.

Signs

Signs are another concern. Some cities have regulated signs and do not allow new or larger ones. Some businesses have used these laws to get publicity. For example, a car dealer who was told to take down a large number of American flags on his lot filed a federal lawsuit and rallied the community behind him.

ADA Compliance Compliance with the ADA is another concern when buying a commercial building. Find out from the building department if the building is in compliance or what needs to be done to put it in compliance. If you remodel, the requirements may be more strict.

NOTE: *When dealing with public officials, keep in mind that they do not always know what the law is, or do no accurately explain it. Some are overzealous and try to intimidate people into doing things that are not required by law. Read the requirements yourself and question the officials if they seem to be interpreting it incorrectly. Seek legal advice if officials refuse to reexamine the law or move away from an erroneous position.*

On the other hand, consider that keeping them happy may be worth the price. If you are already doing something they have overlooked, do not make a big deal over a little thing they want changed, or they may subject you to a full inspection or audit.

CHECK GOVERNMENTAL REGULATIONS

When looking for a site for your business, investigate the different governmental regulations in your area. For example, a location just outside the city or county limits might have a lower licensing fee, a lower sales tax rate, or less strict sign requirements.

Licensing Your Business

The federal and state legislatures and local governments have an interest in protecting consumers from bad business practices. In order to ensure that consumers are protected from unscrupulous business people and to require a minimum level of service to the public, the federal, state, and local governments have developed hundreds of licensing requirements that cover occupations and services ranging from attorneys to barbers to day care providers.

OCCUPATIONAL LICENSES AND ZONING

Some California counties and cities require you to obtain an occupational license. If you are in a city, you may need both a city and a county license. Businesses that do work in several cities, such as builders, must obtain a license from each city in which they do work. This does not have to be done until you actually begin a job in a particular city.

Licensing requirements of county and city governments can be found by checking with your local city and county. An easy way to get this information is at **www.infospace.com**. This site will give you all city and county offices with appropriate telephone numbers and email addresses.

Be sure to find out if zoning allows your type of business before buying or leasing property. The licensing departments will check the zoning before issuing your license.

If you will be preparing or serving food, you will need to check with the local health department to be sure that the premises comply with their regulations. In some areas, if food has been served on the premises in the past, there is no problem getting a license. If food has never been served on the premises, then the property must comply with all the newest regulations. This can be very costly.

Home Businesses

Problems occasionally arise when people attempt to start businesses in their homes. Small, new businesses cannot afford to pay rent for commercial space, and cities often try to forbid business in residential areas. Getting a county occupational license or advertising a fictitious name often gives notice to the city that a business is being conducted in a residential area.

Some people avoid the problem by starting their businesses without occupational licenses, figuring that the penalties for not having a license (if they are caught) are less expensive than the cost of office space. Others get the county license and ignore the city rules. If a person regularly parks commercial trucks and equipment on his or her property, has delivery trucks coming and going, or has employee cars parked along the street, there will probably be complaints from neighbors and the city will probably take legal action. However, if a person's business consists merely of making phone calls out of the home and keeping supplies there, the problem may never become an issue.

If a problem does arise regarding a home business that does not disturb the neighbors, a good argument can be made that the zoning law that prohibits the business is unconstitutional. When zoning laws were first instituted, they were not meant to stop people from doing things in a residence that had historically been part of the life in a residence. Consider an artist. Should a zoning law prohibit a person from sitting at home and painting pictures? Does selling them for a living there make a difference? Can the government force the artist to rent commercial space just because the artist decides to sell the paintings?

Similar arguments can be made for many home businesses. For hundreds of years people performed income-producing activities in their homes. On the other hand, court battles with a city are expensive and probably not worth the effort for a small business. The best course of action is to keep a low profile. Using a post office box for the business is sometimes helpful in diverting attention away from the residence.

STATE-REGULATED PROFESSIONS

Many professionals require special state licenses. You will probably be called upon to produce such a license when applying for an occupational license.

If you are in a regulated profession, you should be aware of the laws that apply to your profession. You can find out about regulated professions and regulating agencies at your local public library or county law library.

CALIFORNIA STATE LICENSING

California requires some type of license for almost every business. There is a list of the various boards that control the granting, monitoring, suspension, and revocation of licenses. (Cal. Bus. and Prof. Code, Section 101.) The California Technology Trade and Commerce Agency (**http://commerce.ca.gov/state/ttca/ttca_homepage.jsp**) gives you access to permits and licenses.

FEDERAL LICENSES

Few businesses require federal registration. If you are in any of the types of businesses in the following list, you should check with the federal agency listed with it.

- ✪ Radio or television stations or manufacturers of equipment emitting radio waves:

Federal Communications Commission
445 12th Street, SW
Washington, DC 20554
www.fcc.gov

○ Manufacturers of alcohol, tobacco, or firearms:

Bureau of Alcohol, Tobacco, Firearms, and Explosives
Office of Public and Governmental Affairs
650 Massachusetts Avenue, NW
Room 8290
Washington, DC 20226
www.atf.treas.gov

○ Securities brokers and providers of investment advice:

Securities and Exchange Commission
100 F Street, NW
Washington, DC 20549
www.sec.gov

○ Manufacturers of drugs and processors of meat:

Food and Drug Administration
5600 Fishers Lane
Rockville, MD 20857
www.fda.gov

○ Interstate carriers:

Surface Transportation Board
1925 K Street, NW
Washington, DC 20423
www.stb.dot.gov

○ Exporters:

Bureau of Industry and Security
Department of Commerce
14th Street & Constitution Avenue, NW
Washington, DC 20230
www.bis.doc.gov

Contract Laws

As a business owner, you will need to know the basics of forming a simple contract for your transactions with both customers and vendors. There is a lot of misunderstanding about what the law is, and people may give you erroneous information. Relying on it can cost you money. This chapter will give you a quick overview of the principles that apply to your transactions and the pitfalls to avoid. If you face more complicated contract questions, consult a law library or an attorney familiar with small business law.

TRADITIONAL CONTRACT LAW

The simplest definition of a *contract* is: if you promise to do something and the law says that you cannot change your mind and refuse to do it, you have made a contract. This is, obviously, not a technical definition, and there are exceptions. However, the point is that you should not agree to do something unless you have given it some thought.

One of the first things taught in law school is that a contract is not legal unless three elements are present: *offer*, *acceptance*, and *consideration*. The rest of the semester dissects exactly what may be a valid offer, acceptance, and consideration. For your purposes, the important things to remember are the following.

✪ If you make an offer to someone, it may result in a binding contract, even if you change your mind or find out it was a bad deal for you.

✪ Unless an offer is accepted and both parties agree to the same terms, there is no contract.

✪ A contract does not always have to be in writing. Some laws require certain contracts to be in writing, but as a general rule, an oral contract is legal. The problem is proving that the contract existed.

✪ Without *consideration* (the exchange of something of value or mutual promises), there is not a valid contract.

Basic Contract Rules

Some of the most important rules for the business owner are as follows.

✪ *An advertisement is not an offer.* Suppose you put an ad in the newspaper offering "New IBM computers only $995," but there is a typo in the ad and it says $9.95. Can people come in and say "I accept, here's my $9.95," creating a legal contract? Fortunately, no. Courts have ruled that an ad is not an offer that a person can accept. It is an invitation to come in and make offers, which the business can accept or reject.

✪ *The same rule applies to the price tag on an item.* If someone switches price tags on your merchandise, or if you accidentally put the wrong price on it, you are not required by law to sell it at that price. However, many merchants honor a mistaken price, because refusing to do so would constitute bad will and probably lose a customer. If you intentionally put a lower price on an item, intending to require a buyer to pay a higher price, you may be in violation of *bait and switch* laws.

✪ *When a person makes an offer, several things may happen.* It may be accepted, creating a legal contract; it may be rejected; it may expire before it has been accepted; or, it may be withdrawn before acceptance. A contract may expire either by a date made in the offer ("This offer remains open until noon on January 29, 2007") or after a reasonable amount of time. What is *reasonable* is a factual question that a court must decide. If someone makes you an offer to sell goods, clearly you cannot come back five years later and accept. Can you accept a week or a month later and create a legal contract? That depends on the type of goods and the circumstances.

✪ *A person accepting an offer cannot add any terms to it.* If you offer to sell a car for $1,000 and the other party says he or she accepts as long as you put new tires on it, there is no contract. An acceptance with changed terms is considered a rejection and a counteroffer.

✪ *When someone rejects your offer and makes a counteroffer, a contract can be created by your acceptance of the counteroffer.*

These rules can affect your business on a daily basis. Suppose you offer to sell something to one customer over the phone, and five minutes later another customer walks in and offers you more for it. To protect yourself, you should call the first customer and withdraw your offer before accepting the offer of the second customer. If the first customer accepts before you have withdrawn your offer, you may be sued if you sold the item to the second customer. (Be sure to see the subsection on "Firm Offers" on page 65.)

Exceptions There are a few exceptions to the basic rules of contracts. Some of the important exceptions you need to know are as follows.

✪ *Consent to a contract must be voluntary.* If it is made under a threat, the contract is not valid. If a business refuses to give a person's car back unless the customer pays $500 for changing the oil, the customer could probably sue and get the $500 back.

✪ *Contracts to do illegal acts or acts against public policy are not enforceable.* If an electrician signs a contract to put some wiring in a house that is not legal, the customer could probably not force him or her to do it, because the court would refuse to require an illegal act.

✪ *If either party to an offer dies, then the offer expires and cannot be accepted by the heirs.* If a painter is hired to paint a portrait and dies before completing it, his wife, for example, cannot finish it and require payment. However, a corporation does not die, even if its owners die. If a corporation is hired to build a house and the owner dies, the heirs may take over the corporation, finish the job, and require payment.

✪ *Contracts made under misrepresentation are not enforceable.* For example, if someone tells you a car has 35,000 miles on it and you later discover it has 135,000 miles, you may be able to rescind the contract for fraud and misrepresentation.

✪ *If there was a serious mutual mistake a contract may be rescinded.* For example, if both you and the seller thought the car had 35,000 miles on it and both relied on that assumption, the contract could be rescinded if the car had 135,000 miles on it. However, if the seller knew the car has 135,000 miles on it, but you assumed it had 35,000 and did not ask, you probably could not rescind the contract.

Do not rely on these rules to be accurate in every situation. There are both many exceptions as well as interpretations of the facts. If you have a serious contract dispute, contact a lawyer.

STATUTORY CONTRACT LAW

The previous section discussed the basics of contract law. These are not usually stated in statutes, but are the legal principles decided by judges over the past hundreds of years. In recent times, the legislatures have made numerous exceptions to these principles. In most cases, these laws have been passed when the legislature felt that traditional law was not fair.

Statutes of Frauds

All states have laws providing that certain types of contracts must be in writing in order to be enforceable in court. A law stating that a certain type of contract must be in writing is called a *statute of frauds*. California's statutes of frauds are set out in California Civil Code (Cal. Civ. Code), Section 1624 and California Commercial Code (Cal.

Com. Code), Sections 2201 through 2210. According to California Civil Code, Section 1624(a),the following contracts will not be enforced by a court unless they are in writing:

✪ an agreement that by its terms is *not to be performed within one year* from the making thereof;

✪ a special promise to answer for the *debt, default, or miscarriage of another*, except in the cases provided for in Section 2794;

> **NOTE:** *Section 2794 sets out exceptions that are rather complicated. The general rule to remember is that if you agree to pay someone else's debt to benefit yourself rather than the debtor, you do not need a contract in writing.*

✪ an agreement authorizing or employing an agent, broker, or any other person *to purchase or sell real estate*, or to lease real estate for a longer period than one year, or to procure, introduce, or find a purchaser or seller of real estate or a lessee or lessor of real estate where the lease is for a longer period than one year, for compensation or a commission;

✪ an agreement that by its terms is *not to be performed during the lifetime* of the promisor;

✪ an agreement by a purchaser of real property to pay an indebtedness secured by a *mortgage or deed of trust* upon the property purchased, unless assumption of the indebtedness by the purchaser is specifically provided for in the conveyance of the property;

✪ a contract, promise, undertaking, or commitment to loan money or to *grant or extend credit*, in an amount greater than $100,000, not primarily for personal, family, or household purposes, made by a person engaged in the business of lending or arranging for the lending of money or extending credit; and,

✪ an agreement for the leasing of a proprety for a longer period than *one year*, or for the sale of real property or of an interest therein. Such an agreement, if made by an agent of the party sought to be charged, is invalid, unless the authority of the agent is in writing, subscribed by the party sought to be charged.

Also, California Commercial Code, Section 2201 provides:

(1) Except as otherwise provided in this section, a contract for the sale of goods for the price of five hundred dollars ($500) or more is not enforceable by way of action or defense unless there is some writing sufficient to indicate that a contract for sale has been made between the parties and signed by the party against whom enforcement is sought or by his or her authorized agent or broker. A writing is not insufficient because it omits or incorrectly states a term agreed upon, but the contract is not enforceable under this paragraph beyond the quantity of goods shown in the writing.

In order for a contract to be written, it is not necessary that there be the type of document that most people think of when they use the word *contract*. All that is required is that there be some type of writing that shows the basic terms of the agreement, and that the writing be signed by the person being sued for not complying. Such a writing is frequently referred to as a *memorandum* of the agreement. It may be on a single sheet of paper or on two or more pieces of paper (including a series of notes or letters between the two parties that outline the terms of the agreement).

The person who is to be forced to comply is called *the party to be charged*. Therefore, if you read legal texts about contracts, you will usually see references to the requirement that there be "a memorandum of the agreement, signed by the party to be charged or by that party's agent." The writing does not need to be signed by the person who is trying to enforce the agreement—only by the person against whom the writing is being enforced.

There are several exceptions to the statutes of frauds, some of which are fairly complicated. For example, there can be exceptions for those who are considered merchants. The easiest way to avoid problems is to use written contracts for all matters that you consider important. Also, do not make verbal agreements with the idea that you can always change your mind. These agreements may be enforceable, even those listed in the statutes of frauds.

Firm Offers
The *Uniform Commercial Code* (UCC), simply called the *Commercial Code* in California law, covers, among other things, the sale of goods. This is true if you have a one-time garage sale or a large business. The difference is that there are stricter rules for a merchant. A merchant is one who regularly deals in the goods in question. If you had a jewelry store, for example, you would be considered a merchant if you sold a customer a ring. However, if you sold one of your display cases, you would not be considered a merchant because you do not regularly sell display cases.

A very important exception to general contract law created by the code is the *merchant's firm offer*. As the name states, it applies only to merchants. The importance of the law is that it creates an irrevocable offer without consideration. In plain words, if you make a written, signed offer and state that it will remain open, it must remain open for the time stated (or a reasonable time if no time is stated), not to exceed three months. (Cal. Commercial Code Sec. 2205 (a).)

If you wrote to a customer, for example, saying that you will be selling widget model 1234 for the reduced price of $10 for the next month, you must hold that price even though the cost of the widget to you doubles the next day. This is why you always see a note in a sale offer saying that the offer may be withdrawn at any time. It is not because the company making the offer plans to withdraw it. It is a protection against the unexpected. Of course, if your customer writes back (or calls you) and says that he or she does not want any widget, model 1234, your offer has been rejected and it terminates. It is not likely to happen, since there is no reason for a customer to contact you if he or she does not want the product.

NOTE: *Do not think you can avoid this situation by not signing the offer. The law defines a signature as any mark made to authenticate the document. This would include your letterhead.*

Consumer Protection Law
Due to the alleged unfair practices by some types of businesses, laws have been passed controlling the types of contracts they may use. Most notable among these are health clubs and door-to-door

solicitations. The laws covering these businesses usually give the consumer a certain time to cancel the contract. These laws are described in Chapter 13.

PREPARING YOUR CONTRACTS

Before you open your business, you should obtain or prepare the contracts or policies you will use in your business. In some businesses, such as a restaurant, you will not need much. Perhaps you will want a sign near the entrance stating "shirt and shoes required" or "diners must be seated by 10:30 p.m."

However, if you are a building contractor, you will need detailed contracts to use with your customers. If you do not clearly spell out your rights and obligations, you may end up in court and could lose thousands of dollars in profits.

The best way to have an effective contract is to have an attorney experienced in the subject prepare one to meet the needs of your business. However, since this may be too expensive for your new operation, you may want to go elsewhere. Three sources for the contracts you will need are other businesses like yours, trade associations, and legal forms books. You should obtain as many different contracts as possible, compare them, and decide which terms are most comfortable for you.

Insurance

There are few laws requiring you to have insurance, but if you do not have insurance, you may face liability that could ruin your business. You should be aware of the types of insurance available and weigh the risks of a loss against the cost of a policy.

Be aware that there can be a wide range of prices and coverage in insurance policies. You should get at least three quotes from different insurance agents and ask each one to explain the benefits of his or her policy.

Insurance is one of the few areas of starting a business that absolutely requires expert advice. You can keep your own books, do your own hiring, order your materials, and do your own marketing, but you cannot write your own insurance policies.

Find an insurance agent who specializes in small business insurance. The most important things to remember are the following.

- ✪ *Most agents are anxious to sell you insurance.* Over-insuring can be very expensive, especially when you have not started deriving any income from your business. Always ask if the insurance is required.

✪ *You can insure against almost anything.* If the policy does not cover the particular situation you are concerned about, ask about a rider or endorsement. If the answer you get from the agent does not satisfy you, talk to another company.

✪ *Shop wisely.* The best places to start are industry trade groups. Insurance agents familiar with your industry know exactly what you need. Your trade association may have someone you can consult for advice. SCORE is another good source—retired executives usually have the answers or know where to get them. (see Chapter 1.)

The types of insurance discussed in the rest of the chapter are either required or usually recommended.

WORKERS' COMPENSATION

California Labor Code requires every employer except the state to have workers' compensation insurance. (Cal. Lab. Code Sect. 3700.) For a private business, this is done either through an insurance policy from one of the many private insurers who write such policies, or through self-insurance. If you plan to self-insure, you are beyond the scope of this book.

The *State Compensation Insurance Fund* (SCIF), commonly known as State Fund, writes the most policies. The following is how they describe themselves.

> *The California State Fund is a nonprofit, public enterprise fund that operates like a mutual insurance carrier. Unused premium, in excess of operating expenses, claims costs and expenses, and necessary surplus are returned in the form of dividends to policyholders. State Fund has returned in excess of $4.8 billion to its policyholders since its founding—far and away the largest premium return among carriers.*

For a list of local offices, go to the website at **www.scif.com**.

California Division of Workers' Compensation

The law is subject to frequent changes. The California Workers' Compensation Institute (CWCI) offers a sixteen-page booklet called *An Employer's Guide to California Workers' Compensation*, as well as many other informative publications. Order online at **www.cwci.org**, or contact them at:

> 1111 Broadway
> Suite 2350
> Oakland, CA 94607
> 510-251-9470

The State of California Division of Workers' Compensation publishes changes in the law as well as other helpful information. Their headquarters is located at:

> 1515 Clay Street
> 17ᵗʰ Floor
> Oakland, CA 94612
> 510-286-7100

LIABILITY INSURANCE

In most cases, you are not required to carry liability insurance. A notable exception is the limited liability partnership (LLP), which must have liability insurance. There are different amounts required, depending upon the purpose of the LLP (i.e., legal services, accountancy, architecture). The amounts range from $500,000 to $10,000,000. If this applies to your business, see the California Corporations Code, beginning with Section 16956.

Liability insurance can be divided into two main areas—coverage for injuries on your premises and by your employees, and coverage for injuries caused by your products or services.

Coverage for the first type of injury is usually very reasonably priced. Injuries in your business or by your employees (such as in an auto accident) are covered by standard premises or auto policies. However, coverage for injuries caused by products may be harder to find and more expensive.

Asset Protection If insurance is unavailable or unaffordable, you can go without and use a corporation and other asset protection devices to protect yourself from liability. The best way to find out if insurance is available for your type of business is to check with other businesses. If there is a trade group for your industry, their newsletter or magazine may contain ads for insurers.

Umbrella Policy As a business owner, you will be a more visible target for lawsuits, even if there is little merit to them. Lawyers know that a *nuisance suit* is often settled for thousands of dollars. Because of your greater exposure, you should consider getting a *personal umbrella policy*. This is a policy that covers you for claims of up to a million—or even two or five million—dollars, and is very reasonably priced.

HAZARD INSURANCE

One of the worst things that can happen to your business is a fire, flood, or other disaster. With lost customer lists, inventory, and equipment, many businesses have been forced to close after such a disaster.

The premium for insurance protection from such disasters is usually reasonable, and could protect you from loss of your business. You can even get *business interruption* insurance, which will cover your loss of income while your business is getting back on its feet.

HOME BUSINESS INSURANCE

There is a special insurance problem for home businesses. Most homeowner and tenant insurance policies do not cover business activities. In fact, under some policies, you may be denied coverage if you used your home for a business.

If you merely use your home to make business phone calls and send letters, you will probably not have a problem and not need extra coverage. However, if you own equipment or have dedicated a portion of your home exclusively to the business, you could have a problem. Check with your insurance agent for the options that are available to you.

If your business is a sole proprietorship, and you have, say, a computer that you use both personally and for your business, it would probably be covered under your homeowners policy. However, if you incorporated your business and bought the computer in the name of the corporation, coverage might be denied. If a computer is your main business asset, you could get a special insurance policy in the company name covering just the computer.

AUTOMOBILE INSURANCE

If you or any of your employees will be using an automobile for business purposes, be sure that such use is covered. Sometimes a policy may contain an exclusion for business use. Be sure your liability policy covers you if one of your employees causes an accident while running a business errand.

HEALTH INSURANCE

While new businesses can rarely afford health insurance for their employees, the sooner they can obtain it, the better chance they will have to find and keep good employees. As a business owner, you certainly need insurance for yourself (unless you have a working spouse who can cover the family), and you can sometimes get a better rate if you purchase a small business package.

The *Health Insurance Plan of California* (known as *Pacific Health Advantage* or *PacAdvantage*) was established by the legislature in 1993 to provide affordable health coverage to small businesses. Their website is **www.pacadvantage.org**. The phone number for employers is 877-735-5742.

EMPLOYEE THEFT

If you fear that employees may be able to steal from your business, you may want to have them bonded. This means that you pay an insurance company a premium to guarantee employees' honesty, and if they cheat you, the insurance company pays you damages. This can cover all existing and new employees.

Your Business and the Internet

The Internet has opened up a world of opportunities for businesses. It was not long ago that getting national visibility cost a fortune. Today, a business can set up a Web page for a few hundred dollars, and with some clever publicity and a little luck, millions of people around the world will see it.

This new world has new legal issues and new liabilities. Not all of them have been addressed by laws or by the courts. Before you begin doing business on the Internet, you should know the existing rules and the areas where legal issues exist.

DOMAIN NAMES

A *domain name* is the address of your website. For example, www.apple.com is the domain name of Apple Computer Company. The last part of the domain name, the ".com" (or "dot com") is the *top-level domain*, or TLD. Dot com is the most popular, but others are currently available in the United States, including .net and .org. (Originally, .net was only available to network service providers and .org only to nonprofit organizations, but regulations have eliminated those requirements.)

It may seem like most words have been taken as a dot-com name, but if you combine two or three short words or abbreviations, a nearly unlimited number of possibilities are available. For example, if you have a business dealing with automobiles, most likely someone has already registered automobile.com and auto.com. You can come up with all kinds of variations, using adjectives or your name, depending on your type of business:

autos4u.com	joesauto.com	autobob.com
myauto.com	yourauto.com	onlyautos.com
greatauto.com	autosfirst.com	usautos.com
greatautos.com	firstautoworld.com	4autos.com

One site that provides both low-cost registrations and suggestions for name variations is **www.registerfly.com**.

When the Internet first began, some individuals realized that major corporations would soon want to register their names. Since the registration was easy and cheap, people registered names they thought would ultimately be used by someone else.

At first, some companies paid high fees to buy their names from the registrants. One company, Intermatic, filed a lawsuit instead of paying. The owner of the domain name they wanted had registered numerous domain names, such as britishairways.com and ussteel.com. The court ruled that since Intermatic owned a trademark on the name, the registration of their name by someone else violated that trademark, and that Intermatic was entitled to it.

Since then, people have registered names that are not trademarks, such as CalRipkin.com, and have attempted to charge the individuals with those names to buy their domain. In 1998, Congress passed the *Anti-Cybersquatting Consumer Protection Act*, making it illegal to register a domain with no legitimate need to use it.

This law helped a lot of companies protect their names, but then some companies started abusing it and tried to stop legitimate users of names similar to theirs. This is especially likely against small companies. An organization that has been set up to help small companies protect their domains is the *Domain Name Rights Coalition*. Its website is

www.netpolicy.com. Some other good information on domain names can be found at **www.bitlaw.com/internet/domain.html**.

Registering a domain name for your own business is a simple process. There are many companies that offer registration services. For a list of those companies, visit the site of the *Internet Corporation for Assigned Names and Numbers* (ICANN) at **www.icann.org**. You can link directly to any member's site and compare the costs and registration procedures required for the different top-level domains.

WEB PAGES

There are many new companies eager to help you set up a website. Some offer turnkey sites for a low, flat rate, while custom sites can cost tens of thousands of dollars. If you have plenty of capital, you may want to have your site handled by one of these professionals. However, setting up a website is a fairly simple process, and once you learn the basics, you can handle most of it in-house.

If you are new to the Web, you may want to look at **www.learn thenet.com** and **www.webopedia.com**, which will familiarize you with the Internet jargon and give you a basic introduction to the Web.

Site Setup   There are seven steps to setting up a website: site purpose, design, content, structure, programming, testing, and publicity. Whether you do it yourself, hire a professional site designer, or employ a college student, the steps toward creating an effective site are the same.

Before beginning your own site, you should look at other sites, including those of major corporations and of small businesses. Look at the sites of all the companies that compete with you. Look at hundreds of sites and click through them to see how they work (or do not work).

Site purpose. To know what to include on your site, you must decide what its purpose will be. Do you want to take orders for your products or services, attract new employees, give away samples, or show off your company headquarters? You might want to do several of these things.

Site design. After looking at other sites, you can see that there are numerous ways to design a site. It can be crowded, or open and airy; it can have several windows (frames) open at once or just one; and, it can allow long scrolling or just click-throughs.

You will have to decide whether the site will have text only; text plus photographs and graphics; or, text plus photos, graphics, and other design elements, such as animation or Java script. Additionally, you will begin to make decisions about colors, fonts, and the basic graphic appearance of the site.

Site content. You must create the content for your site. For this, you can use your existing promotional materials, new material just for the website, or a combination of the two. Whatever you choose, remember that the written material should be concise, free of errors, and easy for your target audience to read. Any graphics (including photographs) and written materials not created by you require permission. You should obtain such permission from the lawful copyright holder in order to use any copyrighted material. Once you know your site's purpose, look, and content, you can begin to piece the site together.

Site structure. You must decide how the content (text plus photographs, graphics, animation, etc.) will be structured—what content will be on which page, and how a user will link from one part of the site to another. For example, your first page may have the business name and then choices to click on, such as "about us," "opportunities," or "product catalog." Have those choices connect to another page containing the detailed information, so that a user will see the catalog when he or she clicks on "product catalog." Your site could also have an option to click on a link to another website related to yours.

Site programming and setup. When you know nothing about setting up a website, it can seem like a daunting task that will require an expert. However, *programming* here means merely putting a site together. There are inexpensive computer programs available that make it very simple.

Commercial programs such as Microsoft FrontPage, Dreamweaver, Pagemaker, Photoshop, MS Publisher, and PageMill allow you to set up Web pages as easily as laying out a print publication. These programs will convert the text and graphics you create into HTML, the programming language of the Web. Before you choose Web design software and design your site, you should determine which Web hosting service you will use. Make sure that the design software you use is compatible with the host server's system. The Web host is the provider who will give you space on their server and who may provide other services to you, such as secure order processing and analysis of your site to see who is visiting and linking to it.

If you have an America Online (AOL) account, you can download design software and a tutorial for free. You do not have to use AOL's design software in order to use this service. You are eligible to use this site whether you design your own pages, have someone else do the design work for you, or use AOL's templates. This service allows you to use your own domain name and choose the package that is appropriate for your business.

If you have used a page layout program, you can usually get a simple Web page up and running within a day or two. If you do not have much experience with a computer, you might consider hiring a college student to set up a Web page for you.

Site testing. Some of the website setup programs allow you to thoroughly check your new site to see if all the pictures are included and all the links are proper. There are also websites you can go to that will check out your site. Some even allow you to improve your site, such as by reducing the size of your graphics so they download faster. Use a major search engine listed on page 78 to look for companies that can test your site before you launch it on the Web.

Site publicity. Once you set up your website, you will want to get people to look at it. *Publicity* means getting your site noticed as much as possible by drawing people to it.

The first thing to do to get noticed is to be sure your site is registered with as many *search engines* as possible. These are pages that people use to find things on the Internet, such as Yahoo and Google. They do not automatically know about you just because you created a website. You must tell them about your site, and they must examine and catalog it.

For a fee, there are services that will register your site with numerous search engines. If you are starting out on a shoestring, you can easily do it yourself. While there are hundreds of search engines, most people use a dozen or so of the bigger ones. If your site is in a niche area, such as genealogy services, then you would want to be listed on any specific genealogy search engines. Most businesses should be mainly concerned with getting on the biggest ones.

By far the biggest and most successful search engine today is Google (**www.google.com**). Some of the other big ones are:

www.altavista.com	www.hotbot.com
www.excite.com	www.lycos.com
www.fastsearch.com	www.metacrawler.com
www.go.com	www.northernlight.com
www.goto.com	www.webcrawler.com

Most of these sites have a place to click to "add your site" to their system. Some sites charge hundreds of dollars to be listed. If your site contains valuable information that people are looking for, you should be able to do well without paying these fees.

Getting Your Site Known

A *meta tag* is an invisible subject word added to your site that can be found by a search engine. For example, if you are a pest control company, you may want to list all of the scientific names of the pests you control and all of the treatments you have available, but you may not need them to be part of the visual design of your site. List these words as meta tags when you set up your page so people searching for those words will find your site.

Some companies thought that a clever way to get viewers would be to use commonly searched names, or names of major competitors, as meta tags to attract people looking for those big companies. For example, a small delivery service that has nothing to do with UPS or FedEx might use those company names as meta tags so people looking for them would find the smaller company. While it may sound like a good idea, it has been declared illegal trademark infringement. Today, many companies have computer programs scanning the Internet for improper use of their trademarks.

Once you have made sure that your site is passively listed in all the search engines, you may want to actively promote your site. However, self-promotion is seen as a bad thing on the Internet, especially if its purpose is to make money.

Newsgroups are places on the Internet where people interested in a specific topic can exchange information. For example, expectant mothers have a group where they can trade advice and experiences. If you have a product that would be great for expectant mothers, that would be a good place for it to be discussed. However, if you log into the group and merely announce your product, suggesting people order it from your website, you will probably be *flamed* (sent a lot of hate mail).

If you join the group, however, and become a regular, and in answer to someone's problem, mention that you "saw this product that might help," your information will be better received. It may seem unethical to plug your product without disclosing your interest, but this is a procedure used by many large companies. They hire *buzz agents* to plug their product all over the Internet and create positive *buzz* for the product. So, perhaps it has become an acceptable marketing method and consumers know to take plugs with a grain of salt. Let your conscience be your guide.

Keep in mind that Internet publicity works both ways. If you have a great product and people love it, you will get a lot of business. If you sell a shoddy product, give poor service, and do not keep your customers happy, bad publicity on the Internet can kill your business. Besides being an equalizer between large and small companies, the Internet can be a filtering mechanism between good and bad products.

Spamming   Sending unsolicited email advertising (called *spam*) started out as a mere breach of Internet etiquette (netiquette), but has now become a state and federal crime. The ability to reach millions of people with advertising at virtually no cost was too good for too many businesses to pass up, and this resulted in the clogging of most users' email boxes and near shutdown of some computer systems. Some people ended up with thousand of offers every day.

To prevent this, many states passed anti-spamming laws and Congress passed the CAN-SPAM Act. This law:

- ✪ bans misleading or false headers on email;

- ✪ bans misleading subject lines;

- ✪ requires allowing recipients to opt out of future mailings;

- ✪ requires the email be identified as advertising; and,

- ✪ requires the email include a valid physical address.

Each violation can result in up to an $11,000 fine, and the fines can be raised if advertisers violate other rules, such as not harvesting names and not using permutations of existing names. More information can be found on the Federal Trade Commission's website (**www.ftc.gov**).

In addition, you may be sued by the attorney general of California and anyone who receives the unsolicited advertising. Liability in California can be as high as $1,000,000. The applicable statutes are Sections 17529 and 17538 of the Business and Professions Code.

Advertising Advertising on the Internet has grown in recent years. At first, small, thin, rectangular ads appeared at the top of websites. These are called *banner ads*. Lately, they have grown bigger, can appear anywhere on the site, and usually blink or show a moving visual.

The fees can be based on how many people view an ad, how many click on it, or both. Some larger companies, such as Amazon.com, have affiliate programs in which they will pay a percentage of a purchase if a customer comes from your site to theirs and makes a purchase. For sites that have thousands of visitors, the ads have been profitable—some sites reportedly make over $100,000 a year.

Example:
One financially successful site is Manolo's Shoe Blog (http://shoeblogs.com). It is written by a man who loves shoes, has a great sense of humor, and writes in endearing broken

English. Because he is an expert in his field, his suggestions are taken by many readers who click through to the products and purchase them.

LEGAL ISSUES

Before you set up a Web page, you should consider the many legal issues associated with it.

Jurisdiction

Jurisdiction is the power of a court in a particular location to decide a particular case. Usually, you have to have been physically present in a jurisdiction or have done business there before you can be sued there. Since the Internet extends your business's ability to reach people in faraway places, there may be instances when you could be subject to legal jurisdiction far from your own state (or country). There are a number of cases that have been decided in this country regarding the Internet and jurisdiction, but very few cases have been decided on this issue outside of the United States.

In most instances, U.S. courts use the pre-Internet test—whether you have been present in another jurisdiction or have had enough contact with someone in the other jurisdiction. The fact that the Internet itself is not a place will not shield you from being sued in another state when you have shipped your company's product there, have entered into a contract with a resident of that state, or have defamed a foreign resident with content on your website.

According to the courts, there is a spectrum of contact required between you, your website, and consumers or audiences. (*Zippo Manufacturing Co. v. Zippo Dot Com, Inc.,* 952 F. Supp. 1119 (W.D. Pa 1997).) The more interactive your site is with consumers, the more you target an audience for your goods in a particular location, and the farther you reach to send your goods out into the world, the more it becomes possible for someone to sue you outside of your own jurisdiction—so weigh these risks against the benefits when constructing and promoting your website.

The law is not even remotely final on these issues. The American Bar Association, among other groups, is studying this topic in detail. At present, no final, global solution or agreement about jurisdictional issues with websites exists.

One way to protect yourself from the possibility of being sued in a far-away jurisdiction would be to state on your website that those using the site or doing business with you agree that "jurisdiction for any actions regarding this site" or your company will be in your home county.

For extra protection, you can have a preliminary page that must be clicked before entering your website. However, this may be overkill for a small business with little risk of lawsuits. If you are in any business for which you could have serious liability, you should review some competitors' sites and see how they handle the liability issue. They often have a place to click for "legal notice" or "disclaimer" on their first page.

You may want to consult with an attorney to discuss the specific disclaimer you will use on your website, where it should appear, and whether you will have users of your site actively agree to this disclaimer or just passively read it. However, these disclaimers are not enforceable everywhere in the world. Until there is global agreement on jurisdictional issues, this may remain an area of uncertainty for some time to come.

Libel   *Libel* is any publication that injures the reputation of another. This can occur in print, writing, pictures, or signs. All that is required for publication is that you transmit the material to at least one other person who is not the person claiming to have libeled. When putting together your website, you must keep in mind that it is visible to millions of people all over the planet, and that if you libel a person or company, you may have to pay damages. Many countries do not have the freedom of speech that we do, and a statement that is not libelous in the United States may be libelous elsewhere. If you are concerned about this, alter the content of your site or check with an attorney about libel laws in the country you think might take action against you.

Copyright Infringement   It is so easy to copy and borrow information on the Internet that it is easy to infringe copyrights without even knowing it. A *copyright* exists for a work as soon as the creator creates it. There is no need to register the copyright or to put a copyright notice on it. Therefore, practically everything on the Internet belongs to someone.

Some people freely give their works away. For example, many people have created Web artwork (*gifs* and *animated gifs*) that they freely allow people to copy. There are numerous sites that provide hundreds or thousands of free gifs that you can add to your Web pages. Some require you to acknowledge the source and some do not. You should always be sure that the works are free for the taking before using them.

Linking and Framing   One way to violate copyright laws is to improperly link other sites to yours, either directly or with framing. *Linking* is when you provide a link that takes the user to the linked site. *Framing* occurs when you set up your site so that when you link to another site, your site is still viewable as a frame around the linked-to site.

While many sites are glad to be linked to others, some—especially providers of valuable information—object. Courts have ruled that linking and framing can be a copyright violation. One rule that has developed is that it is usually okay to link to the first page of a site, but not to link to some valuable information deeper within the site. The rationale for this is that the owner of the site wants visitors to go through the various levels of their site (viewing all the ads) before getting the information. By linking directly to the information, you are giving away their product without the ads.

The problem with linking to the first page of a site is that it may be a tedious or difficult task to find the needed page from there. Many sites are poorly designed and make it nearly impossible to find anything.

If you wish to link to another page, the best solution is to ask permission. Email the Webmaster or other person in charge of the site, if an email address is given, and explain what you want to do. If they grant permission, be sure to print out a copy of their email for your records.

Privacy   Since the Internet is such an easy way to share information, there are many concerns that it will cause a loss of individual privacy. The two main concerns arise when you post information that others consider private, and when you gather information from customers and use it in a way that violates their privacy.

While public actions of politicians and celebrities are fair game, details about their private lives are sometimes protected by law, and details about people who are not public figures are often protected. The laws in each state are different, and what might be allowable in one state could be illegal in another. If your site will provide any personal information about individuals, you should discuss the possibility of liability with an attorney.

Several well-known companies have been in the news lately for violations of their customers' privacy. They either shared what the customer was buying or downloading, or looked for additional information on the customer's computer. To let customers know that you do not violate certain standards of privacy, you can subscribe to one of the privacy codes that have been created for the Internet. These allow you to put a symbol on your site guaranteeing to your customers that you follow the code.

The following are the websites of two organizations that offer this service, and their fees at the time of this publication.

www.privacybot.com	$100
www.bbbonline.com	$200 to $7,000

Protecting Yourself   The easiest way to protect yourself personally from the various possible types of liability is to set up a corporation or limited liability company to own the website. This is not foolproof protection since, in some cases, you could be sued personally as well, but it is one level of protection.

COPPA   If your website is aimed at children under the age of thirteen, or if it attracts children of that age, then you are subject to the federal *Children Online Privacy Protection Act of 1998* (COPPA). This law requires such websites to:

❂   give notice on the site of what information is being collected;

❂   obtain verifiable parental consent to collect the information;

✪   allow the parent to review the information collected;

✪   allow the parent to delete the child's information or to refuse to allow the use of the information;

✪   limit the information collected to only that necessary to participate on the site; and,

✪   protect the security and confidentiality of the information.

HIRING A WEBSITE DESIGNER

If you hire someone to design your website, you should make sure of what rights you are buying. Under copyright law, when you hire someone to create a work, you do not get all rights to that work unless you clearly spell that out in a written agreement.

For example, if your designer creates an artistic design to go on your website, you may have to pay extra if you want to use the same design on your business cards or letterhead. Depending on how the agreement is worded, you may even have to pay a yearly fee for the rights.

If you spend a lot of money promoting your business, and a logo or design becomes important to your image, you would not want to have to pay royalties for the life of your business to someone who spent an hour or two putting together a design. Whenever you purchase a creative work from someone, be sure to get a written statement of what rights you are buying. If you are not receiving all rights for all uses for all time you should think twice about the purchase.

If the designer also is involved with hosting your site, you should be sure you have the right to take the design with you if you move to another host. You should get a backup of your site on a CD in case it is ever lost or you need to move it to another site.

FINANCIAL TRANSACTIONS

The existing services for sending money over the Internet, such as PayPal, usually offer more risk and higher fees than traditional credit card processing. Under their service agreements, you usually must agree that they can freeze your account at any time and can take money out of your bank account at any time. Some do not offer an appeal process. Before signing up for any of these services, you should read their service agreement carefully and check the Internet for other peoples' experiences with them.

For now, the easiest way to exchange money on the Internet is through traditional credit cards. Because of concerns that email can be abducted in transit and read by others, most companies use a secure site in which customers are guaranteed that their card data is encrypted before being sent.

When setting up your website, you should ask the provider if you can be set up with a secure site for transmitting credit card data. If they cannot provide it, you will need to contract with another software provider. Use one of the major search engines listed on page 78 to look for companies that provide credit card services to businesses on the Internet.

As a practical matter, there is very little to worry about when sending credit card data by email. If you do not have a secure site, another option is to allow purchasers to fax or phone in their credit card data. However, keep in mind that this extra step will lose some business unless your products are unique and your buyers are very motivated.

The least effective option is to provide an order form on the site that can be printed out and mailed in with a check. Again, your customers must be really motivated or they will lose interest after finding out this extra work is involved.

FTC RULES

Because the Internet is an instrument of interstate commerce, it is a legitimate subject for federal regulation. The Federal Trade Commission (FTC) first said that all of its consumer protection rules applied to the Internet, but lately it has been adding specific rules and issuing publications. The following publications are available from the FTC website at **www.ftc.gov/bcp/menu-internet.htm** or by mail from:

Consumer Response Center
Federal Trade Commission
600 Pennsylvania, NW
Room H-130
Washington, DC 20580

✪ *Advertising and Marketing on the Internet: The Rules of the Road*

✪ *Appliance Labeling Rule Homepage*

✪ *BBB-Online: Code of Online Business Practices*

✪ *Big Print. Little Print. What's the Deal? How to Disclose the Details*

✪ *Businessperson's Guide to the Mail and Telephone Order Merchandise Rule*

✪ *CAN-SPAM Act: Requirements for Commercial Emailers*

✪ *Complying with the Telemarketing Sales Rule*

✪ *Disclosing Energy Efficiency Information: A Guide for Online Sellers of Appliances*

✪ *Dot Com Disclosures: Information About Online Advertising*

✪ *Electronic Commerce: Selling Internationally. A Guide for Business*

✪ *How to Comply With The Children's Online Privacy Protection Rule*

✪ *Frequently Asked Questions About the Children's Online Privacy Protection Rule*

✪   *Internet Auctions: A Guide for Buyer and Sellers*

✪   *"Remove Me" Responses and Responsibilities: Email Marketers Must Honor "Unsubscribe" Claims*

✪   *Securing Your Server—Shut the Door on Spam*

✪   *Security Check: Reducing Risks to Your Computer Systems*

✪   *Selling on the Internet: Prompt Delivery Rules*

✪   *TooLate.Com: The Lowdown on Late Internet Shipments*

✪   *Website Woes: Avoiding Web Service Scams*

✪   *What's Dot and What's Not: Domain Name Registration Scams*

✪   *You, Your Privacy Policy & COPPA*

FRAUD

Because the Internet is somewhat anonymous, it is a tempting place for those with fraudulent schemes to look for victims. As a business consumer, you should exercise caution when dealing with unknown or anonymous parties on the Internet.

The U.S. Department of Justice, the FBI, and the National White Collar Crime Center jointly launched the Internet Crime Complaint Center (ICCC). If you suspect that you are the victim of fraud online, whether as a consumer or a business, you can report incidents to the ICCC on their website, **www.ic3.gov**. The ICCC is currently staffed by FBI agents and representatives of the National White Collar Crime Center, and will work with state and local law enforcement officials to prevent, investigate, and prosecute high-tech and economic crime online.

Health and Safety Laws

As a reaction to the terrible work conditions prevalent in the factories and mills of the nineteenth century industrial age, Congress and the states developed many laws intended to protect the health and safety of the nation's workers. These laws are difficult to understand and often seem to be very unfair to employers. Therefore, this is an area that you need to pay particular attention to as a new business. Failure to do so can result in terrible consequences for you.

FEDERAL LAWS

The federal government's laws regarding health and safety of workers are far-reaching and very important to consider in running your business, especially if you are a manufacturer or in the oil and gas, food production, or agriculture industries.

OSHA The point of the *Occupational Safety and Health Administration* (OSHA) is to place the duty on the employer to keep the workplace free from recognized hazards that are likely to cause death or serious bodily injury to workers. The regulations are not as cumbersome for small businesses as for larger enterprises. If you have ten or fewer employees, or if you are in a certain type of business, you do not have to keep a record of illnesses, injuries, and exposure to hazardous substances of employees. If you have eleven or more employees, OSHA's rules will apply. One important rule to know is that within forty-eight hours of an on-the-job death of an employee or injury of five or more employees on the job, the area director of OSHA must be contacted.

In California the CAL/OSHA Consultation Service Office is located at:

> 45 Freemond Street
> Suite 1260
> San Francisco, CA 94105
> 415-972-8515

You can also visit their website, **www.osha.gov**, to obtain copies of their publications, *OSHA Handbook for Small Business* (OSHA 2209) and *OSHA Publications and Audiovisual Programs Catalog* (OSHA 2019). They also have a poster that is required to be posted in the workplace. Find it at **www.osha.gov/publications/poster.html**.

The *Hazard Communication Standard* requires that employees be made aware of the hazards in the workplace. (Code of Federal Regulations (C.F.R.), Title 29, Section (Sec.) 1910.1200.) It is especially applicable to those working with chemicals, but this can even include offices that use copy machines. Businesses using hazardous chemicals must have a comprehensive program for informing employees of the hazards and for protecting them from contamination.

For more information, you can contact OSHA at the previously-mentioned addresses, phone numbers, or websites. They can supply a copy of the regulation and a booklet called *OSHA 3084,* which explains the law.

EPA   The *Worker Protection Standard for Agricultural Pesticides* requires safety training, decontamination sites, and of course, posters. The *Environmental Protection Agency* (EPA) will provide information on compliance with this law. They can be reached at 800-490-9198, or on their website at **www.epa.gov**.

They can also be reached by mail at:

U.S. Environmental Protection Agency
75 Hawthorne Street
San Francisco, CA 94105

FDA   The *Pure Food and Drug Act of 1906* prohibits the misbranding or adulteration of food and drugs. It also created the *Food and Drug Administration* (FDA), which has promulgated many regulations and which must give permission before a new drug can be introduced into the market. If you will be dealing with any food or drugs, you should keep abreast of their policies. Their website is **www.fda.gov**. The FDA's small business site is **www.fda.gov/ora/fed_state/small_business**, and their regional small business representative is at:

Food and Drug Administration
Pacific Region
1301 Clay Street
Suite 1180 N
Oakland, CA 94612
510-637-3960
Fax: 510-637-3976

Hazardous   There are regulations that control the shipping and packing of haz-
Materials   ardous materials. For more information, contact:
Transportation

Office of Hazardous Materials Safety
400 Seventh Street, SW
Washington, DC 20590
202-366-0656

For an organizational structure and phone contacts, visit **http://hazmat.dot.gov/contact/org/org&ct.htm**.

CPSC   The *Consumer Product Safety Commission* (CPSC) has a set of rules that cover the safety of products. The commission feels that because its rules cover products, rather than people or companies, they apply to everyone producing such products. However, federal laws do not apply to small businesses that do not affect interstate commerce.

Whether a small business would fall under a CPSC rule would depend on the size and nature of your business.

The CPSC rules are contained in the Code of Federal Regulations, Title 16 in the following parts.

Product	Part
Antennas, CB, and TV	1402
Architectural Glazing Material	1201
Articles Hazardous to Children Under 3	1501
Baby Cribs—Full Size	1508
Baby Cribs—Non-Full Size	1509
Bicycle Helmets	1203
Bicycles	1512
Carpets and Rugs	1630, 1631
Cellulose Insulation	1209, 1404
Cigarette Lighters	1210
Citizens Band Base Station Antennas	1204
Coal and Wood Burning Appliances	1406
Consumer Products Containing Chlorofluorocarbons	1401
Electrically Operated Toys	1505
Emberizing Materials Containing Asbestos (banned)	1305
Extremely Flammable Contact Adhesives (banned)	1302
Fireworks	1507
Garage Door Openers	1211
Hazardous Lawn Darts (banned)	1306
Hazardous Substances	1500
Human Subjects	1028
Lawn Mowers, Walk-Behind	1205
Lead-Containing Paint (banned)	1303
Matchbooks	1202
Mattresses	1632
Pacifiers	1511
Patching Compounds Containing Asbestos (banned)	1304
Poisons	1700
Rattles	1510
Self-Pressurized Consumer Products	1401
Sleepwear—Children's	1615, 1616
Swimming Pool Slides	1207
Toys, Electrical	1505
Unstable Refuse Bins (banned)	1301

Search the CPSC's site at **www.cpsc.gov** for more information on these rules.

Additional Regulations

Every day there are proposals for new laws and regulations. It would be impossible to include every conceivable one in this book. To be up-to-date on the laws that affect your type of business, you should belong to a trade association for your industry and subscribe to newsletters that cover your industry. Attending industry conventions is a good way to learn more about federal regulations and to discover new ways to increase your profits.

CALIFORNIA LAWS

In additional to federal laws, the State of California has statutes and regulations designed to protect the health and safety of workers and consumers.

Hazardous Occupations

California distinguishes between *high hazard employers*, *intermittent worker employers*, and *non-high hazard employers* in determining what is necessary for the employer to do to minimize the risk to employees. The designation is sometimes established not by the type of industry, but by the tasks of the employees.

For further information on workplace safety, publications such as *Injury and Illness Prevention Program* are available on the CAL/OSHA website at **www.dir.ca.gov/dosh/PubOrder.asp**. You can download publications or fill out a form on the site to receive publications by mail. The site also offers consultation online, at CAL/OSHA offices, or at your business. Bringing CAL/OSHA to your business should be a last resort, as they may find more things to fix than you believe are necessary.

Smoking

Smoking is not allowed in any enclosed place of employment in the state. (Cal. Labor Code, Section 6404.5.)

There are still a few exceptions to the smoking laws. However, local laws may prohibit smoking, even if state law allows it. An employer can prohibit smoking in the workplace regardless of the state or local laws. You can set aside a smoking lounge under state law. See the code for the requirements.

Employment and Labor Laws

As they have with health and safety laws, Congress and the states have heavily regulated the actions that employers can take with regard to hiring and firing, improper employment practices, and discrimination. Because the penalties can be severe, educate yourself on the proper actions to take and consult a labor and employment lawyer if necessary, prior to making important employee decisions. You may want to use the **APPLICATION FOR EMPLOYMENT** found on page 247 when potential employees apply for the job.

HIRING AND FIRING LAWS

For small businesses, there are not many rules regarding who you may hire or fire. The ancient law that an employee can be fired at any time (or may quit at any time) still prevails for small businesses. In certain situations and as you grow, however, you will come under a number of laws that affect your hiring and firing practices.

One of the most important things to consider when hiring someone is that if you fire him or her, that fired employee may be entitled to unemployment compensation. If so, your unemployment compensation tax rate will go up and it can cost you a lot of money. Therefore, you should only hire people you are sure you will keep, and you should avoid situations where your former employees can make claims against your company.

One way this can be done is by hiring only part-time employees. The drawback to this is that you may not be able to attract the best employees. When hiring dishwashers or busboys this may not be an issue, but when hiring someone to develop a software product, you do not want him or her to leave halfway through the development.

A better solution is to screen applicants to begin with and only hire those who you feel certain will work out. Of course, this is easier said than done. Some people interview well, but then turn out to be incompetent at the job.

The best record to look for is someone who has stayed a long time at each of his or her previous jobs. Next best is someone who has not stayed as long (for good reasons), but has always been employed. The worst type of hire would be someone who is or has been collecting unemployment compensation.

The reason those who have collected compensation are a bad risk is that if they collect in the future, even if it is not your fault, your employment of them could make you chargeable for their claim. For example, you hire someone who has been on unemployment compensation and he or she works out well for a year, but then quits to take another job and is fired after a few weeks. In this situation, you would be chargeable for most of his or her claim, because the last five quarters of work are analyzed. Look for a steady job history.

Often, the intelligence of an employee is more important than his or her experience. An employee with years of typing experience may be fast, but unable to figure out how to use your new computer, whereas an intelligent employee can learn the equipment quickly and eventually gain speed. Of course, common sense is important in all situations.

The bottom line is that you cannot know if an employee will be able to fill your needs from a résumé and interview. Once you have found someone who you think will work out, offer that person a job with a ninety-day probationary period. If you are not completely satisfied with the employee after the ninety days, offer to extend the probationary period for ninety additional days rather than end the relationship immediately. Of course, all of this should be in writing.

Background Checks

Beware that a former boss of a prospective employee may be a good friend or even a relative. It has always been considered acceptable to exaggerate on résumés, but in recent years, some applicants have been found to be completely fabricating sections of their education and experience. Checking references is important.

Polygraph Tests

Under the federal *Employee Polygraph Protection Act,* you cannot require an employee or prospective employee to take a polygraph test unless you are in the armored car, guard, or pharmaceutical business.

Drug Tests

Under the *Americans with Disabilities Act* (ADA), drug testing can only be required of applicants who have been offered jobs conditioned upon passing the drug test. Random drug testing is no longer used in California. Companies with twenty-five or more employees must make a reasonable effort to accommodate an employee who wants to enter a drug rehabilitation program. Reasonable effort does not mean paying for the program or giving paid time off to the employee. However, if the employee does have accumulated sick time, the employer must allow the employee to use it.

FIRING

In most cases, unless you have a contract with an employee for a set time period, you can fire him or her at any time. This is only fair, since the employee can quit at any time. This type of employment is called *at will.* You should make it clear when offering a job to someone that, upon acceptance, he or she will be an at-will employee. The exceptions to this are if you fired someone based on illegal discrimination, for filing some sort of health or safety complaint, or for refusing your sexual advances.

NEW HIRE REPORTING

In order to track down parents who do not pay child support, a federal law was passed in 1996 that requires the reporting of new hires.

The *Personal Responsibility and Work Opportunity Reconciliation Act of 1996* (PRWORA) provides that such information must be reported by employers to their state government.

Within twenty days of hiring a new employee, an employer must provide the state with information about the employee, including the name, Social Security number, and address. This information can be submitted in several ways, including mail, fax, magnetic tape, or over the Internet. There is a special form that can be used for this reporting; however, an employer can simply use the **EMPLOYEE'S WITHHOLDING ALLOWANCE CERTIFICATE (IRS FORM W-4)** for this purpose. (see form 7, p.267.) Since this form must be filled out for all employees anyway, it would be pointless to use a separate form for the new hire reporting. A copy of the **IRS FORM W-4** is included in Appendix B.

For more information about the program, you can call the Employment Development Department at 888-745-3886.

EMPLOYMENT AGREEMENTS

To avoid misunderstandings with employees, you should use an employment agreement or an employee handbook. These can spell out in detail the policies of your company and the rights of your employees. These agreements can protect your trade secrets and spell out clearly that employment can be terminated at any time by either party.

Make sure that your agreement is fair and clear, because you have the upper hand in this situation and you would not want a court to find that you abused that bargaining power with an unreasonable employee agreement.

If having an employee sign an agreement is awkward, you can usually obtain the same rights by putting the company policies in an employee manual. Each existing and new employee should be given a copy along with a letter stating that the rules apply to all employees, and that by accepting or continuing employment at your company, they agree to abide by the rules. Having an employee sign a receipt for the letter and manual is proof that he or she received it.

One danger of an employment agreement or handbook is that it may be interpreted to create a long-term employment contract. To avoid this, be sure that you clearly state in the agreement or handbook that the employment is at will and can be terminated at any time by either party.

Some other things to consider in an employment agreement or handbook are:

- what the salary and other compensation will be;

- what the hours of employment will be;

- what the probationary period will be;

- that the employee cannot sign any contracts binding the employer; and,

- that the employee agrees to arbitration rather than filing a lawsuit if serious disagreements arise.

INDEPENDENT CONTRACTORS

One way to avoid problems with employees and taxes at the same time is to have all of your work done through independent contractors. This can relieve you of most of the burdens of employment laws, as well as the obligation to pay Social Security and Medicare taxes for the workers.

An independent contractor is, in effect, a separate business that you pay to do a job. You pay them just as you pay any company from which you buy products or services. At the end of the year, if the amount paid exceeds $600, you must issue a 1099 form, which is similar to the W-2 that you would issue to employees.

This may seem too good to be true, and in some situations it is. The IRS does not like arrangements involving independent contractors, because it is too easy for the independent contractors to cheat on their taxes. To limit the use of independent contractors, the IRS has strict regulations on who may and may not be classified as an independent contractor. Also, companies who do not appear to pay enough in wages for their field of business are audited.

Using independent contractors for jobs not traditionally done by independent contractors puts you at high risk for an IRS audit. For example, you could not get away with hiring a secretary as an independent contractor. One of the most important factors considered in determining if a worker can be an independent contractor is the amount of control the company has over his or her work. If you take your typing needs to a typing service, you are obviously dealing with an independent contractor. If you require a person to type in your office during certain hours, and you set the times for lunch and other breaks, you are going to have difficulty classifying that person as something other than an employee.

The IRS has a form you can use in determining if a person is an employee or an independent contractor, called **DETERMINATION OF WORKER STATUS (IRS FORM SS-8)**. It is included in Appendix B of this book, along with instructions. (see form 6, p.261.)

Independent Contractors vs. Employees

In deciding whether to make use of independent contractors or employees, you should weigh the following advantages and disadvantages of hiring an independent contractor.

Advantages.

✪ *Lower taxes.* You do not have to pay Social Security, Medicare, unemployment, or other employee taxes.

✪ *Less paperwork.* You do not have to handle federal withholding deposits or the monthly employer returns to the state or federal government.

✪ *Less insurance.* You do not have to pay workers' compensation insurance or insurance against their possible liabilities.

✪ *More flexibility.* You can use independent contractors only when you need them.

Disadvantages.

✪ *IRS scrutiny.* The IRS and state tax offices are strict about which workers can be qualified as independent contractors. They will audit companies whose use of independent contractors does not appear to be legitimate.

✪ *Stiff penalties.* If your use of independent contractors is found to be improper, you may have to pay back taxes and penalties, and may have problems with your pension plan.

✪ *Greater risk of lawsuit.* While employees may be covered by workers' compensation, independent contractors are not. You must have insurance to protect you should you be sued if one is injured, harassed, etc.

✪ *Fewer rights to the work.* If you are paying someone to produce a creative work (writing, photography, artwork), you receive fewer rights to the work of an independent contractor.

✪ *Less control.* You have less control over the work of an independent contractor and less flexibility in terminating him or her if you are not satisfied that the job is being done the way you require.

✪ *Less loyalty.* You have less loyalty from an independent contractor who works sporadically for you and possibly others than you have from your own full-time employees.

For some businesses, the advantages outweigh the disadvantages. For others, they do not. Consider your business plans and the consequences from each type of arrangement. Keep in mind that it will be easier to start with independent contractors and switch to employees than to hire employees and have to fire them to hire independent contractors.

TEMPORARY WORKERS

Another way to avoid the hassles of hiring employees is to get workers from a temporary agency. In this arrangement, you may pay a higher amount per hour for the work, but the agency will take care of all of the tax and insurance requirements. Since these can be expensive and time-consuming, the extra cost may be well worth it.

Whether or not temporary workers will work for you depends upon the type of business you are in and tasks you need performed. For such jobs as sales management, you would probably want someone who will stay with you long-term and develop relationships with the buyers, but for order fulfillment, temporary workers might work out well.

Another advantage of temporary workers is that you can easily stop using those who do not work out well for you. Conversely, if you find one who is ideal, you may be able to hire him or her on a full-time basis.

In recent years, a new wrinkle has developed in the temporary worker area. Many large companies are beginning to use them because they are so much cheaper than paying the benefits demanded by full-time employees. For example, Microsoft Corp. had as many as 6,000 temporary workers, some of whom worked for them for years. Some of the temporary workers won a lawsuit that declared they are really employees and are entitled to the same benefits of other employees (such as pension plans).

The law is not yet settled in this area, regarding what arrangements will result in a temporary worker being declared an employee. That will take several more court cases, some of which have already been filed. A few things you can do to protect yourself include the following.

❂   Be sure that any of your benefit plans make it clear that they do not apply to workers obtained through temporary agencies.

❂   Do not keep the same temporary workers for longer than a year.

❂   Do not list temporary workers in any employee directories or hold them out to the public as your employees.

❂   Do not allow them to use your business cards or stationery.

✪ Pay temporary workers who work for you for ninety or more nonconsecutive days the same as employees you have doing similar work. If this creates an unwanted increased cost, limit employment to less than ninety days for the same worker. Consider, however, that a person who knows your company and the job from working there for ninety days or more often may be worth the increase.

CHILD AND SPOUSAL SUPPORT

If an employee owes support to a spouse or child, you may receive a *wage assignment,* requiring you to deduct the support amount from his or her wages. For further information, contact the California Department of Child Support Services. You can read their handbook at **www.childsup.cahwnet.gov**.

The site will also allow you to obtain the address of local offices. Click on "contact local offices" and click on your county. In 2006, the system will be changed with the creation of the *State Disbursement Unit* (SDU). The SDU will handle all child support disbursements. The website will keep you informed of the changes, and the SDU will send you notice by mail. Until then, the wage assignment you receive will give instructions as to where to send the money.

DISCRIMINATION LAWS

There are numerous federal laws forbidding discrimination based upon race, sex, pregnancy, color, religion, national origin, age, or disability. The laws apply to both hiring and firing, and to employment practices such as salaries, promotions, and benefits. Most of these laws only apply to an employer who has fifteen or more employees for twenty weeks of a calendar year, or has federal contracts or subcontracts. Therefore, you most likely will not be required to comply with the law immediately upon opening your business. However, there are similar state laws that may apply to your business that have a lower employee threshold.

One exception to the fifteen or more employees rule is the *Equal Pay Act*. This act applies to employers with two or more employees, and requires that women be paid the same as men in the same type of job.

Employers with fifteen or more employees are required to display a poster regarding discrimination. This poster is available from the Equal Employment Opportunity Commission on their website at **www.dol.gov/esa/regs/compliance/posters/eeo.htm**. Employers with one hundred or more employees are required to file an annual report with the EEOC.

Discriminatory Interview Questions

When hiring employees, some questions are illegal or inadvisable to ask. The following data *should not* be collected on your employment application or in your interviews, unless the information is somehow directly tied to the duties of the job.

✪ Do not ask about an applicant's citizenship or place of birth. However, after hiring an employee, you must ask about his or her right to work in this country.

✪ Do not ask a female applicant her maiden name. You can ask if she has been known by any other name in order to do a background check.

✪ Do not ask if applicants have children, plan to have them, or have child care. You can ask if an applicant will be able to work the required hours.

✪ Do not ask if the applicant has religious objections for working Saturday or Sunday. You can mention if the job requires such hours and ask whether the applicant can meet this job requirement.

✪ Do not ask an applicant's age. You can ask if an applicant is age 18 or over, or if it is a liquor-related job, you can ask if the applicant is age 21 or over.

✪ Do not ask an applicant's weight.

✪ Do not ask if an applicant has AIDS or is HIV positive.

- Do not ask if the applicant has filed a workers' compensation claim.

- Do not ask about the applicant's previous health problems.

- Do not ask if the applicant is married or whether the spouse would object to the job, hours, or duties.

- Do not ask if the applicant owns a home, furniture, or car, as it is considered racially discriminatory.

- Do not ask if the applicant was ever arrested. You can ask if the applicant was ever convicted of a crime.

ADA Under the Americans with Disabilities Act (ADA), employers who do not make *reasonable accommodations* for disabled employees will face fines of up to $100,000, as well as other civil penalties and civil damage awards.

While the goal of creating more opportunities for the disabled is a good one, the result has put all of the costs of achieving this goal on businesses that are faced with disabled applicants. In fact, studies done since the law was passed have shown that employers have hired fewer disabled applicants than before the law was passed, possibly due to the costs of reasonable accommodations and the fear of being taken to court.

The ADA is very vague. When it passed, some feared it could be taken to ridiculous lengths—such as forcing companies to hire blind applicants for jobs that require reading, and then forcing them to hire people to read for the blind employees. In the years since its enactment, some of the critics' fears have been met. In some famous rulings, the EEOC said:

- rude, disruptive, and chronically late employees could be protected by the ADA if they had some type of mental disability;

- recovering drug addicts and alcoholics are protected by the ADA;

- obesity can be a disability covered by the ADA;

✪ workers who are disturbed by the sight of other workers because of emotional imbalance must be given private work areas; and,

✪ airlines cannot discriminate against persons blind in one eye when hiring pilots.

When the ADA was passed, it was estimated that three million Americans were blind, deaf, or in wheelchairs, but it has been estimated that the ADA now applies to forty-nine million Americans with every type of physical or mental impairment. Of the ADA cases that go to court, 92% are won by businesses. While this may sound good, considering the cost of going to court, the expense of this litigation is devastating for the businesses. Many of these lawsuits occur because the law is worded so vaguely.

The ADA currently applies to employers with fifteen or more employees. Employers who need more than fifteen employees might want to consider contracting with independent contractors to avoid problems with this law, particularly if the number of employees is only slightly larger than fifteen.

For more information on how this law affects your business, see the U.S. Department of Justice website at **www.usdoj.gov/crt/ada/business.htm**.

Tax Benefits   There are three types of tax credits to help small businesses with the burden of these laws.

✪ Businesses can deduct up to $15,000 a year for making their premises accessible to the disabled and can depreciate the rest. (Internal Revenue Code (I.R.C.) Section 190.)

✪ Small businesses (under $1,000,000 in revenue and under thirty employees) can get a tax credit each year for 50% of the cost of making their premises accessible to the disabled, but this only applies to the amount between $250 and $10,500.

✪ Small businesses can get a credit of up to 40% of the first $6,000 of wages paid to certain new employees who qualify through the **PRE-SCREENING NOTICE AND CERTIFICATION REQUEST (IRS FORM 8850)**. (see form 11, p.283.)

Records

To protect against potential claims of discrimination, all employers should keep detailed records showing reasons for hiring or not hiring applicants, and for firing employees.

California Law

California prohibits discrimination in employment based on race, religious creed, color, national origin, ancestry, physical disability, mental disability, medical condition, marital status, sex, or sexual orientation. (Cal. Gov't. Code Sec. 12940 (a).)

You may refuse to hire or may fire an employee whose physical, mental, or medical condition renders that person unable to perform the essential duties of the job, or would endanger the health and safety of others, even with reasonable accommodations. (Cal. Gov't. Code Sec. 12940 (a) (1) and (2).)

You may cause spouses to work in different departments or facilities for reasons of supervision, safety, security, or morale. (Cal. Gov't. Code Sec. 12940 (a) (3) (A).)

You may also favor Vietnam Era veterans in hiring, even though it discriminates. (Cal. Gov't. Code Sec. 12940 (a) (4).)

SEXUAL HARASSMENT

As an employer, you can be liable for the acts of your employees. One of the types of acts that employers have been help liable for is sexual harassment of customers, employees, and others. While you cannot control every act of every employee, if you indicate to employees that such behavior is unacceptable and set up a system to resolve complaints, you will do much to protect yourself against lawsuits.

The EEOC has held the following in sexual harassment cases.

- The victim as well as the harasser may be a woman or a man.

- The victim does not have to be of the opposite sex.

- ✪ The harasser can be the victim's supervisor, an agent of the employer, a supervisor in another area, a coworker, or a nonemployee.

- ✪ The victim does not have to be the person harassed, but could be anyone affected by the offensive conduct.

- ✪ Unlawful sexual harassment may occur without economic injury to or discharge of the victim.

- ✪ The harasser's conduct must be unwelcome.

Some of the actions that have been considered harassment include:

- ✪ displaying sexually explicit posters in the workplace;

- ✪ requiring female employees to wear revealing uniforms;

- ✪ rating the sexual attractiveness of female employees as they pass male employees' desks;

- ✪ continued sexual jokes and innuendos;

- ✪ demands for sexual favors from subordinates;

- ✪ unwelcomed sexual propositions or flirtation;

- ✪ unwelcomed physical contact; and,

- ✪ whistling or leering at members of the opposite sex.

In 1993, the United States Supreme Court ruled that an employee can make a claim for sexual harassment even without proof of a specific injury. However, lower federal courts in more recent cases have dismissed cases where no specific injury was shown. These new cases may indicate that the pendulum has stopped moving toward expanded rights for the employee.

On the other hand, another recent case ruled that an employer can be liable for the harassment of an employee by a supervisor—even if the employer was unaware of the supervisor's conduct—if the employer did not have a system in place to allow complaints against harassment. This area of law is still developing, but to avoid a possible lawsuit, you should be aware of the things that could potentially cause liability and avoid them.

Some things a business can do to protect against claims of sexual harassment include the following.

- ✪ Distribute a written policy against all kinds of sexual harassment to all employees.

- ✪ Encourage employees to report all incidents of sexual harassment.

- ✪ Ensure there is no retaliation against those who complain.

- ✪ Make clear that your policy is zero tolerance.

- ✪ Explain that sexual harassment includes both requests for sexual favors and a work environment that some employees may consider hostile.

- ✪ Allow employees to report harassment to someone other than their immediate supervisor, in case that person is involved in the harassment.

- ✪ Promise as much confidentiality as possible to complainants.

California Law California law prohibits sexual harassment. (Cal. Gov't. Code Sec. 12940.)

Common Law It is possible for an employee to sue for sexual harassment in civil court. However, this is difficult and expensive, and would only be worthwhile where there were substantial damages or money to be won.

WAGE AND HOUR LAWS

The *Fair Labor Standards Act* (FLSA) applies to all employers who are engaged in *interstate commerce* or in the production of goods for interstate commerce (anything that will cross the state line), and all employees of hospitals, schools, residential facilities for the disabled or aged, or public agencies. It also applies to all employees of enterprises that gross $500,000 or more per year.

While many small businesses might not think they are engaged in interstate commerce, the laws have been interpreted so broadly that nearly any use of the mails, interstate telephone service, or other interstate services, however minor, is enough to bring a business under the law.

Minimum Wage
The federal wage and hour laws are contained in the federal Fair Labor Standards Act. In 1996, Congress passed and President Clinton signed legislation raising the minimum wage to $5.15 an hour beginning September 1, 1997.

In certain circumstances, a wage of $4.25 may be paid to employees under 20 years of age for a ninety-day training period.

For employees who regularly receive more than $30 a month in tips, the minimum wage is $2.13 per hour. If the employee's tips do not bring him or her up to the full $5.15 minimum wage, then the employer must make up the difference.

California Law
California minimum wage is $6.75 for most employees. There are exceptions for trainees and outside salespersons, who may work on commission. You can download a poster to place in your workplace at **www.dir.ca.gov/wp.asp**.

California law provides for overtime pay of one and one-half times regular hourly pay for hours worked over eight in a twenty-four-hour period or forty hours in a seven-day period. Over twelve hours in a twenty-four hour period requires double pay. (Cal. Lab. Code Secs. 750-752.)

If you hire an employee and make a contract in which the employee agrees not to require overtime pay, you will still have to pay the overtime pay if the employee later decides to file a complaint with the Labor Commission.

If you do hire someone who will be working extra hours and is willing to forgo overtime pay, you can form a contract that says that the employee's normal pay would be less if overtime were being paid. For example, say the normal rate of pay is $2,500 per month. Because the employee will not receive overtime, the rate of pay is $3,000 per month. Consult an attorney to draw up the contract.

Regardless of the contract, if the amount paid is less than overtime pay would have been, your employee can collect the difference, as well as attorney's fees and other costs of suit.

Overtime The general rule is that employees who work more than forty hours a week must be paid time-and-a-half for hours worked over forty. However, there are many exemptions to this general rule based on salary and position. These exceptions were completely revised in 2004, and an explanation of the changes, including a tutorial video, are available at **www.dol.gov/esa**. For answers to questions about the law, call the Department of Labor at 866-4-USA-DOL (866-487-2365).

California requires overtime for nonexempt employees for work over eight hours per day or forty hours per week. The law reads as follows.

Eight hours of labor constitutes a day's work. Any work in excess of eight hours in one workday and any work in excess of 40 hours in any one workweek and the first eight hours worked on the seventh day of work in any one workweek shall be compensated at the rate of no less than one and one-half times the regular rate of pay for an employee. Any work in excess of 12 hours in one day shall be compensated at the rate of no less than twice the regular rate of pay for an employee. In addition, any work in excess of eight hours on any seventh day of a workweek shall be compensated at the rate of no less than twice the regular rate of pay of an employee. Nothing in this section requires an employer to combine more than one rate of overtime compensation in order to calculate the amount to be paid to an employee for any hour of overtime work. (Cal. Labor Code Sec. 510a.)

The law makes exceptions for what are called *alternative workweek schedules*. For example, an employee works four days per week, ten hours per day. There are limitations. If you want to set up some unusual schedule, contact the Department of Labor for approval.

Exempt Employees

While nearly all businesses are covered, certain employees are exempt from the FLSA. Exempt employees include those who are considered executives, administrators, managers, professionals, computer professionals, and outside salespeople.

Whether or not one of these exceptions applies to a particular employee is a complicated legal question. Thousands of court cases have been decided on this issue, but they have given no clear answers. In one case, a person could be determined to be exempt because of his or her duties, but in another, a person with the same duties could be found not exempt.

One thing that is clear is that the determination is made on the employee's function—not just the job title. You cannot make a person exempt by calling that person a manager if his or her duties are nonmanagerial. For more information, see the Department of Labor website **www.dol.gov/esa/whd/flsa**, or contact their offices at:

U.S. Department of Labor
Frances Perkins Building
200 Constitution Avenue, NW
Washington, DC 20210
866-4-USA-DOL

Local offices can be contacted at the following locations.

(Serving San Bernardino county and portions of Los Angeles and Riverside counties)

U.S. Department of Labor
East Los Angeles District Office
ESA Wage and Hour Division
100 North Barranca Street
Suite 850
West Covina, CA 91791
626-966-0478

(Serving Kern, Santa Barbara, San Luis, Obispo, and Ventura counties, and portions of Los Angeles county)

U.S. Department of Labor
Los Angeles District Office
ESA Wage and Hour Division
915 Wilshire Boulevard
Suite 960
Los Angeles, CA 90017
818-240-5274

U.S. Department of Labor
Sacramento District Office
ESA Wage and Hour Division
2800 Cottage Way
Room W-1836
Sacramento, CA 95825
916-978-6123

(Serving Imperial, Orange, and San Diego counties, and portions of Riverside county)

U.S. Department of Labor
San Diego District Office
ESA Wage and Hour Division
5675 Ruffin Road
Suite 310
San Diego, CA 92123
619-557-5606

U.S. Department of Labor
San Francisco District Office
ESA Wage and Hour Division
455 Market Street
Suite 800
San Francisco, CA 94105
415-744-5590

U.S. Department of Labor
San Jose Area Office
ESA Wage and Hour Division
60 South Market Street
Suite 420
San Jose, CA 95113
408-291-7730

You can obtain information on the Department of Labor's *Employment Law Guide* online at **www.dol.gov/asp/programs/guide/main.htm**.

PENSION AND BENEFIT LAWS

There are no laws requiring small businesses to provide any types of special benefits to employees. Such benefits are given to attract and keep good employees. With pension plans, the main concern is if you do start one, it must comply with federal tax laws.

There are no federal or California laws that require employees be given holidays off. You can require them to work Thanksgiving and Christmas, and can dock their pay or fire them for failing to show up. Of course, you will not have much luck keeping employees with such a policy.

Holidays   Most companies give full-time employees a certain number of paid holidays, such as: New Year's Day (January 1); Memorial Day (last Monday in May); Fourth of July; Labor Day (first Monday in September); Thanksgiving (fourth Thursday in November); and, Christmas (December 25). Some employers include other holidays, such as: Martin Luther King, Jr.'s birthday (January 15); President's Day; and, Columbus Day. If one of the holidays falls on a Saturday or Sunday, many employers give the preceding Friday or following Monday off.

For example, in 2005 California state employees get the following holidays off:

New Year's Day	(January 1)
Martin Luther King, Jr.	(third Monday in January)
Abraham Lincoln's Birthday	(February 12)
George Washington's Birthday	(third Monday in February)
Cesar Chavez Day	(March 31)
Memorial Day	(last Monday in May)
Independence Day	(July 4th)
Labor Day	(first Monday in September)
Columbus Day	(second Monday in October)
Veterans Day	(November 11)
Thanksgiving Day	(last Thursday in November)
Friday following Thanksgiving	
Christmas Day	(December 25)

However, the fact that these are designated state holidays does not mean anything. In fact, not even the state government is closed on all of these days.

Sick Days

There is no federal or California law mandating that an employee be paid for time that he or she is home sick. The situation seems to be that the larger the company, the more paid sick leave is allowed. Part-time workers rarely get sick leave, and small business sick leave is usually limited for the simple reason that they cannot afford to pay for time that employees do not work.

Some small companies have an official policy of no paid sick leave, but when an important employee misses a day because he or she is clearly sick, it is paid.

Breaks

Federal law does not require employers to provide any coffee breaks or lunch breaks. California law requires meal periods and breaks for hourly (nonexempt) employees. (Cal. Labor Code Sec. 512a.)

The law reads as follows.

An employer may not employ an employee for a work period of more than five hours per day without providing the employee with a meal period of not less than 30 minutes, except that if the total work period per day of the employee is no more than six hours, the meal period may be waived by mutual consent of both the employer and employee. An employer may not employ an employee for a work period of more than 10 hours per day without providing the employee with a second meal period of not less than 30 minutes, except that if the total hours worked is no more than 12 hours, the second meal period may be waived by mutual consent of the employer and the employee only if the first meal period was not waived.

Pension Plans and Retirement Accounts

Few small new businesses can afford to provide pension plans for their employees. The first concern of a small business is usually how the owner can shelter income in a pension plan without having to set up a pension plan for an employee. Under most pension plans, this is not allowed.

IRA. Any individual can put up to $4,000 ($5,000 if age 50 or over) in an *Individual Retirement Account* (IRA). Unless the person, or his or her spouse, is covered by a company pension plan and has income over a certain amount, the amount put into the account is fully tax deductible.

Roth IRA. Contributions to a Roth IRA are not tax deductible, but when the money is taken out, it is not taxable. People who expect to still have taxable income when they withdraw from their IRA can benefit from these.

SEP IRA, SAR-SEP IRA, SIMPLE IRA. With these types of retirement accounts, a person can put a much greater amount into a retirement plan and can deduct it from their taxable income. Employees must also be covered by such plans, but certain employees are exempt, so it is sometimes possible to use these for the owners alone. The best source for more information is a mutual fund company (such as Vanguard, Fidelity, or Dreyfus) or a local bank, which can set up the plan and provide you with all of the rules. These have an advantage over qualified plans (discussed below), since they do not have the high annual fees.

Qualified Retirement Plans. Qualified retirement plans are 401(k) plans, Keogh plans, and corporate retirement plans. These are covered by the *Employee Retirement Income Security Act* (ERISA), which is a complicated law meant to protect employee pension plans. Congress did not want employees who contributed to pension plans all their lives ending up with nothing if the plan went bankrupt. The law is so complicated and the penalties so severe that some companies are cancelling their pension plans. Applications for new plans are a fraction of what they were previously. However, many banks and mutual funds have created *canned plans*, which can be used instead of drafting one from scratch. Still, the fees for administering them are steep. Check with a bank or mutual fund for details.

FAMILY AND MEDICAL LEAVE LAW

To assist business owners in deciding what type of leave to offer their employees, Congress passed the *Family and Medical Leave Act of 1993* (FMLA). This law requires an employee to be given up to twelve weeks of unpaid leave when:

- ✪ the employee or employee's spouse has a child;

- ✪ the employee adopts a child or takes in a foster child;

- ✪ the employee needs to care for an ill spouse, child, or parent; or,

- ✪ the employee becomes seriously ill.

The law only applies to employers with fifty or more employees. Also, the top 10% of an employer's salaried employees can be denied this leave because of the disruption in business their loss could cause.

California Law   California also has a law concerning family and medical leave. (Cal. Gov't. Code, Section 12945.2.) The California law is similar to the federal law in many respects.

- ✪ Leave is available for the same reasons as the federal law.

✪ It only applies to employers with fifty or more employees within seventy-five miles of the work site where the employee seeking the leave is employed.

✪ It provides that key employees may be replaced if their absence has a serious detrimental effect on the business.

Most people reading this book will not be opening their business with fifty or more employees. However, if you are among those few who do plan to start with, or very rapidly grow to, fifty employees, you should obtain a copy of both the federal and California family and medical leave laws, and become familiar with them.

If the California law applies, it basically provides that an employee:

with more than 12 months of service with the employer, and who has at least 1,250 hours of service with the employer during the previous 12-month period, [may] take up to a total of 12 work-weeks in any 12-month period for family care and medical leave.

Generally, this runs concurrent with the federal law.

Employees who pay into *State Disability Insurance* (SDI) are now entitled to up to six weeks of partial salary (about 55% for most employees), which is paid by the state Employment Development Department (EDD), not the employer. Visit the EDD website at **www.edd.ca.gov** for details. This does not affect existing law, and a better deal for the employee can be negotiated with the employer.

CHILD LABOR LAWS

The federal Fair Labor Standards Act also contains rules regarding the hiring of children. The basic rules are that children under 16 years old may not be hired at all except in a few jobs, such as acting and newspaper delivery, and those under 18 may not be hired for dangerous jobs. Children may not work more than three hours a day or eighteen hours a week in a school week, or more than eight hours a day or forty hours a week in a nonschool week. If you plan to hire children, you should check the federal Fair Labor Standards Act, which is in United

States Code (U.S.C.), Title 29, and the related regulations, which are in the Code of Federal Regulations (C.F.R.), Title 29.

California Law

California child labor laws are discussed here a bit more extensively, not only because they may be helpful in your business (most likely to convince you that it is too much trouble to hire minors), but also because they are interesting. The laws regarding using babies in movies, fourteen-year-old professional baseball players, door-to-door begging, and candy selling are probably ones that you will not see in many other states. First, the laws relating generally to various age groups are summarized. Second, laws that apply to certain jobs or industries are discussed. Finally, a few general things about hiring minors are mentioned. Unless otherwise indicated, all references are to sections of the California Labor Code (Cal. Lab. Code).

All minors. No minor may be employed or permitted to work in any occupation declared particularly hazardous for the employment of minors between 16 and 18 years of age, or declared detrimental to their health or well-being. (29 C.F.R., Sec. 570, Subpart E, and Cal. Lab. Code, Section 1293.1(b).)

There are special exceptions for minors with newspaper routes. Minors may enter a newspaper plant, except for areas where printing presses are located, if they are engaged in the processing and delivery of newspapers. (Cal. Lab. Code, Section 1294.1(c).) They are also allowed to make deliveries by foot, bicycle, public transportation, or by an automobile driven by a person 16 years of age or older. (Cal. Lab. Code, Section 1294.4.) No minor under age 12 may be employed or permitted to work in or in connection with the occupation of selling or distributing newspapers, magazines, periodicals, or circulars. (Cal. Lab. Code, Section 1298(a).)

No minor under the age of 18 may be employed or permitted to work as a messenger for any telegraph, telephone, or messenger company, or for the United States government or any of its departments while operating a telegraph, telephone, or messenger service, in the distribution, transmission, or delivery of goods or messages in cities of more than 15,000 inhabitants before 6:00 a.m. or after 9:00 p.m. (Cal. Lab. Code, Section 1297.)

No person under the age of 16 may work in any of the following capacities (Cal. Lab. Code, Section 1292(a), (b), and (c) and Section 1293):

✪ adjusting any belt to any machinery;

✪ sewing or lacing machine belts in any workshop or factory;

✪ oiling, wiping, or cleaning machinery, or assisting therein;

✪ operating or assisting in the operation of any of the following machines:

- circular or band saws; wood shapers; wood jointers; planers; sandpaper or wood-polishing machinery; wood turning or boring machinery;

- picker machines or machines used in picking wool, cotton, hair, or other material; carding machines; leather-burnishing machines; laundry machinery;

- printing-presses of all kinds; boring or drilling presses; stamping machines used in sheet metal and tinware, in paper and leather manufacturing, or in washer and nut factories; metal or paper-cutting machines; paper-lace machines;

- corner-staying machines in paper-box factories; corrugating rolls, such as are used in corrugated paper, roofing, or washboard factories;

- dough brakes or cracker machinery of any description;

- wire or iron straightening or drawing machinery; rolling-mill machinery; power punches or shears; washing, grinding, or mixing machinery; calendar rolls in paper and rubber manufacturing; steam-boilers; in proximity to any hazardous or unguarded belts, machinery, or gearing;

✪ upon any railroad, whether steam, electric, or hydraulic;

✪ upon any vessel or boat engaged in navigation or commerce within the jurisdiction of the state;

✪ in, about, or in connection with any processes in which dangerous or poisonous acids are used, in the manufacture or packing of paints, colors, white or red lead, or in soldering;

✪ in occupations causing dust in injurious quantities, in the manufacture and use of dangerous or poisonous gases, or in the manufacture or preparation of compositions with dangerous or poisonous gases, or in the manufacture or use of compositions of lye in which the quantity is injurious to health;

✪ on scaffolding, in heavy work in the building trades, in any tunnel or excavation, or in, about, or in connection with any mine, coal breaker, coke oven, or quarry;

✪ in assorting, manufacturing, or packing tobacco;

✪ operating any automobile, motorcar, or truck;

✪ in any occupation dangerous to the life or limb, or injurious to the health or morals of the minor;

✪ in any occupation declared particularly hazardous for the employment of minors below the age of 16 years in C.F.R., Title 29, Section 570.71 of Subpart E-1 of Part 570;

✪ in any occupation excluded from the application of C.F.R., Title 29, Section 570.33 of Subpart C of part 570 and paragraph (b) of Section 570.34;

✪ as a messenger for any telegraph, telephone, or messenger company, or for the United States government or any of its departments while operating a telegraph, telephone, or messenger service, in the distribution, transmission, or delivery of goods or messages in cities of more than 15,000 inhabitants; and,

✪   door-to-door sales of newspaper or magazine subscriptions, or of candy, cookies, flowers, or other merchandise or commodities, if those activities are more than fifty miles from the minor's place of residence.

Minors ages 14 and 15. Some sections of the law state the type of jobs minors may hold. Minors who are 14 and 15 years of age may be employed in any occupation not otherwise prohibited by law, including, but not limited to, the following:

✪   office and clerical work, including the operation of office machines;

✪   cashiering, selling, modeling, art work, work in advertising departments, window trimming, and comparative shopping;

✪   price marking and tagging by hand or by machine, assembling orders, patching, and shelving;

✪   bagging and carrying out customer's orders;

✪   errand and delivery work by foot, bicycle, and public transportation;

✪   cleanup work, including the use of vacuum cleaners and floor waxers, and maintenance of grounds, but not including the use of power-driven mowers and cutters;

✪   kitchen work and other work involved in preparing and serving food and beverages, including the operation of machines and devices used in the performance of this work, such as dishwashers, toasters, dumbwaiters, popcorn poppers, milkshake blenders, and coffee grinders; and,

✪   cleaning vegetables and fruits, and wrapping, sealing, labeling, weighing, pricing, and stocking goods when performed in areas physically separate from areas where meat is prepared for sale and outside freezers or meat coolers.

Minors under age 12. No minor under the age of 12 may be employed or permitted to work or accompany or be permitted to accompany an employed parent or guardian, in any of the following capacities:

❂ in an agricultural zone of danger (defined as on or about moving equipment, in or about unprotected chemicals, on or about any unprotected water hazard, or any other hazards determined by the Department of Industrial Relations);

❂ in any of the occupations declared hazardous for employment of minors below age 16 in C.F.R., Title 29, Section 570.71; or,

❂ in or in connection with the occupation of selling or distributing newspapers, magazines, periodicals, or circulars. (Cal. Lab. Code, Section 1298.)

Minors under age 6. No minor under the age of 6 may be permitted to engage in the door-to-door sales or street sales of candy, cookies, flowers, or any other merchandise or commodities. (Cal. Lab. Code, Section 1308.1(a).)

The following laws relate to the employment of minors in certain types of jobs or industries.

Gas stations. Minors 16 and 17 years of age may work in gas service stations in the following activities. (Cal. Lab. Code, Section 1294.5):

❂ dispensing gas or oil;

❂ courtesy service;

❂ car cleaning, washing, and polishing; or,

❂ activities specified in Cal. Lab. Code, Section 1294.3.

They may not perform work that involves the inflation of any tire mounted on a rim equipped with a removable retaining ring. Minors under the age of 16 years may be employed in gas service stations to perform only those activities specified under the heading "Minors ages 14 and 15" on page 122.

Entertainment industry. As would be expected in California, there are special rules for children employed in the entertainment industry. The consent of the labor ccommissioner is required for any of the following (Cal. Lab. Code, Section 1308.5):

✪ the employment of any minor under the age of 16 in the presentation of any drama or legitimate play, or in any radio broadcasting or television studio;

✪ the employment of any minor between the ages of 12 and 15 in any other performance, concert, or entertainment;

✪ the appearance of any minor between the ages of 8 and 15 in any performance, concert, or entertainment during the public school vacation;

✪ allowing any minor between the ages of 8 and 18 (who is permitted by California law to be employed as an actor, actress, or performer) in a theater, motion picture studio, radio broadcasting studio, or television studio, before 10:00 p.m., in the presentation of a performance, play, or drama continuing from an earlier hour until after 10:00 p.m., to continue his or her part in such presentation between the hours of 10:00 p.m. and midnight;

✪ the appearance of any minor under the age of 16 in any entertainment which is noncommercial in nature;

✪ the employment of any minor artist under the age of 16 in the making of phonograph recordings;

✪ the employment of any minor under the age of 16 as an advertising or photographic model; or,

✪ the employment or appearance of any minor under the age of 16 pursuant to a contract approved by the superior court under the California Family Code (Cal. Fam. Code), beginning with Section 6750.

No minor may be employed in the entertainment industry more than eight hours in one day of twenty-four hours, or more than forty-eight hours in one week, or before 5:00 a.m., or after 10:00 p.m. on any day preceding a school day. However, a minor may work these hours during any evening preceding a nonschool day until 12:30 a.m. of the nonschool day. (Cal. Lab. Code, Section 1308.7.) (A *school day* is any day in which a minor is required to attend school for 240 minutes or more.)

No infant under the age of one month may be employed on any motion picture set or location unless a licensed physician and surgeon who is board-certified in pediatrics provides written certification that the infant is at least fifteen days old and, in his or her medical opinion, the infant was carried to full term, was of normal birth weight, is physically capable of handling the stress of filmmaking, and the infant's lungs, eyes, heart, and immune system are sufficiently developed to withstand potential risks. (Cal. Lab. Code, Section 1308.8.)

The law does not prohibit the appearance of a minor:

- in any radio or television broadcasting exhibition, where the minor receives no compensation directly or indirectly, where the engagement of the minor is limited to a single appearance lasting not more than one hour, and where no admission fee is charged for the radio broadcasting or television exhibition, or

- at any event during a calendar year, occurring on a day in which school attendance is not required or on the day preceding such a day, lasting four hours or less, where a parent or guardian of the minor is present, for which the minor does not directly or indirectly receive any compensation.

Professional baseball. Minors 14 years of age and older may be employed during certain hours to perform sports-attending services in professional baseball. (29 C.F.R., Sec. 570.35 (b).) The minor must obtain the written approval of either the school district, the school in which the minor is enrolled, or the county board of education of the county in which that school district is located. The hours are limited to outside of school hours until 12:30 a.m. during any evening preceding a nonschool day, and until 10:00 p.m. during any evening preceding a school day. The child may not work more than five hours on any school day, more than eighteen hours in any week while school is in session, more than eight hours on a nonschool day, or more than forty hours in any week that school is not in session. However, a 16- or 17-year-old may be employed outside of school hours for up to five hours on any school day. (Cal. Lab. Code, Section 1295.5.)

Education and training exceptions. Certain prohibitions for dangerous activities do not apply to any of the following (Cal. Lab. Code, Section 1295):

- ✪ courses of training in vocational or manual training schools or in-state institutions;

- ✪ apprenticeship training programs and work experience education programs, established pursuant to certain provisions of the Education Code;

- ✪ student-learners in a bona fide vocational agriculture program; or,

- ✪ minors 14 or 15 years of age who hold certificates of completion of either a tractor operation or a machine operation program, and who are working in the occupations for which they have been trained.

Permits, inspections, and penalties. By hiring a minor, you open yourself up to additional permit requirements, inspections, and penalties. For example, permits of some type are required for the following:

- ✪ the employment of a minor as a musician at a concert or other musical entertainment, or as a performer in any form of entertainment (Cal. Lab. Code, Section 1308.5);

- ✪ any person age 18 or older who transports, or provides direction or supervision during transportation of, a minor under age 16 to any location more than ten miles from the minor's residence (except for the minor's parent or guardian; a person solely providing transportation for hire, who is not otherwise subject to this requirement; and, persons acting on behalf of a trustee, charitable corporation, or certain other entities defined in the California Government Code); or who directs or supervises a minor for the purpose of facilitating the minor's participation in door-to-door sales of any merchandise or commodity. This requires an initial registration fee of up to $100 and an annual renewal fee of up to $50 (Cal. Lab. Code, Section 1308.2); and,

✪ any individual, association, corporation, or other entity that employs or uses, either directly or indirectly through third persons, minors under 16 years of age in door-to-door sales at any location more than ten miles from the minor's residence. This requires an initial registration fee of up to $350 and an annual renewal fee of up to $200. (Cal. Lab. Code, Section 1308.3.)

If you employ a minor, your business will be subject to inspections by the county attendance supervisor and probation officer according to the labor commissioner's office. (Cal. Lab. Code, Section 1302.) If you are required to have a permit, you may be required to show it at any time. You may also be required to maintain certain kinds of records for government inspectors, and may be required to give them access to your payroll records.

Penalties for violating the various child labor laws mentioned above range from fines of $1,000 to $10,000, or imprisonment for up to six months, or both.

IMMIGRATION LAWS

There are strict penalties for any business that hires aliens who are not eligible to work. You must verify both the identity and the employment eligibility of anyone you hire by using the **EMPLOYMENT ELIGIBILITY VERIFICATION (IRS FORM I-9)**. (see form 4, p.249.) Both you and the employee must fill out the form, and you must check an employee's identification cards or papers. Fines for hiring illegal aliens range from $250 to $2,000 for the first offense, and up to $10,000 for the third offense. Failure to maintain the proper paperwork may result in a fine of up to $1,000. The law does not apply to independent contractors with whom you may contract, and it does not penalize you if the employee used fake identification.

There are also penalties that apply to employers of four or more persons for discriminating against eligible applicants because they appear foreign or because of their national origin or citizenship status.

Appendix B has a list of acceptable documentation, a blank form, and instructions. (see form 4, p.249.) The blank form can also be downloaded at **www.uscis.gov/graphics/formsfee/forms/i-9.htm**.

For more information, call 800-357-2099. For the *Handbook for Employers and Instructions for Completing Form I-9,* check the *United States Citizenship and Immigration Services* (USCIS) website at **www.uscis.gov**.

NOTE: *As of this writing, Congress is debating immigration reform. The law and its enforcement may be different by the time you read this, so check the USCIS website for updates.*

Foreign Employees
If you wish to hire employees who are foreign citizens and are not able to provide the proper documentation, they must first obtain a work visa from USCIS.

Work visas for foreigners are not easy to get. Millions of people around the globe would like to come to the U.S. to work, but the laws are designed to keep most of them out to protect the jobs of American citizens.

Whether or not a person can get a work visa depends on whether there is a shortage of U.S. workers available to fill the job. For jobs requiring few or no skills, it is practically impossible to get a visa. For highly skilled jobs, such as nurses and physical therapists, and for those of exceptional ability, such as Nobel Prize winners and Olympic medalists, obtaining a visa is fairly easy.

There are several types of visas, and different rules for different countries. For example, NAFTA has made it easier for some types of workers to enter the U.S. from Canada and Mexico. For some positions, the shortage of workers is assumed by the USCIS. For others, a business must first advertise a position available in the United States. Only after no qualified persons apply can it hire someone from another country.

The visa system is complicated and subject to regular change. If you wish to hire a foreign worker, you should consult with an immigration specialist or a book on the subject.

California Law   California law requires that any contract made with a foreign worker (i.e., one who is not a U.S. citizen but is legally entitled to work) must be written in the language of the worker and must contain all the material terms of employment, including pay, housing, transportation, and any other benefits the worker will receive.

The type of business you have will determine the scrutiny you will be under. For example, if you are in landscaping, it is almost expected that you will hire people illegally in the country. Since fake documentation is easy to get, most landscaping businesses simply lose their workers if there is a raid and do not face penalties.

However, if you are dealing as a contractor with government security or sensitive computer information, be sure that your foreign workers comply with all immigration laws.

HIRING OFF THE BOOKS

Because of the taxes, insurance, and red tape involved with hiring employees, some new businesses hire people *off the books*. They pay them in cash and never admit they are employees. While the cash paid in wages would not be tax deductible, they consider this a smaller cost than compliance. Some even use off the books receipts to cover it.

Except when your spouse or child is giving you some temporary help, this is a terrible idea. Hiring people off the books can result in civil fines, loss of insurance coverage, and even criminal penalties. When engaged in dangerous work, like roofing or using power tools, you are risking millions of dollars in potential liability if a worker is killed or seriously injured. It may be more costly and time-consuming to comply with the employment laws, but if you are concerned with long-term growth with less risk, it is the wiser way to go.

FEDERAL CONTRACTS

Companies that do work for the federal government are subject to several laws.

The *Davis-Bacon Act* requires contractors engaged in U.S. government construction projects to pay wages and benefits that are equal to or better than the prevailing wages in the area.

The *McNamara-O'Hara Service Contract Act* sets wages and other labor standards for contractors furnishing services to agencies of the U.S. government.

The *Walsh-Healey Public Contracts Act* requires the Department of Labor to settle disputes regarding manufacturers supplying products to the U.S. government.

MISCELLANEOUS LAWS

In addition to the broad categories of laws affecting businesses, there are several other federal and state laws that you should be familiar with.

Federal Law   Federal law regulates affirmative action, layoffs, unions, and informational posters.

Affirmative action. In most cases, the federal government does not tell employers who they must hire. The only situation in which a small business would need to comply with affirmative action requirements would be if it accepted federal contracts or subcontracts. These requirements could include hiring minorities or veterans of the conflict in Vietnam.

Layoffs. Companies with one-hundred or more full-time employees at one location are subject to the *Worker Adjustment and Retraining Notification Act*. This law requires a sixty-day notification prior to certain layoffs and has other strict provisions.

Unions. The *National Labor Relations Act of 1935* gives employees the right to organize a union or to join one. (29 U.S.C. Secs. 151 et seq.)

There are things employers can do to protect themselves, but you should consult a labor attorney or a book on the subject before taking action that might be illegal and result in fines.

Poster laws. Poster laws require certain posters to be displayed to inform employees of their rights. Not all businesses are required to display all posters, but the following list should be of help.

- ✪ All employers must display the wage and hour poster available from the U.S. Department of Labor at **www.dol.gov/esa**.

- ✪ Employers with fifteen or more employees for twenty weeks of the year must display the sex, race, religion, and ethnic discrimination poster, as well as the age discrimination poster available from the EEOC at **www.eeoc.gov/publications.html**.

- ✪ Employers with federal contracts or subcontracts of $10,000 or more must display the sex, race, religion, and ethnic discrimination poster, plus a poster regarding veterans of the conflict in Vietnam (available from the local federal contracting office).

- ✪ Employers with government contracts subject to the *Service Contract Act* or the *Public Contracts Act* must display a notice to employees working on government contracts available from the Employment Standards Division at **www.dol.gov/esa/whd**.

Advertising and Promotion Laws

Because of the unscrupulous and deceptive advertising techniques of some companies, as well as the multitude of con artists trying to steal from innocent consumers, numerous federal and state statutes have been enacted that make it unlawful to use improper advertising and promotional techniques in soliciting business.

ADVERTISING LAWS AND RULES

The federal government regulates advertising through the *Federal Trade Commission* (FTC). The rules are contained in the *Code of Federal Regulations* (C.F.R.). You can find these rules in most law libraries and many public libraries. If you plan on doing any advertising that you think may be questionable, you might want to check the rules. As you read the rules, you will probably think of many violations you see every day.

Federal rules do not apply to every business, and small businesses that operate only within the state and do not use the postal service may be exempt. However, many of the federal rules have been adopted into law by the State of California. Therefore, a violation could be prosecuted by the state rather than the federal government.

Some of the important rules are summarized in this section. If you wish to learn more details about the rules, you should obtain copies from your library.

Deceptive Pricing   (C.F.R., Title 16, Ch. I, Part 233.) When prices are being compared, it is required that actual and not inflated prices are used. For example, if an object would usually be sold for $7, you should not first offer it for $10 and then start offering it at 30% off. It is considered misleading to suggest that a discount from list price is a bargain if the item is seldom actually sold at list price. If most surrounding stores sell an item for $7, it is considered misleading to say it has a retail value of $10, even if there are some stores elsewhere selling it at that price.

Bait Advertising   (C.F.R., Title 16, Ch. I, Part 238.) Bait advertising is placing an ad when you do not really want the respondents to buy the product offered, but want them to switch to another item.

Use of "Free," "Half-Off," and Similar Words   (C.F.R., Title 16, Ch. I, Part 251.) Use of words such as "free," "1¢ sale," and the like must not be misleading. This means that the regular price must not include a markup to cover the free item. The seller must expect to sell the product without the free item at some time in the future.

Substantiation of Claims   (C.F.R., Title 16; Federal Regulations (F.R.), Title 48, Page 10471 (1983).) The FTC requires that advertisers be able to substantiate their claims. Some information on this policy is contained on the Internet at **www.ftc.gov/bcp/guides/ad3subst.htm**.

Endorsements   (C.F.R., Title 16, Ch. I, Part 255.) The FTC forbids endorsements that are misleading. An example is a quote from a film review that is used in such a way as to change the substance of the review. It is not necessary to use the exact words of the person endorsing the product, as long as the opinion is not distorted. If a product is changed, an endorsement that does not apply to the new version cannot be used. For some items, such as drugs, claims cannot be used without scientific proof. Endorsements by organizations cannot be used unless one is sure that the membership holds the same opinion.

Unfairness
(15 U.S.C. Section 45.) Any advertising practices that can be deemed to be *unfair* are forbidden by the FTC. An explanation of this policy is located on the Internet at **www.ftc.gov/bcp/policystmt/ad-unfair.htm**.

Negative Option Plans
(C.F.R., Title 16, Ch. I, Part 425.) When a seller uses a sales system in which the buyer must notify the seller if he or she does not want the goods, the seller must provide the buyer with a form to decline the sale and at least ten days in which to decline. Bonus merchandise must be shipped promptly, and the seller must promptly terminate shipment for any who so request after completion of the contract.

Laser Eye Surgery
(15 U.S.C. Sections 45, 52–57.) Under the laws governing deceptive advertising, the FTC and the FDA are regulating the advertising of laser eye surgery. Anyone involved in this area should obtain a copy of these rules. They are located on the Internet at **www.ftc.gov/bcp/guides/eyecare2.htm**.

Food and Dietary Supplements
(21 U.S.C. Section 343.) Under the *Nutritional Labeling Education Act of 1990*, the FTC and the FDA regulate the packaging and advertising of food and dietary products. Anyone involved in this area should obtain a copy of these rules. They are located on the Internet at **www.ftc.gov/bcp/menu-health.htm**.

Jewelry and Precious Metals
(F.R., Title 61, Page 27212.) The FTC has numerous rules governing the sale and advertising of jewelry and precious metals. Anyone in this business should obtain a copy of these rules. They are located on the Internet at **www.ftc.gov/bcp/guides/jewel-gd.htm**.

California Laws
California law regulating advertising is contained in several different codes, especially the Civil Code and the Business and Professional Code. The gist of these laws is that you can advertise almost anything if you tell the truth, fully inform the public of the nature of the product or service, and inform the public about the risks or costs involved.

Under the California Civil Code (Cal. Civ. Code), Section 1770, it is forbidden to make any misrepresentations of goods or services to the public, including the following:

- passing off goods or services as those of another;

- misrepresenting the source, sponsorship, approval, or certification by another;

- misrepresenting the affiliation, connection, or association with, or certification by, another;

- using deceptive representations or designations of geographic origin in connection with goods or services;

- representing that goods or services have sponsorship, approval, characteristics, ingredients, uses, benefits, or quantities, that they do not have or that a person has a sponsorship, approval, status, affiliation, or connection that he or she does not have;

- representing that goods are original or new if they have deteriorated unreasonably or are altered, reconditioned, reclaimed, used, or secondhand;

- representing that goods or services are of a particular standard, quality, or grade, or that goods are of a particular style or model, if they are of another;

- disparaging the goods, services, or business of another by false or misleading representation of fact;

- advertising goods or services with intent not to sell them as advertised;

- advertising goods or services with intent not to supply reasonably expected demand, unless the advertisement discloses a limitation of quantity;

- advertising furniture without clearly indicating that it is unassembled if that is the case;

✪ advertising the price of unassembled furniture without clearly indicating the assembled price of that furniture, if the same furniture is available assembled from the seller;

✪ making false or misleading statements of fact concerning reasons for, existence of, or amounts of price reductions;

✪ representing that a transaction confers or involves rights, remedies, or obligations that it does not have or involve, or that are prohibited by law;

✪ representing that a part, replacement, or repair service is needed when it is not;

✪ representing that the subject of a transaction has been supplied in accordance with a previous representation when it is not;

✪ representing that the consumer will receive a rebate, discount, or other economic benefit, if the earning of the benefit is contingent on an event to occur subsequent to the consummation of the transaction;

✪ misrepresenting the authority of a salesperson, representative, or agent to negotiate the final terms of a transaction with a consumer;

✪ inserting an unconscionable provision in the contract; or,

✪ advertising that a product is being offered at a specific price plus a specific percentage of that price unless (1) the total price is set forth in the advertisement, which may include, but is not limited to, shelf tags, displays, and media advertising, in a size larger than any other price in that advertisement, or (2) the specific price plus a specific percentage of that price represents a markup from the seller's costs or from the wholesale price of the product. This does not apply to in-store advertising by businesses open only to members or cooperative organizations organized pursuant to the California Corporations Code (Cal. Corp. Code), beginning with Section

12000, where more than 50% of purchases are made at the specific price set forth in the advertisement.

The California Business and Professions Code (Cal. Bus. and Prof. Code), Sections 17530 through 17539.6, cover a wide range of advertising and sales prohibitions, and requirements applying to specific professions or products, including:

❂ retail sale of caskets, alternative containers, or outer burial containers by someone other than a funeral director (Cal. Bus. and Prof. Code, Sec. 17530.7);

❂ secondhand, used, defective, or blemished merchandise; merchandise known as *seconds*; or, merchandise that has been rejected by its manufacturer as not first class (Cal. Bus. and Prof. Code, Sec. 17531);

❂ the sale of surplus materials, as defined in the federal *Surplus Property Act of 1944* (50 U.S.C. Sec. 1622) and California Business and Professions Code, Sec. 17531.5; and the use of words such as "Army," "Navy," "United States," "Federal," "treasury," "procurement," "G.I.," or others, which have a tendency to lead the public to believe, contrary to fact, that there is some official relationship to the United States Government; or that all of the articles are such surplus materials; or that the articles are of higher quality and lower prices than those elsewhere obtainable (Cal. Bus. and Prof. Code, Sec. 17533.5);

❂ mailed solicitation materials that contain a seal, insignia, trade or brand name, or any other term or symbol that reasonably could be interpreted or construed as implying any state or local government connection, approval, or endorsement (Cal. Bus. and Prof. Code, Sec. 17533.6);

❂ use of the words "Made in the U.S.A.," "Made in America," "U.S.A.," or similar words when the merchandise or any article, unit, or part thereof, has been entirely or substantially made, manufactured, or produced outside of the United States (Cal. Bus. and Prof. Code, Sec. 17533.7);

✪ advertisements for a prize or gift, with the intent to offer a sales presentation (Cal. Bus. and Prof. Code, Sec. 17533.8);

✪ advertisements for the sale of tear gas, tear gas devices, and tear gas weapons (Cal. Bus. and Prof. Code, Sec. 17533.9); and,

✪ advertisements for the sale of anabolic steroids. (Cal. Bus. and Prof. Code, Sec. 17533.10.)

INTERNET SALES LAWS

There are not yet specific laws governing Internet transactions that are different from laws governing other transactions. The FTC feels that its current rules regarding deceptive advertising, substantiation, disclaimers, refunds, and related matters must be followed by Internet businesses, and that consumers are adequately protected by them. See the first three pages of this chapter, under "Advertising Laws and Rules," for that information.

For some specific guidelines on Internet advertising, see the FTC's site at **www.ftc.gov/bcp/conline/pubs/buspubs/ruleroad.htm**.

Most California Code Sections regarding advertising simply include the Internet in the list of advertising media.

EMAIL ADVERTISING

The Controlling the Assault of Non-Solicited Pornography And Marketing Act of 2003 (CANSPAM) has put numerous controls on how you can use email to solicit business for your company. Some of the prohibited activities under the Act are:

✪ false or misleading information in an email;

✪ deceptive subject heading;

✪ failure to include a functioning return address;

- ✪ mailing to someone who has asked not to receive solicitations;

- ✪ failure to include a valid postal address;

- ✪ omitting an opt-out procedure;

- ✪ failure to clearly mark the email as advertising; and,

- ✪ including sexual material without adequate warnings.

Some of the provisions contain criminal penalties as well as civil fines.

For more information on the CANSPAM Act, see **www.gigalaw.com canspam**. For text of the Act and other spam laws around the world, see **www.spamlaws.com**.

HOME SOLICITATION LAWS

The Federal Trade Commission has rules governing door-to-door sales. In any such sale, it is a deceptive trade practice to fail to furnish a receipt explaining the sale (in the language of the presentation), as is failure to give notice that there is a right to back out of the contract within three days, known as a *right of rescission*. The notice must be supplied in duplicate, must be in at least 10-point type, and must be captioned either "Notice of Right to Cancel" or "Notice of Cancellation." The notice must be worded as the example on page 141 illustrates.

NOTICE OF CANCELLATION

_____
(Date)

YOU MAY CANCEL THIS TRANSACTION, WITHOUT ANY PENALTY OR OBLIGATION, WITHIN THREE BUSINESS DAYS FROM THE ABOVE DATE.

IF YOU CANCEL, ANY PROPERTY TRADED IN, ANY PAYMENTS MADE BY YOU UNDER THE CONTRACT OR SALE, AND ANY NEGOTIABLE INSTRUMENT EXECUTED BY YOU WILL BE RETURNED TO YOU WITHIN 10 BUSINESS DAYS FOLLOWING RECEIPT BY THE SELLER OF YOUR CANCELLATION NOTICE, AND ANY SECURITY INTEREST ARISING OUT OF THE TRANS-ACTION WILL BE CANCELLED.

IF YOU CANCEL, YOU MUST MAKE AVAILABLE TO THE SELLER AT YOUR RESIDENCE, IN SUBSTANTIALLY AS GOOD CONDITION AS WHEN RECEIVED, ANY GOODS DELIVERED TO YOU UNDER THIS CONTRACT OR SALE; OR YOU MAY, IF YOU WISH, COMPLY WITH THE INSTRUCTIONS OF THE SELLER REGARDING THE RETURN SHIPMENT OF THE GOODS AT THE SELLER'S EXPENSE AND RISK.

IF YOU DO MAKE THE GOODS AVAILABLE TO THE SELLER AND THE SELLER DOES NOT PICK THEM UP WITHIN 20 DAYS OF THE DATE OF YOUR NOTICE OF CANCELLATION, YOU MAY RETAIN OR DISPOSE OF THE GOODS WITHOUT ANY FURTHER OBLIGATION. IF YOU FAIL TO MAKE THE GOODS AVAILABLE TO THE SELLER, OR IF YOU AGREE TO RETURN THE GOODS AND FAIL TO DO SO, THEN YOU REMAIN LIABLE FOR PER-FORMANCE OF ALL OBLIGATIONS UNDER THE CONTRACT.

TO CANCEL THIS TRANSACTION, MAIL OR DELIVER A SIGNED AND DATED COPY OF THIS CANCELLATION NOTICE OR ANY OTHER WRITTEN NOTICE, OR SEND A TELEGRAM, TO _____(name of seller), AT _____(address of seller's place of business) NOT LATER THAN MIDNIGHT OF _____ (date).

I HEREBY CANCEL THIS TRANSACTION.

_____   _____
(Buyer's signature)   (Date)

The seller must complete the notice and orally inform the buyer of the right to cancel. He or she cannot misrepresent the right to cancel, assign the contract until the fifth business day, or include a confession of judgment in the contract. For more specific details, see the rules contained in the Code of Federal Regulations, Title 16, Chapter I, Part 429.

California Law

California Civil Code, Sections 1689.5 through 1693 cover a home solicitation contract or offer. These sections cover all transactions that:

- are for the sale, rental, or lease of goods, services, or both;

- involve an amount of at least $25 (including all charges, interest, etc.); and,

- are made other than at the seller's regular place of business.

The law specifically does not apply to:

- any contract under which the buyer has the right to rescind under the federal *Consumer Credit Protection Act* or

- any contract for repair services with a licensed contractor if the contract price is less than $100, the negotiation was initiated by the buyer, and the contract contains a written and dated statement signed by the prospective buyer stating that the negotiation between the parties was initiated by the prospective buyer.

Written agreement. According to California Civil Code, Section 1689.7, the contract or offer must:

- be written in the same language as principally used in the oral sales presentation;

- be dated and signed by the buyer; and,

- contain in immediate proximity to the space reserved for the buyer's signature a conspicuous statement in a size equal to at least 10-point bold type, as follows:

You, the buyer, may cancel this transaction at any time prior to midnight of the third business day after the date of this transaction. See the attached notice of cancellation form for an explanation of this right.

Right to cancel. Any such sale described above may be cancelled by the buyer by written notice, in any form, deposited in the mail any time before midnight of the third business day after the sales day. Business days do not include Sunday, New Year's Day, Washington's Birthday, Memorial Day, Independence Day, Labor Day, Columbus Day, Veterans Day, Thanksgiving Day, and Christmas Day.

The code specifically provides for a seven-day right to cancel for sales of a personal emergency response unit. (Cal. Civ. Code Sec. 1689.6.) The code also provides for repairs made after a disaster, unless the repairs are necessary for the safety of the buyer or the buyer's property. (Cal. Civ. Code Sec. 1689.14.)

The code also provides for a three-day right to cancel after a sale made at a seminar. The importance of this law is that these sales may be cancelled even if made at the seller's place of business. (Cal. Civ. Code Sec. 1689.20.)

The agreement or offer to purchase must be accompanied by a completed form, in duplicate, captioned "Notice of Cancellation." It must be attached to the agreement or offer to purchase and be easily detachable. The statement must be in at least 10-point type and written in the same language used in the contract. An example of the statement is on page 141.

Seller's duty upon cancellation. Within ten days after cancellation, the seller must return any payments made by the buyer and any note or other evidence of indebtedness. If the down payment included goods traded in, the goods must be returned to the buyer in substantially as good condition as when received. Until the seller has complied with the above obligations, the buyer may retain possession of goods delivered by the seller, and the buyer has a lien on the goods. (Cal. Civ. Code Sec. 1689.10.)

If the seller has performed any services prior to cancellation, the seller is not entitled to compensation. If the seller's services result in the alteration of property of the buyer, the seller must restore the property to substantially as good condition as it was at the time the services were rendered. (Cal. Civ. Code Sec. 1689.11(c).)

Buyer's duty upon cancellation. Within twenty days after cancellation, the buyer, upon demand of the seller, must tender to the seller any goods delivered by the seller pursuant to the sale or offer, but the buyer is not obligated to tender the goods at any place other than his or her own address. If the seller fails to demand possession of goods within twenty days after cancellation, the goods become the property of the buyer without obligation to pay for them. (Cal. Civ. Code, Sec. 1689.11(a).)

The buyer has a duty to take reasonable care of the goods in his or her possession both prior to cancellation and during the twenty-day period following. During the twenty-day period, except for the buyer's duty of care, the goods are at the seller's risk. (Cal. Civ. Code Sec. 1689.11(b).)

You cannot get the buyer to waive these rights, so including waiver language in a contract or receipt will not work, because it will be void and unenforceable. (Cal. Civ. Code Sec. 1689.12.)

TELEPHONE SOLICITATION LAWS

Telephone solicitations are governed by the *Telephone Consumer Protection Act* (47 U.S.C. Sec. 227) and the Federal Communications Commission (FCC) rules implementing the Act (C.F.R., Title 47, Sec. 64.1200). Violators of the act can be sued for $500 damages by consumers and can be fined $10,000 by the FCC. Some of the requirements under the law include the following.

- ✪ Calls can only be made between 8 a.m. and 9 p.m.

- ✪ Solicitors must keep a *do not call* list and honor requests not to call.

- There must be a written policy that the parties called are told the name of the caller, the caller's business name and phone number or address, that the call is a sales call, and the nature of the goods or services.

- Personnel must be trained in the policies.

- Recorded messages cannot be used to call residences.

In 2003, the FCC introduced the national *Do Not Call Registry*, in which individuals could register their telephone numbers and prohibit certain telephone solicitors from calling the registered numbers. Once a person registers a telephone number, it remains on the registry for five years. Telemarketing firms can receive heavy fines for violating the registry statute, with fines ranging up to $11,000 per violation. Not all telephone solicitations are barred, however. The following solicitors may still contact a person whose telephone number has been entered in the registry:

- calls from companies with which the registered person has a prior business relationship;

- calls for which the recipient has given written consent;

- calls that do not include advertisements; and,

- calls from charitable organizations.

It is illegal under the Act to send advertising faxes to anyone who has not consented to receiving such faxes or is not an existing customer.

California Law   The California Business and Professions Code, Sections 17511 through 17513, cover telephone solicitations. These sections apply both to unsolicited calls and those made in response to a mailing. The typical mailing is one that tells the person receiving the mail to call for a free prize of some sort.

The exceptions to the law are too numerous to discuss. Some important ones involve potential purchasers you are already dealing with and calling to try to set up an appointment. If you plan to solicit by phone, you must register with the Department of Justice, Consumer Law Section. A form giving information about yourself and your company must be filled out, and a fee paid. At that time, you can determine if you qualify for an exemption.

If a buyer wants to sue a telephone solicitor and is not able to find him or her, serving the state's attorney general will constitute valid service.

Telephone sales falling under the law require written notice of the three-day right to cancel. The form that must be furnished to the purchaser in on page 147. No information may be added to the form and it must be in the same language in which the solicitation was made.

NOTICE OF BUYER'S RIGHT OF CANCELLATION

You may cancel this transaction, without any penalty or obligation, within three business days following your receipt of this notice of cancellation and the receipt of any products, or in the case of services, within three business days following receipt of the attached notice of confirmation.

If you cancel, any payments made by you or authorized by you, pursuant to any telephonic solicitation and purchase agreement shall be returned to you within ten days following receipt by the seller of your cancellation notice.

If you cancel, you must make available to the seller at your residence, in substantially as good condition as when received, any goods delivered to you under this contract, agreement, or sale, or you may, if you wish, comply with the instructions of the seller regarding the return shipment of the goods at the seller's expense and risk.

If you do make the goods available to the seller and the seller does not pick them up within twenty days of the date of your notice of cancellation, you may retain or dispose of the goods without any further obligation. If you fail to make the goods available to the seller, or if you agree to return the goods to the seller and fail to do so, then you remain liable for the performance of all obligations under the contract.

To cancel this transaction, mail or deliver a signed and dated copy of this cancellation notice, or any other written notice, or send a telegram to _____ (name of seller), at _____ (address of seller's place of business) not later than midnight of the third business day after receipt of the products and this notice of cancellation.

I HEREBY CANCEL THIS TRANSACTION.

_____

DATE

_____

BUYER'S SIGNATURE

PRICING, WEIGHTS, AND LABELING

All food products are required to have labels displaying information on the product's nutritional values, such as calories, fat, and protein. For most products, the label must be in the required format so that consumers can easily compare products. However, if such a format will not fit on the product label, the information may be in another format that is easily readable.

Federal rules require metric measurement be included on products. Under these rules, metric measures do not have to be the first measurement on the container, but they must be included. Food items that are packaged as they are sold (such as delicatessen items) do not have to contain metric labels.

California Law   The California Business and Professions Code, Section 12655, describes the legislature's intent to have unit pricing by labeling products by their price per ounce, per pound, per gallon, or their metric equivalent, or by per one-hundred square feet or per hundred count.

Sections 7100 through 7106 of the California Civil Code require item pricing for grocery items in stores using an automatic checkout system on at least 85% of the items. There are many exceptions, and the law does not apply to stores where there are not more than two permanent employees other than the owner or the owner's parents or children.

The Business and Professions Code contains numerous provisions on labeling, including the following.

- ✪ Sections 22900–22927 deal specifically with agriculture, utility, and industrial equipment sold by retailers under agreements with manufacturers and distributors. If this applies to you, check with the manufacturer or distributor as well as reading the code sections.

- ✪ Sections 12500–12517 require a certificate of approval for all designs of weighing and measuring devices used for a commercial purpose.

✪ Sections 12200–12214 describe the office of the *county sealer* who is appointed by each county's board of supervisors. The more common name for the county sealer is the *weights and measures inspector*.

✪ Sections 12300–12314 provide the standards (metric) for anyone contracting with the state.

✪ Sections 12100–12108 give the general authority for weights and measures to the Department of Agriculture. The Department oversees, instructs, and makes suggestions to the county sealers. It also may make inspections or accept the inspections of county sealers.

Sections 12601 through 12615.5 of the California Business and Professions Code describe how packaged commodities must be labeled. The gist of the law is to require labeling so that the consumer knows both what and how much is in the package. The law applies to any person engaged in the packaging or labeling of any commodity for distribution or sale, or for any person (other than a common carrier for hire, a contract carrier for hire, or a freight forwarder for hire) engaged in the distribution of any packaged or labeled commodity. The law does not apply to wholesale or retail distributors, unless they (1) are engaged in the packaging or labeling, (2) specify the manner of packaging or labeling, or (3) have knowledge of the violation of any labeling law requirements. (Cal. Bus. and Prof. Code Sec. 12602.)

According to California Business and Professions Code, Section 12603, the packaging must:

✪ bear a label specifying the identity of the commodity and the name and place of business of the manufacturer, packer, or distributor, and

✪ separately and accurately state the net quantity of the contents (in terms of weight or mass, measure, numerical count, or time), in a uniform location on the principal display panel of the label, using the most appropriate units of both the customary inch-pound system of measure and the metric system.

However, on a random package labeled in terms of pounds and decimal fractions of the pound, the statement may be carried out to not more than three decimal places and is not required to include a metric system. Also, the requirements concerning the metric system do not apply to nonconsumer packages, or foods that are packaged at the retail store level.

The label may not use any qualifying words or phrases in conjunction with the statement of net quantity; the words "minimum," "when packaged," or, words of similar import; or, qualify any unit of weight, measure, or count by any term that tends to exaggerate the amount (such as "jumbo," "giant," or "full"). (Cal. Bus. and Prof. Code, Sec. 12605.)

California Business and Professions Code, Section 12606, applies to the labeling of packaging and containers that are not subject to Section 403(d) of the *Federal Food, Drug and Cosmetic Act*. (21 U.S.C. Sec. 343(d).) No container may have a false bottom, false sidewalls, false lid or covering, or be in any way constructed or filled so as to facilitate the perpetration of deception or fraud. (Cal. Bus. and Prof. Code Sec. 12606(a).)

No container or packaging may be made, formed, or filled so as to be misleading. (Cal. Bus. and Prof. Code Sec. 12606(b).) A container that does not allow the consumer to fully view its contents is considered to be filled so as to be misleading if it contains nonfunctional *slack fill* (the difference between the actual capacity of a container and the volume of product it contains). The law gives fifteen situations in which slack fill is acceptable. Some of these situations are:

✪ where necessary to protect the contents;

✪ where there is unavoidable product settling during shipping and handling;

✪ where necessary to provide space for mandatory and necessary labeling information;

✪ where the product is packaged in a decorative or presentational container that has value independent of its function to hold the product (such as a gift combined with a container intended for use after the product is consumed), or a durable commemorative or promotional package, or along with a free gift;

✪ where the package size is necessary to discourage pilfering, facilitate handling, or accommodate tamper-resistant devices;

✪ where space is necessary for mixing, adding, shaking, or dispensing liquids or powders;

✪ where the packaging contains a product delivery or dosing device, if the device is readily apparent to the consumer; and,

✪ where the exterior packaging or immediate product container encloses computer hardware or software designed to serve a particular computer function, if the particular computer function to be performed is clearly and conspicuously disclosed on the exterior packaging.

California Business and Professions Code, Section 12606.2 has similar provisions that apply to food containers that are subject to Section 403 (d) of the Federal Food, Drug and Cosmetic Act.

Toys Every manufacturer, wholesaler, jobber, distributor, or other person who packages children's toys for sale to a retailer must clearly state on the outside of the package that the toy is unassembled if that is the case. If toys are packaged in another state, such labeling is the responsibility of the first wholesaler, jobber, distributor, or other person who has possession or control of the toys in California. (Cal. Bus. and Prof. Code Sec. 17531.1.)

If you will be involved in packaging your product, you should obtain a copy of these laws and become familiar with them.

Payment and Collection

Depending on the business you are in, you may be paid by cash, checks, credit cards, or some sort of financing arrangement, such as a promissory note or mortgage. Both state and federal laws affect the type of payments you collect, and failure to follow the laws can cost you considerably.

CASH

Cash is probably the easiest form of payment and it is subject to few restrictions. The most important one is that you keep an accurate accounting of your cash transactions and that you report all of your cash income on your tax return. Recent efforts to stop the drug trade have resulted in some serious penalties for failing to report cash transactions and for money laundering. The laws are so sweeping that even if you deal in cash in an ordinary business, you may violate the law and face huge fines and imprisonment.

The most important law to be concerned with is the one requiring the filing of the **REPORT OF CASH PAYMENTS OVER $10,000 (IRS FORM 8300)**. (A copy of form 8300 can be found at **www.irs.gov** or in Appendix B on page 277.) If one person pays you with $10,000 or more in cash, you are required to file this form. A transaction does not have to happen in one day. If a person brings you smaller amounts of cash that add up to $10,000 and the government can construe them as one transaction, then the form must be filed. Under this law, *cash* also includes travelers' checks and money orders, but not cashiers' checks or bank checks.

CHECKS

It is important to accept checks in your business. While there is a small percentage that will be bad, most checks will be good, and you will be able to accommodate more customers. To avoid having problems with checks, you should follow these rules.

- Accept only preprinted checks.

- Accept only checks drawn on local banks.

- Have the checks signed in your presence.

- Verify the sufficient funds with the bank on checks over a certain amount. If you are not selling big ticket items, you may want to set a maximum amount that you will accept.

- Do not accept third-party checks. The person who gives you the check should be the drawer.

- Ask to see a picture identification, such as a driver's license, California identification card, or military identification card.

Common sense always applies. Once you get to know your customers, you may relax your procedures a little.

You are not required by law to accept checks. (Cal. Civ. Code Sec.1725(d).) However, if you do accept checks, you may not:

- require a customer to provide a credit card as a condition of acceptance of the check, or record the number of the credit card;

✪ require a customer to sign a statement agreeing to allow his or her credit card to be charged to cover the check if it is returned as no good;

✪ record a credit card number; or,

✪ contact a credit card issuer to determine if the amount of any credit available to the person paying with a check will cover the amount of the check.

The penalty for an intentional violation is a fine of $250 for the first violation and $1,000 for each subsequent violation. However, no fine may be assessed if the business shows that the violation was not intentional and resulted from a bona fide error. If you are unsure about something regarding this law, contact an attorney.

However, a business accepting checks may:

✪ require the production of reasonable forms of identification, other than a credit card, which may include a driver's license or a California state identification card, or where one of these is not available, another form of photo identification;

✪ request, but not require, a purchaser to voluntarily display a credit card as an indication of creditworthiness or financial responsibility, or as an additional identification, provided that the only information recorded is the type of card, the issuer of the card, and the expiration date of the card. If you request the display of a credit card, you must inform the customer, by either of the following methods, that displaying the credit card is not a requirement for check writing:

  • by posting the following notice in a conspicuous location in the unobstructed view of the public within the premises where the check is being written, clearly and legibly: "Check writing ID: credit card may be requested but not required for purchases," or

- by training and requiring sales clerks or retail employees requesting the credit card to inform all check-writing customers that they are not required to display a credit card to write a check;

✪ request production of, or record, a credit card number as a condition for cashing a check that is being used solely to receive cash back;

✪ request, receive, or record a credit card number in lieu of requiring a deposit to secure payment in event of default, loss, damage, or other occurrence;

✪ require, verify, and record the purchaser's name, address, and telephone number; and,

✪ request or record a credit card number on a negotiable instrument used to make a payment on that credit card account.

Bad Checks   A payee of a check passed on insufficient funds can collect a service charge of not more that $25 on the first check passed and not more than $35 on each subsequent check. (Cal. Civ. Code Sec.1719.)

In addition, the payee can send a certified letter to the person who passed the check demanding payment for the amount of the check, the service charge, and the cost of the certified mailing. The letter must contain the provisions of the California Civil Code, Section 1719, the amount of the check, and the amount of the service charge. If payment is not made within thirty days from the date the written demand was mailed, the payee may collect three times the amount of the check (*treble damages*), subject to a minimum of $100 and a maximum of $1,500. If the payee collects treble damages, no service charge or mailing charge may be added. See California Civil Code, Section 1719, for forms and more details about what is required to bring the payee to court and win.

A customer can have *insufficient funds* by lacking funds in his or her account, not having an open account, or stopping payment on the check. However, stop payments do not constitute insufficient funds if there is a good faith dispute as to the transaction. Similarly, it would not constitute insufficient funds if there is written confirmation of an error or delay caused by the bank, or a delay in the regularly scheduled transfer or posting of a direct deposit of a Social Security or government benefit assistance payment.

Refunds After Accepting a Check

A popular scam is for a person to purchase something by using a check and then come back the next day demanding a refund. After making the refund, the business discovers the initial payment check bounced. Do not make refunds until checks clear.

REFUNDS

If you do not have a full refund or exchange policy for at least seven days after purchase, you must conspicuously display your policy. The California Civil Code Section 1723, reproduced below, gives the exact details. The rule is a common sense one. If you mark an item *as is* or *no return accepted*, you are okay. Foods or any items that could cause a health problem if resold are not subject to the rule. The customer must provide proof of purchase and return the item in the original package.

1723. (a) Every retail seller which sells goods to the public in this state that has a policy as to any of those goods of not giving full cash or credit refunds, or of not allowing equal exchanges, or any combination thereof, for at least seven days following purchase of the goods if they are returned and proof of their purchase is presented, shall conspicuously display that policy either on signs posted at each cash register and sales counter, at each public entrance, on tags attached to each item sold under that policy, or on the retail seller's order forms, if any. This display shall state the store's policy, including, but not limited to, whether cash refund, store credit, or exchanges will be given for the full amount of the purchase price; the applicable time period; the types of merchandise which are covered by the policy; and any other conditions which govern the refund, credit, or exchange of merchandise.

(b) This section does not apply to food, plants, flowers, perishable goods, goods marked "as is," "no returns accepted," "all

sales final," or with similar language, goods used or damaged after purchase, customized goods received as ordered, goods not returned with their original package, and goods which cannot be resold due to health considerations.

A retailer violating this law is liable to the buyer for the amount of the purchase if the buyer returns, or attempts to return, the goods on or before the thirtieth day after purchase. However, even if you post a strict policy, you may want to balance the potential loss of taking back an item against the loss of a customer.

CREDIT CARDS

In our buy now, pay later society, charge cards can add greatly to your sales potential, especially with large, discretionary purchases. For MasterCard, Visa, and Discover, the fees are about 2%, and this amount is easily paid for by the extra purchases that the cards allow. American Express charges 4–5%. (You may decide this is not worth paying, since almost everyone who has an American Express card also has another card.)

For businesses that have a retail outlet, there is usually no problem getting merchant status, which allows you to process credit card payments. Most commercial banks can handle it. Discover can also set you up to accept their card as well as MasterCard and Visa, and they will wire the money into your bank account daily.

Mail Order Businesses

For mail order businesses, especially those operating out of the home, it is much harder to get merchant status because of the number of scams in which large amounts are charged, no products are shipped, and the company folds.

Today, things are a little better. Some companies are even soliciting merchants. However, beware of those that charge exorbitant fees (such as $5 or $10 per order for "processing"). American Express will accept mail order companies operating out of the home. However, not as many people have their cards as others.

Some companies open a small storefront (or share one) to get merchant status, then process mostly mail orders. The processors usually do not want to accept you if you will do more than 50% mail order business; however, if you do not have many complaints, you may be allowed to process mostly mail orders. Whatever you do, keep your charge customers happy so that they do not complain.

California's credit card statutes are found in the *Song-Beverly Credit Card Act of 1971*. (Cal. Civ. Code Secs. 1747 through 1748.7.) You may want to put in an hour or two reading this if you plan to offer sales by credit card. The major points of this law that relate to offering credit through a major credit card company are summarized below. If you plan to offer your own credit, as opposed to merely using one or more of the major credit card companies, you will need to know and understand the entire Act.

Running Charges Through Another Business

You might be tempted to try to run your charges through another business. This may be all right if you actually sell your products through the other businesses, but if you run your business charges through that account, the other business may lose its merchant status. People who bought a book by mail from you and then find a charge on their statement from a florist shop will probably call the credit card company saying that they never bought anything from the florist shop. If you have too many of these, the account will be closed.

A new money-making scheme by the credit card companies is to offer business credit cards that the merchants are charged a higher fee for accepting. To make these more profitable, the credit card companies are telling customers they are not allowed to use their personal credit cards for business purposes. To keep your processing fees down, you can tell your customers you prefer personal, not business, credit cards.

Further, California law says that the person who processes the card for payment must furnish the goods or services that are the subject of the charge. (Cal. Civ. Code Sec. 1748.7.) There are a few exceptions, including:

✪ where a person furnishes goods or services on the business premises of a general merchandise retailer (defined as any person or entity, regardless of the form of organization, that has continuously offered for sale or lease more than one hundred different types of goods or services to the public in California throughout a period that includes the immediately preceding five years);

✪ where there is a franchisee/franchisor relationship; or,

✪ where less than $500 of credit card charges in any one year period are processed through a retailer's account.

Surcharges and Discounts

The California Civil Code forbids charging a surcharge to a customer for using a credit card. (Cal. Civ. Code Sec. 1748.1(a).) This does not apply if a retailer only accepts credit cards for payment of telephone orders and only accepts cash at a public store or other facility of the same retailer. (Cal. Civ. Code Sec. 1748.1(b).) The law does allow you to sell items at a discount for cash, but the discount must be the same for all customers. (Cal. Civ. Code Sec. 1748.1(a).) Charges for third-party credit card guarantee services, if added to the price charged if cash were paid, are considered prohibited surcharges, even if they are payable directly to the third party or are charged separately. (Cal. Civ. Code Sec. 1748.1(d).) Furthermore, a credit card issuer cannot prevent a retailer from offering a discount for cash. (Cal. Civ. Code Sec. 1748.)

Identification and Personal Information

Under California Civil Code Section 1747.8, if you accept a credit card, you may not do any of the following:

✪ request or require the cardholder to write any personal identification information, such as address and telephone number, on the credit card transaction form or otherwise;

✪ request or require the cardholder to provide personal identification information, which you or your employee writes on the credit card transaction form or otherwise; or,

✪ utilize a credit card form that contains preprinted spaces specifically designated for filling in personal identification information of the cardholder.

However, you may request or require personal identification information:

✪   when the credit card is being used as a deposit to secure payment in the event of default, loss, damage, or other similar occurrence;

✪   when the credit card is being used for cash advance transactions;

✪   when you are contractually obligated to provide personal identification information in order to complete the credit card transaction, or are obligated to collect and record the personal identification information by federal law or regulation; or,

✪   when personal identification information is required for a special purpose incidental but related to the individual credit card transaction, including, but not limited to, information relating to shipping, delivery, servicing, or installation of the purchased merchandise, or for special orders.

Further, you may require the buyer to display another form of positive identification, provided that none of the information contained thereon is written or recorded on the credit card transaction form or otherwise. If the cardholder pays for the transaction with a credit card number and does not make the credit card available upon request to verify the number, the cardholder's driver's license number or identification card number may be recorded on the credit card transaction form or otherwise.

Violations are punishable by a fine of up to $250 for the first violation and $1,000 for subsequent violations. However, no fine may be assessed if the defendant shows that the violation was not intentional and resulted from a bona fide error. Check with an attorney if you are in this situation.

Receipts for Credit Card Purchases   In California, you may not print more than the last five digits of the credit card account number or the expiration date on any receipt provided to the cardholder. (Cal. Civ. Code Sec. 1747.09.) This requirement applies to receipts that are electronically printed, and not to transactions in which the sole means of recording the person's credit card number is by handwriting or by an imprint or copy of the credit card.

Billing Errors   Any billing error made by the retailer must be corrected within sixty days from the date on which an inquiry concerning a billing error was mailed by the cardholder. (Cal. Civ. Code Sec. 1747.60.) Failure to correct the billing error within this period makes the retailer liable to the cardholder for the amount by which the outstanding balance of the cardholder's account is greater than the correct balance, plus any interest, finance charges, service charges, or other charges on the obligation giving rise to the billing error. Also, any cardholder injured by a willful violation may sue for damages, and judgment may be entered for three times the amount of actual damages, plus attorney's fees and costs. A card issuer is not liable for a billing error made by a retailer, and a retailer is not liable for a billing error made by a card issuer. (Cal. Civ. Code Sec. 1747.65.)

DEBIT CARDS

The debit card has become more popular in the last few years. Rather than extending credit for a purchase, the amount is taken directly from the buyer's bank account. This takes away the risk of the buyer not paying the credit card bill. The procedure is basically the same, but instead of checking to see if the buyer has sufficient credit for the purchase, you check to verify that the buyer has enough money in the bank to cover the purchase.

GIFT CARDS

Although gift cards have been around for many years, they emerged as a major purchase in the holiday season of 2005. Merchants were finally able to convince people that there really was a difference between giving cash and a gift card, and while cash was a thoughtless gift, a gift card was a way to ensure that the recipient got what he or she wanted.

There are two types of gift cards. The first is good at a specific business. An example would be giving a card for dinner at a restaurant you know the recipient enjoys. The second is like a credit or debit card. It is good anywhere the card is accepted. All the major credit card companies have gift cards. While you establish which credit cards you will accept, check the issuer's gift card costs and procedures. Costs are basically the same as a credit card transaction, and verifying the usable amount on the gift card is similar to checking a credit or debit card transaction.

VERIFYING TRANSACTIONS

Verifying transactions from checks, credit cards, debit cards, or gift cards can be done manually or automatically. Manual verification usually requires that you take an imprint of the card. You then telephone the company (Visa, MasterCard, etc.) and punch in the card number. The card is then accepted or declined. An acceptance number is given, which is your evidence that the card was accepted.

Automatic verification requires renting or buying a terminal. You then feed the check or swipe the card into the terminal and that is it—the card is accepted or declined. The cost of a terminal varies depending on the speed of the machine. Expect to spend at least $500. Leasing will cost upwards of $30 per month. Whether you rent or buy, you will still pay a transaction fee.

If your business has relatively few sales, such as a major appliance store, the cheaper manual verification should be sufficient. If you are going to have a line at your checkout counter, you may need the faster automatic terminal.

FINANCING LAWS

Some businesses can more easily make sales if they finance the purchases themselves. If the business has enough capital to do this, it can earn extra profits on the financing terms. Nonetheless, because of abuses, many consumer protection laws have been passed by both the federal and state governments.

Regulation Z Two important federal laws regarding financing are called the *Truth in Lending Act* and the *Fair Credit Billing Act*. These are implemented by what is called *Regulation Z* (commonly known as *Reg. Z*), issued by the Board of Governors of the Federal Reserve System.

(1 C.F.R., Vol. 12, p.226.) This is a very complicated law, and some have said that no business can be sure to be in compliance with it.

The regulation covers all transactions in which four conditions are met:

1. credit is offered;

2   the offering of credit is regularly done;

3. there is a finance charge for the credit or there is a written agreement with more than four payments; and,

4. the credit is for personal, family, or household purposes.

It also covers credit card transactions where only the first two conditions are met. It applies to leases if the consumer ends up paying the full value and keeping the item leased. It does not apply to the following transactions:

✪   transactions with businesses or agricultural purposes;

✪   transactions with organizations such as corporations or the government;

✪   transactions of over $25,000 that are not secured by the consumer's dwelling;

✪   credit involving public utilities;

✪   credit involving securities or commodities; and,

✪   home fuel budget plans.

The way for a small business to avoid Reg. Z violations is to avoid transactions that meet the conditions or to make sure all transactions fall under the exceptions. For many businesses, this is easy. Instead of extending credit to customers, accept credit cards and let the credit card company extend the credit. However, if your customers usually do not have credit cards or if you are in a business that often extends credit, such as used car sales, you should consult a lawyer knowledgeable about Reg. Z or get a copy for yourself at **www.cardreport.com/laws/tila/tila.html**.

California Law   California also has laws regarding financing arrangements. (Cal. Civ. Code Secs. 1810 through 1810.12.) These laws cover disclosure to the consumer of finance charges in an installment sales agreement, what constitutes a finance charge, and other guidelines. Anyone engaged in installment sales in California should carefully review the latest versions of these sections of the Civil Code. There are several other code sections that apply to specific businesses, such as home improvements, automotive repair, and real estate. Check with your industry association to see if any such special financing laws apply to you.

The California Commercial Code covers debt secured by collateral. If you are going to hold the goods until the debt is paid, or be able to repossess the goods for nonpayment, you will need to use a security agreement and financing statement.

USURY

Usury is the charging of an illegally high rate of interest. California's usury law in contained in Article 15 of the state constitution. The legal rate of interest is 7%, but parties may agree in writing to a rate up to 10% for those things used primarily for personal, family, or household purposes. Real estate is not included.

For other purposes, the maximum rate is the higher of 10% or 5% above the prevailing loan rate of the Federal Reserve Bank of San Francisco's as of the 25th of the month preceding the loan.

There are many businesses exempt from usury laws, such as banks, savings and loans, finance companies, pawnbrokers, and mortgage brokers. Check your industry association for your status.

The penalty for charging interest in excess of the legal rate is that the borrower does not have to pay any interest and the lender has to repay double the amounts received. Charging or receiving interest at a rate of over 25% but less than 45% is a misdemeanor, and charging or receiving interest of 45% or greater is a felony. The borrower may also sue for damages, costs, punitive damages, and attorney's fees.

COLLECTIONS

The *Fair Debt Collection Practices Act of 1977* bans the use of deception, harassment, and other unreasonable acts in the collection of debts. It has strict requirements whenever someone is collecting a debt for someone else. If you are in the collection business, you must get a copy of this law.

The Federal Trade Commission has issued some rules that prohibit deceptive representations, such as pretending to be in the motion picture industry, the government, or a credit bureau, or using questionnaires that do not say that they are for the purpose of collecting a debt. (16 C.F.R. Sec. 137.)

California Law   The *Rosenthal Fair Debt Collection Practices Act* specifies prohibited methods of collecting debts in California. (Cal. Civ. Code, beginning with Section 1788.) These prohibited practices are summarized below. The general idea is that you cannot use force or threat of force; lie by pretending to be someone you are not, such as a police officer, government official, or attorney; or, tell others of the debt, such as employers or relatives of the debtor, unless there is a reason to tell them, such as trying to locate the debtor or to enforce a garnishment after a judgment.

Under the Rosenthal Fair Debt Collection Practices Act, a debt collector may not:

- use or threaten to use physical force or violence, or any criminal means, to cause harm to anyone's person, reputation, or property;

- threaten to (falsely) accuse the debtor of committing a crime;

- communicate or threaten to communicate to any person the fact that a debtor has engaged in conduct, other than the failure to pay a consumer debt, that will defame the debtor;

- ✪ threaten to sell or assign a consumer debt to another person, with an accompanying false representation that sale or assignment would result in the debtor losing any defense to the debt;

- ✪ threaten any person that nonpayment of the consumer debt may result in the arrest of the debtor or the seizure, garnishment, attachment, or sale of any property, or the garnishment or attachment of wages of the debtor, unless such action is in fact contemplated by the debt collector and permitted by the law;

- ✪ threaten to take any action against the debtor that is prohibited by law;

- ✪ use obscene or profane language;

- ✪ place telephone calls without disclosing the caller's identity, although an employee of a licensed collection agency may use a registered alias name, as long as he or she correctly identifies the agency he or she represents;

- ✪ cause expense to any person for long-distance telephone calls, telegram fees, or charges for other similar communications, by misrepresenting to such person the purpose of such telephone call, telegram, or similar communication;

- ✪ cause a telephone to ring repeatedly or continuously to annoy the person called;

- ✪ communicate, by telephone or in person, with the debtor with such frequency as to be unreasonable and to constitute harassment of the debtor under the circumstances;

- ✪ communicate with the debtor's employer regarding a consumer debt, unless necessary to the collection of the debt, or unless the debtor or the debtor's attorney consented in writing to such communication;

    NOTE: *A communication is necessary to the collection of the debt only if it is made for the purposes of verifying the debtor's employment, locating the debtor, or effecting* *garnishment of wages after judgment; or, in the case of a medical debt, to discover the existence of medical insurance. Any such communication, other than in the case of a medical debt by a health care provider or its agent for the purpose of discovering the existence of medical insurance, must be in writing, unless such written communication receives no response within fifteen days and may be made only as many times as is necessary to the collection of the debt. Communications to a debtor's employer regarding a debt may not contain language that would be improper if the communication were made to the debtor. One communication solely for the purpose of verifying employment may be oral without prior written contact.*

✪ communicate information regarding a consumer debt to any member of the debtor's family, other than the debtor's spouse, or the parents or guardians of the debtor who is either a minor or who resides in the same household with such parent or guardian, prior to obtaining a judgment against the debtor, except where the purpose of the communication is to locate the debtor, or where the debtor or his or her attorney has consented in writing to such communication;

✪ communicate to any person any list of debtors that discloses the nature or existence of a consumer debt, commonly known as *deadbeat lists*, or advertising any consumer debt for sale by naming the debtor;

✪ communicate with the debtor by means of a written communication that displays or conveys any information about the consumer debt or the debtor other than the name, address, and telephone number of the debtor and the debt collector, and that is intended both to be seen by another person and to embarrass the debtor (however, information may be provided to a consumer reporting agency or to any other person reasonably believed to have a legitimate business need for such information);

✪   communicate with the debtor other than in the name of the debt collector or the person on whose behalf the debt collector is acting;

✪   make any false representation that any person is an attorney or counselor at law;

✪   communicate with a debtor in the name of an attorney at law or upon stationery or like written instruments bearing the name of the attorney, unless such communication is by an attorney or has been approved or authorized by such attorney;

✪   represent that any debt collector is vouched for, bonded by, affiliated with, or is an instrumentality, agent, or official of any federal, state, or local government, or any agency of federal, state, or local government, unless the collector is actually employed by the particular governmental agency in question and is acting on behalf of such agency in the debt collection matter;

✪   falsely represent that the consumer debt may be increased by the addition of attorney's fees, investigation fees, service fees, finance charges, or other charges if such fees or charges may not legally be added to the existing obligation;

✪   falsely represent that information concerning a debtor's failure or alleged failure to pay a consumer debt has been or is about to be referred to a consumer reporting agency;

✪   falsely represent that a debt collector is a consumer reporting agency;

✪   falsely represent that collection letters, notices, or other printed forms are being sent by or on behalf of a claim, credit, audit, or legal department;

✪   falsely represent the true nature of the business or services being rendered by the debt collector;

- ✪ falsely represent that a legal proceeding has been, is about to be, or will be instituted unless payment of a consumer debt is made;

- ✪ falsely represent that a consumer debt has been, is about to be, or will be sold, assigned, or referred to a debt collector for collection or any communication by a licensed collection agency to a debtor demanding money unless the claim is actually assigned to the collection agency;

- ✪ obtain an affirmation of a consumer debt that has been discharged in bankruptcy without clearly and conspicuously disclosing to the debtor, in writing, at the time such affirmation is sought, the fact that the debtor is not legally obligated to make an affirmation;

- ✪ collect or attempt to collect from the debtor the whole or any part of the debt collector's fee or charge for services rendered, or other expense incurred by the debt collector in the collection of the consumer debt, except as permitted by law;

- ✪ initiate communications, other than statements of account, with the debtor with regard to the consumer debt, when the debt collector has been notified in writing by the debtor's attorney that the debtor is represented by the attorney with respect to the consumer debt, and such notice includes the attorney's name and address, and a request that all communications regarding the consumer debt be addressed to the attorney, unless the attorney fails to answer correspondence, return telephone calls, or discuss the obligation in question. This does not apply where prior approval has been obtained from the debtor's attorney, or where the communication is a response in the ordinary course of business to the debtor's inquiry;

- ✪ collect or attempt to collect a consumer debt by means of judicial proceedings when the debt collector knows that service of process, where essential to jurisdiction over the debtor or his property, has not been legally effected;

- ✪ collect or attempt to collect a consumer debt, other than one already reduced to judgment, by means of judicial proceedings in a county other than the county in which the debtor has incurred the debt or the county in which the debtor resides at the time such proceedings are instituted, or resided at the time the debt was incurred; or,

❂ send a communication that simulates legal or judicial process or gives the appearance of being authorized, issued, or approved by a governmental agency or attorney when it is not. (Any violation of the provisions of this is a misdemeanor and punishable by imprisonment for up to six months, or by a fine of up to $2,500, or both.)

Also, a licensed collection agency may not send any communication to a debtor demanding money unless the claim is actually assigned to the collection agency.

chapter 15

Business Relations

At both the federal and state levels, there exist many laws regarding how businesses relate to one another. Some of the more important ones are discussed in this chapter.

THE UNIFORM COMMERCIAL CODE

The *Uniform Commercial Code* (UCC) is a set of laws regulating numerous aspects of doing business. A national group drafted this set of uniform laws to avoid having a patchwork of different laws around the fifty states. Although some states modified some sections of the laws, the UCC is basically the same in most of the states. California's version is simply called the Commercial Code (Cal. Com. Code), and is fairly easy to understand. It is a good idea to obtain a copy (you can download it over the Internet). The purpose of the UCC is to make it easier for people to do business. The UCC takes contract law and changes those areas that would be difficult to use in millions of trans-actions taking place daily.

For example, a buyer sends an order (an *offer*). The seller sends back a confirmation that the order has been received and will be filled (an *acceptance*). Under contract law, the acceptance must exactly match the offer for a contract to be formed. Suppose the printed portion of the seller's confirmation does not exactly match the buyer's printed portion of the order. The UCC looks at whether the difference is minor or important. If it is not a *material* change, the UCC says it becomes part of the contract if there is no objection. There are other rules, but this gives you the general idea of what the UCC is trying to accomplish.

The UCC applies to everyone. If you buy something at your neighbor's yard sale, the Code applies. However, the Code applies higher standards to those in business—merchants. A *merchant* is someone who deals regularly in the goods involved or has special knowledge of them (expertise). For example, a sawmill sold a saw to another sawmill. In a lawsuit that followed, the question arose as to whether the seller was a merchant. The answer was no, because sawmills do not regularly sell saws.

Article 2 of the UCC covers the sale of goods, which are usually defined as moveable items. Some are obvious—a car or pencil would be a good. However, there are times when you may not be sure if the item is covered by the Code. Those things covered by other laws are real estate, services, and *paper rights*, such as stocks and bonds.

When you hire a roofer to install a new roof on your building, there is a combination of product and service involved. Also, once the roof is installed, it is real estate. This type of situation will not come up often, but if it does and you are not sure how or if the UCC applies, see a lawyer.

Other sections of the UCC that you should know concern warranties, negotiable instruments (like checks and notes), letters of credit, secured transactions, shipping terms, sale on approval, and sale or return. Some of the things that you should know will be discussed, but covering the entire UCC is beyond the scope of this book.

Banking

If you are starting a business, you should pick a bank to use. Sit down with whomever is going to handle your account and go over negotiable instruments. Ask what you should know about both the law and the bank's policy. If you are selling items that you will repossess if payments are not made, ask them about that as well. A good banker knows the UCC and can be a valuable asset to your business.

Usage of Trade   One area that may be of even greater importance is called *usage of trade*. This means that you can be responsible for contract language that may not mean what you think it means. There was a case where a biscuit company contracted to buy 100,000 sacks of potatoes. When the time for performance came, the buyer only took about 60,000 sacks. The seller sued. The court held that in this industry, the promise to buy a certain amount is only an approximation of the amount that the buyer will need, and the buyer did not breach the contract by taking the smaller amount. The moral of the story is that you must know your industry and how contracts are interpreted. If you are not sure, put right in your contract that it will be controlled by the plain meaning of the words and that usage of trade shall not be used to interpret the contract.

Shipping Terms and Payment   The California Commercial Code sets out rules for the place of delivery, and time and method of payment.

> *Section 2308. Unless otherwise agreed*
> *(a) The place for delivery of goods is the seller's place of business or if he has none his residence; but*
> *(b) In a contract for sale of identified goods which to the knowledge of the parties at the time of contracting are in some other place, that place is the place for their delivery; and*
> *(c) Documents of title may be delivered through customary banking channels.*

If you are going to ship goods, it is important that you are familiar with shipping terms. Abbreviations such as F.O.B. (free on board), F.A.S. (free alongside), C.I.F. (cost, insurance, and freight), C and F or CF (cost and freight), and Ex-Ship (delivery from the carrying vessel) mean different things as to when the title and risk of loss will pass from the seller to the buyer. (Cal. Com. Code Secs. 2319 through 2322.) Even if insurance is involved, it is important to know which party has to deal with the insurance company.

The code also provides for the time and method of payment.

> *Section 2310. Unless otherwise agreed*
> *(a) Payment is due at the time and place at which the buyer is to receive the goods even though the place of shipment is the place of delivery; and*

> (b) If the seller is authorized to send the goods he may ship them under reservation, and may tender the documents of title, but the buyer may inspect the goods after their arrival before payment is due unless such inspection is inconsistent with the terms of the contract (Section 2513); and
>
> (c) If delivery is authorized and made by way of documents of title otherwise than by subdivision (b) then payment is due at the time and place at which the buyer is to receive the documents regardless of where the goods are to be received; and
>
> (d) Where the seller is required or authorized to ship the goods on credit the credit period runs from the time of shipment but postdating the invoice or delaying its dispatch will correspondingly delay the starting of the credit period.

Note that the code states *unless otherwise agreed*. It is important to know that parties to a contract can set any terms that they desire, so long as they are not illegal, against public policy, or so unfair that they are unconscionable.

Sale on Approval

A *sale on approval* is one where the buyer is going to use the goods for a certain period to decide whether to keep them. If you are going to sell products on approval, there are a few things you should know.

You have seen ads saying, "Try it for ten days. If you are not satisfied, return it and owe nothing." Suppose during those ten days the goods are destroyed, stolen, or the buyer declares bankruptcy. What are the rights of the seller? (Cal. Com. Code Sec. 2326.) If you sell on approval, you retain title and risk of loss until the goods are accepted and paid for. This is good if the buyer declares bankruptcy. You still own the goods and the buyer's creditors cannot get them. However, if the goods are stolen or damaged through no fault of the buyer, it is you who must bear the loss. Talk to your insurance agent about this possibility.

Sale or Return

Sale or return (also called *sale and return*) is a sale to someone who will resell the goods. Say you manufacture bathing suits. You sell to stores with the agreement that they may return any unsold suits at the end of the season. This encourages them to buy more suits.

In a sale or return, the buyer has title and risk of loss. If the buyer declares bankruptcy, you lose the goods and become a general creditor for any unpaid balance. If they are stolen or damaged, it is the buyer's problem. You are still entitled to payment in full. (Cal. Com. Code Sec. 2327.)

WARRANTIES

There are several types of warranties. You can find them at Cal. Com. Code Secs. 2311 through 2317 and Cal. Civ. Code Secs. 1792 through 1795.7. These are summarized below.

Warranty of Title

When you sell (or lease) goods, you warrant that you have the right to do so. In other words, if you sell goods, you warrant that you own the goods or are acting as an agent for the owner. You also warrant that there is no one who is owed money for the goods or has any other claim to them.

Suppose you find something and decide to sell it. You know there is an owner somewhere. You cannot warrant that you are the owner. You must let the buyer know that you are not giving this warranty. Simply saying that the goods are sold *as is* will not do it. You must *specifically disclaim* the warranty. You can do this by letting the buyer know that you found the goods or by saying that there is no *warranty of title* given.

Express Warranties

Express warranties are warranties given with words (oral or written). The words must first pertain to the goods themselves. A promise about delivery terms would not be a warranty. A description ("when it arrives, it will be painted green"), sample or model ("it is going to look just like this model"), or promise ("if it breaks, I will fix it") is a warranty. What is not a warranty is a nonfactual opinion ("I think you are going to like it").

Implied Warranties

Implied warranties are automatic warranties. You give them just by selling (or leasing) the goods. Some examples of implied warranties include the warranty of merchantablity and warranty of fitness for a particular purpose.

Warranty of merchantability. The warranty of merchantability is a warranty given only by a merchant. The main idea of the warranty is that the goods are what the ordinary buyer would think they are. If you sell a camera, you warrant that it has a lens, a shutter, a place to put the film, and that under normal circumstances, it will take pictures. If you sell a toaster, you warrant that it will make toast. The product must also be adequately labeled and packaged. When you disclaim the *warranty of merchantability*, you are really saying that you do not know if the product will work. Merchants do not usually do this.

Warranty of fitness for a particular purpose. The warranty of fitness for a particular purpose is a warranty of which you should be careful. If a seller knows or has reason to know of the buyer's use of the product, and the buyer is relying on the seller's recommendation, the seller gives a warranty that the product is fit for the buyer's purpose. The seller can either tell the buyer that the product will do what the buyer wants or simply hand the buyer the product.

Example 1:
A buyer walks into your camera shop and asks to buy a lens that will take a picture of a small animal at one hundred yards. You take a lens off the shelf and hand it to the buyer. You are giving the buyer the warranty. There may be nothing wrong with the lens, but if it will not take a picture of a small animal at one hundred yards, you have breached your warranty.

Example 2:
A buyer comes into your paint store and tells you that she has run out of paint in the middle of painting a room. The buyer hands you a sample of the paint she has been using. You know that you not only have to sell her paint that is fit for its ordinary use (warranty of merchantability), but paint that will match exactly the paint she has been using (warranty of fitness for a particular purpose).

Implied warranties may be disclaimed by selling the product *as is* or *with all faults*. You may also specifically state that there is no warranty of merchantability (conspicuously if in writing) or no warranty of fitness for a particular purpose (conspicuously and only in writing).

Limited Warranties

You may limit your warranties instead of disclaiming them. They may be limited to time, such as a thirty-day warranty, or to part of the product, such as the drive train of a car. Always limit your warranty in some way, even if you want to give a complete warranty.

Federal Warranties

In 1975, the federal government got involved in warranties with the *Magnuson-Moss Warranty Act*. There are two things you must know about the Act. First, the Act provides for attorney's fees to be paid by the seller for breach of warranty. This means that the buyer could afford to sue for the toaster that would not make toast. This means that no matter how small an amount is involved, pay attention—you could end up paying thousands in lawyer's fees over the toaster.

Although the Act defines a *full warranty*, to this day, no one is quite sure what a full warranty is. This is why even warranties that seem to cover everything are called *limited*.

There are many other features to the Magnuson-Moss Act. If someone is threatening to sue for *breach of warranty* and you do not want to give in, see a lawyer.

LIMITATION OF REMEDIES

You may limit remedies of the buyer. You could, for example, say that the buyer may exchange the item sold, but not get a refund. Limitations of remedies are generally upheld if reasonable. For example, you give the buyer a new item five times and each one is defective. The court would probably say that your remedy has failed and allow the buyer a refund or other remedy. You may not limit remedies when the product has caused physical injury.

Example:

A tire company limited its warranty to replacement of the tire. After six nuns were killed in an accident because of a defective tire, the company's defense was that the only liability was for a new tire. You do not have to be a lawyer to guess the result. Death or injury cannot be defended by a limitation on the warranty.

COMMERCIAL DISCRIMINATION

The *Robinson-Patman Act of 1936* prohibits businesses from injuring competition by offering the same goods at different prices to different buyers. This means that the large chain stores should not be getting a better price than your small shop. It also requires that promotional allowances must be made on proportionally the same terms to all buyers.

As a small business, you may be a victim of Robinson-Patman Act violation, but fighting a much larger company in court would probably be too expensive for you. Your best bet, if an actual violation has occurred, would be to see if you could get the government to prosecute it. For more information on what constitutes a violation, see the Federal Trade Commission and the Department of Justice's joint site at **www.ftc.gov/bc/compguide**.

California Law The California Business and Professions Code covers the deliberate attempt to ruin a competitor.

It is unlawful for any person engaged in the production, manufacture, distribution or sale of any article or product to create locality discriminations with the intent to destroy the competition of any regular established dealer in such article or product, or to prevent the competition of any person who intends and attempts to become such a dealer. Nothing in this section prohibits the meeting in good faith of a competitive price. (Cal. Bus. and Prof. Code Sec. 17040.)

RESTRAINING TRADE

One of the earliest federal laws affecting business is the *Sherman Antitrust Act of 1890*. The purpose of the law was to protect competition in the marketplace by prohibiting monopolies.

Examples of some things that are prohibited are:

✪   agreements between competitors to sell at the same prices;

✪   agreements between competitors on how much will be sold or produced;

✪   agreements between competitors to divide up a market;

✪   refusing to sell one product without a second product; or,

✪   exchanging information among competitors, which results in similarity of prices.

As a small business, you will probably not be in a position to violate the Sherman Act, but you should be aware of it if a larger competitor tries to put you out of business. Fighting a much larger company in court would probably be too expensive for you, but if an actual violation has occurred, you might be able to get the government to prosecute it. For more information on what constitutes a violation, see the website by the Federal Trade Commission and the Department of Justice at **www.ftc.gov/bc/compguide**.

California Law   California's Business and Professions Code contains several provisions relating to restraint of trade, including the following sections.

✪   Section 16720 prohibits trusts. A trust, as defined in this section, is closer to what the average person would call a conspiracy. When two or more persons combine capital, skill, or acts to restrict trade or create unfair competition, it is a trust. This includes price fixing and limiting production to keep prices high.

✪   Section 16721 makes it unlawful to exclude anyone from a business transaction on the basis of a policy expressed in any document or writing that requires discrimination against another person on the basis of the person's sex, race, color, religion, ancestry, or national origin, or on the basis that the person conducts or has conducted business in a particular location. However, to confuse things, the law also states:

Nothing in this section shall be construed to prohibit any person, on the basis of his or her individual ideology or preferences, from doing business or refusing to do business with any other person consistent with law.

✪   Section 16725 makes it clear that industry associations that try to improve industry standards and promote trade are allowed.

✪   Section 16727 prohibits the setting of a price, or giving rebates or discounts to a buyer in exchange for the buyer's agreement not to buy elsewhere.

✪   Section 16728 gives an exemption to *motor carriers of property* (as defined in the California Vehicle Code Section 34601), which may voluntarily elect to participate in uniform cargo liability rules, uniform bills of lading or receipts for property being transported, uniform cargo credit rules, joint line rates or routes, classifications, mileage guides, and pooling. This is to comply with federal law. (49 U.S.C. Sec. 14501 (c).) The election may be made by either participating in an agreement pursuant to 49 U.S.C. Sec. 13703, or by filing a notice and certain documents with the Department of Motor Vehicles.

INTELLECTUAL PROPERTY PROTECTION

As a business owner, you should know enough about intellectual property law to protect your own creations and to keep from violating the rights of others. Intellectual property is the product of human creativity, such as writings, designs, inventions, melodies, and processes. They are things that can be stolen without being physically taken. For example, if you write a book, someone can steal the words from your book without stealing a physical copy of it.

As the Internet grows, intellectual property is becoming more valuable. Business owners should take the action necessary to protect their companies' intellectual property. Additionally, business owners should know intellectual property law to be sure that they do not violate the rights of others. Even an unknowing violation of the law can result in stiff fines and penalties.

The following are the types of intellectual property and the ways to protect them.

Patent   A *patent* is protection given to new and useful inventions, discoveries, and designs. To be entitled to a patent, a work must be completely new and unobvious. A patent is granted to the first inventor who files for the patent. Once an invention is patented, no one else can make use of that invention, even if they discover it independently after a lifetime of research. A patent protects an invention for seventeen years; for designs, it is protected for three and one-half, seven, or fourteen years. Patents cannot be renewed. The patent application must clearly explain how to make the invention, so that when the patent expires, others will be able to freely make and use the invention. Patents are registered with the *United States Patent and Trademark Office* (PTO). Examples of things that would be patentable would be mechanical devices or new drug formulas.

In recent years, patents have been used to protect things such as computer programs and business methods, including Amazon's one-click ordering. Few cases challenging these patents have gotten through the court system, so it is too early to tell if they will hold up. About half the patents that reach the Supreme Court are held to be invalid.

Copyright   A *copyright* is protection given to original works of authorship, such as written works, musical works, visual works, performance works, or computer software programs. A copyright exists from the moment of creation, but one cannot register a copyright until it has been fixed in tangible form. Also, one cannot copyright titles, names, or slogans. A copyright currently gives the author and his or her heirs exclusive right to the work for the life of the author plus seventy years.

Copyrights first registered before 1978 last for ninety-five years. (This was previously seventy-five years, but was extended twenty years to match the European system.) Copyrights are registered with the Register of Copyrights at the Library of Congress. Examples of works that would be copyrightable are books, paintings, songs, poems, plays, drawings, and films.

Trademark   A *trademark* is protection given to a name or symbol used to distinguish one person's goods or services from those of others. It can consist of letters, numerals, packaging, labeling, musical notes, colors, or a combination of these. If a trademark is used on services as opposed to goods, it is called a *service mark*.

A trademark lasts indefinitely if it is used continuously and renewed properly. Trademarks are registered with the United States Patent and Trademark Office and with individual states. (This is explained further in Chapter 3.) Examples of trademarks are the Chrysler name on automobiles, the red border on TIME magazine, and the shape of the Coca-Cola bottle.

Trade Secret

A *trade secret* is some information or process that provides a commercial advantage that is protected by keeping it a secret. Examples of trade secrets may be a list of successful distributors, the formula for Coca-Cola, or some unique source code in a computer program. Trade secrets are not registered anywhere—they are protected by the fact that they are not disclosed. They are protected only for as long as they are kept secret. If you independently discover the formula for Coca-Cola tomorrow, you can freely market it (but you cannot use the trademark "Coca-Cola" on your product to market it).

Unprotected Creations

Some things just cannot be protected—such things as ideas, systems, and discoveries are not allowed any protection under any law. If you have a great idea, such as selling packets of hangover medicine in bars, you cannot stop others from doing the same thing. If you invent a new medicine, you can patent it; if you pick a distinctive name for it, you can register it as a trademark; if you create a unique picture or instructions for the package, you can copyright them. However, you cannot stop others from using your basic business idea of marketing hangover medicine in bars.

Notice the subtle differences between the protective systems available. If you invent something two days after someone else does, you cannot even use it yourself if the other person has patented it. However, if you write the same poem as someone else and neither of you copied the other, both of you can copyright the poem. If you patent something, you can have the exclusive rights to it for the term of the patent, but you must disclose how others can make it after the patent expires. However, if you keep it a trade secret, you have exclusive rights as long as no one learns the secret.

Endless Laws

The state of California and the federal government have numerous laws and rules that apply to every aspect of every type of business. There are even laws governing such things as fence posts, hosiery, rabbit raising, refund policies, frozen desserts, and advertising. Every business is affected by at least one of these laws.

Some activities are covered by both state and federal laws. In such cases, you must obey the stricter of the rules. In addition, more than one agency of the state or federal government may have rules governing your business. Each of these may have the power to investigate violations and impose fines or other penalties.

Penalties for violations of these laws can range from a warning to a criminal fine and even jail time. In some cases, employees can sue for damages. Recently, employees have been given awards of millions of dollars from employers who violated the law. Since ignorance of the law is no excuse, it is your duty to learn which laws apply to your business, or to risk these penalties.

Very few people in business know the laws that apply to their businesses. If you take the time to learn them, you can become an expert in your field and avoid problems with regulators. You can also fight back if one of your competitors uses some illegal method to compete with you.

A list of specialized laws appears on page 187. The laws and rules that affect the most businesses are listed on page 188. You should read through this list and see which ones may apply to your business. Then, go to your public library or law library and read them. Some may not apply to your phase of the business, but if any of them do apply, you should make copies to keep on hand.

No one could possibly know all the rules that affect business, much less comply with them all. (The Interstate Commerce Commission alone has 40 trillion rates on its books telling the transportation industry what it should charge!) However, if you keep up with the important rules, you will stay out of trouble and have more chance of success.

FEDERAL LAWS

The federal laws that are most likely to affect small businesses are rules of the Federal Trade Commission (FTC). The FTC has some rules that affect many businesses, such as the rules about labeling, warranties, and mail order sales. Other rules affect only certain industries.

If you sell goods by mail, you should send for the FTC's booklet, *A Business Guide to the Federal Trade Commission's Mail Order Rule*. If you are going to be involved in a certain industry, such as those listed in this section, or using warranties or your own labeling, you should ask for their latest information on the subject. The address is:

Federal Trade Commission
600 Pennsylvania Avenue, NW
Washington, DC 20580

The rules of the FTC are contained in the Code of Federal Regulations (C.F.R.). Some of the industries covered are the following.

Industry	Part
Adhesive Compositions	235
Aerosol Products Used for Frosting Cocktail Glasses	417
Automobiles (New car fuel economy advertising)	259
Barber Equipment and Supplies	248
Binoculars	402
Business Opportunities and Franchises	436
Cigarettes	408
Decorative Wall Paneling	243
Dog and Cat Food	241
Dry Cell Batteries	403
Extension Ladders	418
Fallout Shelters	229
Feather and Down Products	253
Fiber Glass Curtains	413
Food (Games of Chance)	419
Funerals	453
Gasoline (Octane posting)	306
Gasoline	419
Greeting Cards	244
Home Entertainment Amplifiers	432
Home Insulation	460
Hosiery	22
Household Furniture	250
Jewelry	23
Ladies' Handbags	247
Law Books	256
Light Bulbs	409
Luggage and Related Products	24
Mail Order Insurance	234
Mail Order Merchandise	435
Men's and Boys' Tailored Clothing	412
Metallic Watch Band	19
Mirrors	21
Nursery	18
Ophthalmic Practices	456
Photographic Film and Film Processing	242
Private Vocational and Home Study Schools	254
Radiation Monitoring Instruments	232
Retail Food Stores (Advertising)	424
Shell Homes	230
Shoes	231
Sleeping Bags	400
Tablecloths and Related Products	404
Television Sets	410
Textile Wearing Apparel	423
Textiles	236
Tires	228
Used Automobile Parts	20
Used Lubricating Oil	406
Used Motor Vehicles	455
Waist Belts	405
Watches	245
Wigs and Hairpieces	252

Some other federal laws that affect businesses are as follows.

- ✪ *Alcohol Administration Act*

- ✪ *Child Protection and Toy Safety Act*

- ✪ *Clean Water Act*

- ✪ *Comprehensive Smokeless Tobacco Health Education Act*

- ✪ *Consumer Credit Protection Act*

- ✪ *Consumer Product Safety Act*

- ✪ *Energy Policy and Conservation Act*

- ✪ *Environmental Pesticide Control Act of 1972*

- ✪ *Fair Credit Reporting Act*

- ✪ *Fair Packaging and Labeling Act (1966)*

- ✪ *Flammable Fabrics Act*

- ✪ *Food, Drug, and Cosmetic Act*

- ✪ *Food Safety Enforcement Enhancement Act of 1997*

- ✪ *Fur Products Labeling Act*

- ✪ *Hazardous Substances Act*

- ✪ *Hobby Protection Act*

- ✪ *Insecticide, Fungicide, and Rodenticide Act*

- ✪ *Magnuson-Moss Warranty Act*

- ✪ *Nutrition Labeling and Education Act of 1990*

- ✪ *Poison Prevention Packaging Act of 1970*

- ✪ *Solid Waste Disposal Act*

- ✪ *Textile Fiber Products Identification Act*

- ✪ *Toxic Substance Control Act*

- ✪ *Wool Products Labeling Act*

CALIFORNIA LAWS

California laws are too numerous to try and cover in this book. Unless you are a lawyer who is willing to spend a lot of time on research, you are not going to know all of the law for your new business. This is why industry associations and programs like SCORE are so important. Some advice from a person who is familiar with your type of business is worth more than reading endless laws. Also, see the listing of regulated professions and businesses in Chapter 7.

Bookkeeping and Accounting

It is beyond the scope of this book to explain all the intricacies of setting up a business's bookkeeping and accounting systems. However, it is important to realize that if you do not set up an understandable bookkeeping system, your business will undoubtedly fail.

Without accurate records of where your income is coming from and where it is going, you will be unable to increase your profits, lower your expenses, obtain needed financing, or make the right decisions in all areas of your business. The time to decide how you will handle your bookkeeping is when you open your business—not a year later when it is tax time.

INITIAL BOOKKEEPING

If you do not understand business taxation, you should pick up a good book on the subject, as well as the IRS tax guide for your type of business (proprietorship, partnership, corporation, or limited liability company).

The IRS tax book for small businesses is Publication 334, *Tax Guide for Small Businesses*. There are also instruction booklets for each type of business form, including Schedule C for proprietorships, Form 1120 or 1120S for C corporations and S corporations, and 1165 for partnerships and businesses that are taxed like partnerships (LLCs, LLPs).

Keep in mind that the IRS does not give you the best advice for saving on taxes and does not give you the other side of contested issues. For that, you need a private tax guide or advisor.

The most important thing to do is to set up your bookkeeping so that you can easily fill out your monthly, quarterly, and annual tax returns. The best way to do this is to get copies of the returns—not the totals that you will need to supply—and set up your bookkeeping system to group those totals.

For example, for a sole proprietorship, you will use Schedule C to report business income and expenses to the IRS at the end of the year. Use the categories on that form to sort your expenses. To make your job especially easy, every time you pay a bill, put the category number on the check.

ACCOUNTANTS

Most likely, your new business will not be able to afford hiring an accountant right away to handle your books. Do not be discouraged—doing them yourself will force you to learn about business accounting and taxation. The worst way to run a business is to know nothing about the tax laws and turn everything over to an accountant at the end of the year to find out what is due.

You should know the basics of tax law before making basic decisions, such as whether to buy or rent equipment or premises. You should understand accounting so you can time your financial affairs appropriately. If your business needs to buy supplies, inventory, or equipment, and provides goods or services throughout the year, you need to at least have a basic understanding of the system within which you are working.

Once you can afford an accountant, you should weigh the cost against your time and the risk that you will make an error. Even if you think you know enough to do your own corporate tax return, you should still take it to an accountant one year to see if you have been missing any deductions. You might decide that the money saved is worth the cost of the accountant's services.

COMPUTER PROGRAMS

Today, every business should keep its books by computer. There are inexpensive programs, such as Quicken, that can instantly provide you with reports of your income and expenses, as well as the right figures to plug into your tax returns.

Most programs even offer a tax program each year that will take all of your information and print it out on the current year's tax forms.

TAX TIPS

The following are a few tax tips for small businesses that will help you save money.

- ✪ Usually, when you buy equipment for a business, you must amortize the cost over several years. That is, you do not deduct it all when you buy it, but instead, take, say, 25% of the cost off your taxes each year for four years. (The time is determined by the theoretical usefulness of the item.) However, small businesses are allowed to write off the entire cost of a limited amount of items under Internal Revenue Code (I.R.C.) Sec. 179. If you have income to shelter, use it.

- ✪ Owners of S corporations do not have to pay Social Security or Medicare taxes on the part of their profits that is not considered salary. As long as you pay yourself a reasonable salary, other money you take out is not subject to these taxes.

- ✪ You should not neglect to deposit withholding taxes for your own salary or profits. Besides being a large sum to come up with at once in April, there are penalties that must be paid for failure to do so.

✪   Do not fail to keep track of and remit your employees' withholding. You will be personally liable for them even if you are a corporation.

✪   If you keep track of the use of your car for business, you can deduct 44.5¢ per mile (this may go up or down each year—check with the IRS for current rates). If you use your car for business a considerable amount of the time, you may be able to depreciate it.

✪   If your business is a corporation and if you designate the stock as Section 1244 stock, then if the business fails, you are able to get a much better deduction for the loss.

✪   By setting up a retirement plan, you can exempt up to 20% of your salary from income tax. However, do not use money you might need later. There are penalties for taking it out of the retirement plan.

✪   When you buy things that will be resold or made into products that will be resold, you do not have to pay sales taxes on those purchases.

Paying Federal Taxes

chapter 18

As we all know, the federal government levies many different types of taxes on individuals and businesses. It is very important that you consult an accountant or attorney to properly comply with and take advantage of the incredibly complex federal tax code and regulations. This chapter discusses several of the most important federal taxes that will most likely affect your new business. You can find a **TAX TIMETABLE** in Appendix B on page 243.

INCOME TAX

The manner in which each type of business pays taxes is as follows.

Proprietorship A proprietor reports profits and expenses on Schedule C attached to the usual Form 1040, and pays tax on all of the net income of the business. Each quarter, Form ES-1040 must be filed along with payment of one-quarter of the amount of income tax and Social Security taxes estimated to be due for the year.

Partnership The partnership files a return showing the income and expenses, but pays no tax. Each partner is given a form showing his or her share of the profits or losses, and reports these on Schedule E of Form 1040.

Each quarter, Form ES-1040 must be filed by each partner along with payment of one-quarter of the amount of income tax and Social Security taxes estimated to be due for the year.

C Corporation

A regular corporation is a separate taxpayer, and pays tax on its profits after deducting all expenses, including officers' salaries. If dividends are distributed, they are paid out of after-tax dollars, and the shareholders pay tax a second time when they receive the dividends. If a corporation needs to accumulate money for investment, it may be able to do so at lower tax rates than the shareholders. However, if all profits will be distributed to shareholders, the double-taxation may be excessive unless all income is paid as salaries. C corporations file Form 1120.

S Corporation

A small corporation has the option of being taxed like a partnership. If Form 2553 is filed by the corporation and accepted by the Internal Revenue Service, the S corporation will only file an informational return listing profits and expenses. Then, each shareholder will be taxed on a proportional share of the profits (or be able to deduct a proportional share of the losses). Unless a corporation will make a large profit that will not be distributed, S status is usually best in the beginning. An S corporation files Form 1120S and distributes Form K-1 to each shareholder. If any money is taken out by a shareholder that is not listed as wages subject to withholding, then the shareholder will usually have to file Form ES-1040 each quarter, along with payment of the estimated withholding on the withdrawals.

Limited Liability Companies and Partnerships

Limited liability companies and professional limited liability companies are allowed by the IRS to elect to be taxed either as a partnership or a corporation. To make this election, you file Form 8832, *Entity Classification Election,* with the IRS.

Tax Workshops and Booklets

The IRS conducts workshops to inform businesses about the tax laws. (Do not expect an in-depth study of the loopholes.) If you want to read the manual for the workshop, which is IRS Publication 1066, you can download it from their website at **www.irs.gov**.

WITHHOLDING, SOCIAL SECURITY, AND MEDICARE TAXES

If you need basic information on business tax returns, the IRS publishes a rather large booklet that answers most questions and is available free of charge. Call or write them and ask for Publication No. 334. If you have any questions, look up their toll-free number in the phone book under "United States Government/Internal Revenue Service." If you want more creative answers and tax saving information, you should find a good local accountant. To get started, you will need to be familiar with the following:

- ✪ Employer Identification Number;

- ✪ Employee's Withholding Allowance Certificate;

- ✪ Federal tax deposit coupons;

- ✪ Electronic filing;

- ✪ Estimated Tax Payment Voucher;

- ✪ Employer's quarterly tax return;

- ✪ Wage and Tax Statement;

- ✪ Form 1099 Miscellaneous; and,

- ✪ Earned Income Credit.

Employer Identification Number

If you are a sole proprietor with no employees, you can use your Social Security number for your business. If you are a corporation, a partnership, or a proprietorship with employees, you must obtain an employer identification number. This is done by filing the **APPLICATION FOR EMPLOYER IDENTIFICATION NUMBER (IRS FORM SS-4)**. (see form 5, p.253.) It usually takes a week or two to receive. You will need this number to open bank accounts for the business, so you should file this form a soon as you decide to go into business. The blank form with instructions is in Appendix B.

Employee's Withholding Allowance Certificate

You must have each employee fill out an **EMPLOYEE'S WITHHOLDING ALLOWANCE CERTIFICATE (IRS FORM W-4)** to calculate the amount of federal taxes to be deducted and to obtain their Social Security numbers. (see form 7, p.267.) (The number of allowances on this form is used with IRS Circular E, Publication 15, to figure out the exact deductions.)

Federal Tax Deposit Coupons

After taking withholdings from employees' wages, you must deposit them at a bank that is authorized to accept such funds. If at the end of any month you have over $1,000 in withheld taxes, including your contribution to FICA (Social Security and Medicare), you must make a deposit prior to the 15th of the following month. If on the 3rd, 7th, 11th, 15th, 19th, 22nd, or 25th of any month you have over $3,000 in withheld taxes, you must make a deposit within three banking days.

Electronic Filing

Each year, the IRS requires a few more forms to be filed electronically or over the telephone. When you receive your paper filing forms from the IRS, they will include your options for filing electronically or by telephone. In some cases, electronic filing may save time, but if your business is small and most of your numbers are zeros, it may be faster to mail in the paper forms.

Estimated Tax Payment Voucher

Sole proprietors and partners usually take draws from their businesses without the formality of withholding. However, they are still required to make deposits of income and FICA taxes each quarter. If more than $500 is due in April on a person's 1040 form, then not enough money was withheld each quarter and a penalty is assessed, unless the person falls into an exception. The quarterly withholding is submitted on form 1040-ES on January 15th, April 15th, June 15th, and September 15th each year. If these days fall on a weekend, the due date is the following Monday. The worksheet with Estimated Tax Payment Voucher (Form 1040-ES) can be used to determine the amount to pay. A sample **1040-ES** form can be found on page 236, but there is no blank form in Appendix B because you must obtain the original form from the government.

NOTE: *One of the exceptions to the rule is that if you withhold the same amount as last year's tax bill, then you do not have to pay a penalty. This is usually a lot easier than filling out the 1040-ES worksheet.*

Employer's Quarterly Tax Return

Each quarter, you must file Form 941, reporting your federal withholding and FICA taxes. If you owe more than $1,000 at the end of a quarter, you are required to make a deposit at the end of any month that you have $1,000 in withholding. The deposits are made to the Federal Reserve Bank or an authorized financial institution on Form 501. Most banks are authorized to accept deposits. If you owe more than $3,000 for any month, you must make a deposit at any point in the month in which you owe $3,000. After you file Form SS-4, the 941 forms will be sent to you automatically if you checked the box saying that you expect to have employees.

Wage and Tax Statement

At the end of each year, you are required to issue a W-2 Form to each employee. This form shows the amount of wages paid to the employee during the year, as well as the amounts withheld for taxes, Social Security, Medicare, and other purposes.

Form 1099 Miscellaneous

If you pay at least $600 to a person other than an employee (such as independent contractors), you are required to file a Form 1099-MISC for that person. Along with the 1099s, you must file a Form 1096, which is a summary sheet of all the 1099s you issued.

Many people are not aware of this law and fail to file these forms, but they are required for such things as services, royalties, rents, awards, and prizes that you pay to individuals (but not corporations). The rules for this are quite complicated, so you should either obtain Package 1099 from the IRS or consult your accountant.

Earned Income Credit

Persons who are not liable to pay income tax may have the right to a check from the government because of the Earned Income Credit. You are required to notify your employees of this. You can satisfy this requirement with one of the following:

✪   a W-2 Form with the notice on the back;

✪   a substitute for the W-2 Form with the notice on it;

✪   a copy of Notice 797; or,

✪   a written statement with the wording from Notice 797.

A Notice 797 can be downloaded from the IRS website at **www.irs.gov/ pub/irs-pdf/n797.pdf**.

EXCISE TAXES

Excise taxes are taxes on certain activities or items. Some of the things that are subject to federal excise taxes are tobacco and alcohol, gasoline, tires and inner tubes, some trucks and trailers, firearms, ammunition, bows, arrows, fishing equipment, the use of highway vehicles of over 55,000 pounds, aircraft, wagering, telephone and tele- type services, coal, hazardous wastes, and vaccines. If you are involved with any of these, you should obtain from the IRS publica- tion No. 510, *Information on Excise Taxes*.

UNEMPLOYMENT COMPENSATION TAX

You must pay federal unemployment taxes if you paid wages of $1,500 in any quarter, or if you had at least one employee for twenty calendar weeks. The federal tax amount is 0.8% of the first $7,000 of wages paid each employee. If more than $100 is due by the end of any quarter (if you paid $12,500 in wages for the quarter), then Form 508 must be filed with an authorized financial institution or the Federal Reserve Bank in your area. You will receive Form 508 when you obtain your employer identification number.

At the end of each year, you must file Form 940 or Form 940EZ. This is your annual report of federal unemployment taxes. You will receive an original form from the IRS.

Paying California Taxes

In addition to all the federal taxes, you will also have to be familiar with California taxes. It is a good idea to spend a few extra dollars to consult with an accountant if you are not comfortable with your knowledge after reading the following and getting all the free help available.

SALES AND USE TAX

If you are going to sell or lease personal property that would ordinarily be subject to a retail sales tax, you must obtain a seller's permit. There are two types. The regular permit allows you to purchase inventory without paying sales tax and is called an **APPLICATION FOR SELLER'S PERMIT**. (see form 9, p.271.) The second permit is the same except that it is temporary. If you are going to sell only Christmas trees or have a yard sale, get a temporary permit. Obviously, there are many violations without much enforcement. However, if you are going to have a business like a Christmas tree lot, get a permit. To receive an application for a permit, contact the California State Board of Equalization at 800-400-7115 or one of the local offices listed on pages 205–207. The process takes about one week after submitting the application. The board will send you a packet with instructions. A sample, filled-in form is included in Appendix A. (see form 9, p.233.) A blank one is included in Appendix B.

(see form 9, p.271.) All forms and publications are now available online at **www.boe.ca.gov**. Use the Regulations Order on page 269 to order the sales and use tax regulations for your specific type of business from the Board of Equalization.

Selling to Tax-Exempt Purchasers

The burden of sales tax is placed on the seller. The seller may choose not to collect the tax from the buyer. If you are selling to a buyer who will resell the goods and has a seller's permit, you should obtain a *California Resale Certificate* to avoid having to pay the tax. If you do not have a proper resale certificate form at the time of the sale, get something in writing and signed by the buyer giving the buyer's address, the buyer's seller permit number or note as to the exempt status of the buyer, a description of the goods, and the words *for resale* as sufficient evidence until you can get the proper form.

If the buyer gives a resale certificate and then stores or uses the property other than for inventory or display in the regular course of business, the buyer must pay a *use tax*. The tax must be filed with the tax return for the period during which the property was first stored or used. Get the complete rules when you call for your seller's permit.

The California Revenue and Taxation Code is long and not easily understood. If you have no accounting background, it is wise to consult an accountant for initial setup of your business. If you do not want to spend the money, at least see if a SCORE representative can walk you through it.

UNEMPLOYMENT COMPENSATION TAX

California's Unemployment Insurance Program is much like that of other states, since they all adhere to certain federal standards. The basic idea is that if an employee loses a job through no fault of his or her own, weekly unemployment insurance benefits will be paid temporarily. The payments are made for twenty-six weeks, which can be extended to fifty-two weeks. The employer's tax is paid on up to $7,000 paid to each worker. The tax rate varies based on the prior number of claims against that employer.

The California Employment Development Department handles unemployment compensation. Forms and publications are now available at their website at **www.edd.ca.gov**. You can download the *California Employer's Guide*, which contains over two hundred pages of valuable information, or information can be obtained by phone at 800-300-5616.

TANGIBLE AND INTANGIBLE PROPERTY TAXES

Tangible and intangible taxes are taxes on all personal property used in a business with the exception of inventory. These include such things as dishes, machinery, furniture, tools, signs, carpeting, appliances, laboratory equipment, and just about everything else.

Basic Personal Property

Unlike real property, business personal property is reappraised annually. Each person owning taxable personal property (other than mobile homes) with an aggregate cost of $100,000 or more must file a *Business Property Statement* (BPS) with the County Assessor Department annually. Upon request of the Assessor Department, the owners of all other businesses must file a BPS. The BPS filing includes detailing the cost, by year of acquisition, of all equipment and fixtures, and the cost of supplies on hand at each business location.

Personal property is defined as all property that is not real property. There are two types of personal property: tangible and intangible. Taxable *tangible property* includes such things as machines, equipment, furniture, and tools. Exempt *intangible property* would include stocks and bonds, copyrights, notes, and licenses.

Whether intangible property is exempt or not can be tricky. For example, the California Revenue and Taxation Code states:

> *The value of intangible assets and rights relating to the going concern value of a business using taxable property shall not enhance or be reflected in the value of the taxable property.*

This would include such intangible assets as an exclusive franchise for a certain area, obviously worth a great deal. However, the code goes on to say:

Taxable property may be assessed and valued by assuming the presence of intangible assets or rights necessary to put the taxable property to beneficial or productive use.

Contact your county assessor's office for forms and details if you believe that you should be filing. The California State Board of Equalization (BOE) publication Assessors' Handbook Section 504 gives a complete explanation. Read or download it from **www.boe.ca.gov/proptaxes/ pdf/ah504700.pdf**.

INCOME TAX

California has a state income tax, both for individuals and corporations. The corporate tax is 8.84% with an $800 minimum alternative tax. Form 100 is used for C corporations, and 100S is used for S corporations.

The California Franchise Tax Board can be contacted at:

Franchise Tax Board
P.O. Box 942840
Sacramento, CA 94240
800-852-5711
800-338-0505 (automated)
www.ftb.ca.gov

The *Employment Development Department* (EDD) of California requires that you also file a registration form. A sample filled-in **REGISTRATION FORM FOR COMMERCIAL EMPLOYERS** is in Appendix A. There is also a blank form in Appendix B. (see form 12, p.289.) There is a separate registration form for other industries, so if you are not commercial, do not file this form.

EXCISE TAX

California imposes an excise tax on such items as alcohol, tobacco, and fuel. From time to time there is a temporary tax imposed on top of the excise tax. The Franchise Tax Board can help with information on special tax programs.

Following is a list of field offices for the Board of Equalization's Sales Tax department. Find your city (in boldface) and the rest of the address, as well as phone and fax numbers, follow below it.

STATE TAX FIELD OFFICE LOCATIONS AND ADDRESSES

Bakersfield
1800 30th Street
Suite 380
93301
661-395-2880
Fax: 661-395-2588

Culver City
5901 Green Valley Circle
Suite 200
90230

P.O. Box 3652
90231

310-342-1000
Fax: 310-342-1061

El Centro
1550 West Main Street
92243
760-352-3431
Fax: 760-352-8149

Eureka
707-576-2100
Fax: 707 576-2781

Fresno
5070 North Sixth Street
Suite 110
93710
559-248-4219
Fax: 559-248-4279

Laguna Hills
23141 Moulton Parkway
Suite 100
92653
949-461-5711
Fax: 949-461-5771

Long Beach
100 West Broadway
Suite 305
90802
562-901-2483
Fax: 562-495-9029

Norwalk
12440 East Imperial Highway
Suite 200
90650

P.O. Box 409
90651

562-466-1694
Fax: 562-466-1598

Oakland
1515 Clay Street
Suite 303
94612
510-622-4100
Fax: 510-622-4175

Rancho Mirage
42-700 Bob Hope Drive
Suite 301
92270
760-346-8096
Fax: 760-341-1196

Redding
2881 Churn Creek Road
Suite B
96002

P.O. Box 492529
96049

530-224-4729
Fax: 530-224-4891

Riverside
3737 Main Street
Suite 1000
92501
951-680-6400
Fax: 951-680-6426

Sacramento
3321 Power Inn Road
Suite 210
95826
916-227-6700
Fax: 916-227-6746

Salinas
111 East Navajo Drive
Suite 100
93906
831-443-3003
Fax: 831-443-3131

San Diego
1350 Front Street
Room 5047
92101
619-525-4526
Fax: 619-525-4548

San Francisco
121 Spear Street
Suite 460
94105
415-356-6600
Fax: 415-356-6115

San Jose
250 South Second Street
95113
408-277-1231
Fax: 408-277-1252

San Marcos
334 Via Vera Cruz
Suite 107
92078
760-510-5850
Fax: 760-510-5876

Santa Ana
28 Civic Center Plaza
Room 239
92701
714-558-4059
Fax: 714-558-4904

Santa Rosa
50 D Street
Room 230
95404

P.O. Box 730
95402

707-576-2100
Fax: 707-576-2781

Suisun City
333 Sunset Avenue
Suite 330
94585
707-428-2041
Fax: 707-428-2193

Van Nuys
15350 Sherman Way
Suite 250
91406

P.O. Box 7735
91409

818-904-2300
Fax: 818-901-5252

Ventura
4820 McGrath Street
Suite 260
93003
805-677-2700
Fax: 805-677-2764

West Covina
1521 West Cameron Avenue
Suite 300
91790-2738

P.O. Box 1500
91793-1500

626-480-7200

Out-of-State Field Offices

Sacramento
3321 Power Inn Road
Suite 130
95826

P.O. Box 188268
95818

916-227-6600
Fax: 916-227-6641

Chicago, IL
120 North LaSalle
Suite 1600
60602
312-201-5300
Fax: 312-782-7280

New York, NY
205 East 42nd Street
Suite 1100
10017
212-697-4680
Fax: 212-697-5146

Houston, TX
1155 Dairy Ashford
Suite 550
77079
281-531-3450
Fax: 281-531-3470

Headquarters

Sacramento
450 N Street

P.O. Box 942879
94279

800-400-7115

If you are calling from outside of the forty-eight contiguous states, please call 916-445-6362 to reach our Information Center.

TDD Information

California Relay Telephone Service for the Deaf and Hearing Impaired—From TDD telephones dial 800-735-2929; from voice-operated telephones dial 800-735-2922.

Unless otherwise noted, all offices are open from 8 a.m. to 5 p.m., Monday through Friday, excluding state holidays.

Out-of-State Taxes

As a California business, if you operate your business outside of the borders of the state of California, you not only have to comply with California and federal tax laws, but also with the laws of the states and other countries in which you do business. This can prove to be very complicated.

STATE SALES TAXES

In 1992, the United States Supreme Court struck a blow for the rights of small businesses by ruling that state tax authorities cannot force them to collect sales taxes on interstate mail orders (*Quill Corporation v. North Dakota*). Unfortunately, the court left open the possibility that Congress could allow interstate taxation of mail order sales, and since then several bills have been introduced that would do so.

At present, companies are only required to collect sales taxes for states in which they *do business*. Exactly what business is enough to trigger taxation is a legal question, and some states try to define it as broadly as possible.

If you have an office in a state, you are doing business there, and any goods shipped to consumers in that state are subject to sales taxes. If you have a full-time employee working in the state much of the year, many states will consider you doing business there. In some states, attending a two-day trade show is enough business to trigger taxation for the entire year for every order shipped to the state. One loophole that often works is to be represented at shows by persons who are not your employees.

Because the laws are different in each state, you will have to do some research on a state-by-state basis to find out how much business you can do in a state without being subject to their taxation. You can request a state's rules from its department of revenue, but keep in mind that what a department of revenue wants the law to be is not always what the courts will rule that it is.

BUSINESS TAXES

As a small business just starting out, you are not ready for major expansions. However, a good way to promote your business is through trade shows. Say that you have invented a product that has some relation to automobiles. You want to attend several auto shows in Detroit to promote it.

If you attend only one or two shows per year, you fill out a simple form and pay sales tax on any products that you sold at the show. If you attend three or more shows, you fill out the same form as if you were starting a business in Michigan and have to account for withholding tax if you had workers at the show and use tax as well as sales tax. It might be enough to cause you to attend a maximum of two events per year in Michigan.

Write to the department of revenue of any state with which you have business contacts to see what might trigger your taxation.

INTERNET TAXES

State revenue departments are eager to tax commerce on the Internet. Theories have already been proposed that websites available to state residents mean a company is doing business in a state. Fortunately, Congress has passed a moratorium on taxation of Internet business.

CANADIAN TAXES

The Canadian government expects American companies that sell goods by mail order to Canadians to collect taxes for them and file returns with Revenue Canada, their tax department. Those companies that receive an occasional unsolicited order are not expected to register, and Canadian customers who order things from the U.S. pay the tax plus a $5 fee upon receipt of the goods. Companies that solicit Canadian orders are expected to be registered if their worldwide income is $30,000 or more per year. In some cases, a company may be required to post a bond and to pay for the cost of Canadian auditors visiting its premises and auditing its books. For these reasons, you may notice that some companies decline to accept orders from Canada.

The End...
and the Beginning

If you have read through this whole book, you know more about the rules and laws for operating a California business than most people in business today. However, after learning about all the governmental regulations, you may become discouraged. You are probably wondering how you can keep track of all the laws and how you will have any time left to make money after complying with the laws. It is not that bad. People are starting businesses every day and they are making money—lots of money.

The important thing is that you know the laws and the penalties for violations before making your decision. Knowing the laws will also allow you to use the loopholes in the laws to avoid violations. With this book as your guide, you should be able to navigate business law and make your own business thrive.

Congratulations on deciding to start a business in California!

Glossary

A

acceptance. An agreement that the terms of an offer are acceptable and that the contract can be considered formed. Offer, acceptance, and consideration form a contract.

affirmative action. A movement that attempts to eliminate or remedy past, present, and future acts of discrimination or the effects of discrimination.

articles of incorporation. The document filed with the secretary of state that sets up the bylaws and terms of a corporation.

B

bait advertising. An illegal ploy to entice a customer to buy a higher-priced item by advertising for a lower-priced item, especially where the lower-priced item was never really available.

bulk sales. Selling larger than usual quantities.

C

C corporation. A business where the entity, rather than the shareholders, is taxed.

collections. The part of a business that ensures that payment comes into the business in a timely, accurate manner.

consideration. A thing of value offered between parties that is essential to a contract in order to make it legally enforceable.

copyright. The right to reproduce, sell, display, or perform original work that is expressed in writing, photographs, sound, etc.

corporation. An entity comprised of shareholders, recognized by law as a separate person with rights and duties that a person under the law would have.

D

deceptive pricing. Misleading a consumer into believing that something costs one price, while other hidden costs are added to that price.

discrimination. Denying a person or group, or granting a person or group, privileges based on sex, religion, race, creed, or disability.

domain name. On the Internet, it is the name that identifies a website.

E

endorsements. A way of bolstering the credibility of your product or service, usually by having someone notable make a statement about it or appear on its behalf.

excise tax. Money paid to the government for the manufacture, use or sale of goods, or on licenses and occupation fees.

express warranty. A guarantee overtly made by a seller. It can be a promise ("if it breaks, I will fix it for free"), a description of the goods, or a sample or model.

F

fictitious name. The name a business is known by, or does business as.

G

general partner. A partner who shares profit, loss, and liability. A general partner, unlike a limited partner, may be active in running the business.

goods. Tangible items like a chair or a car. Contracts for goods are controlled by Article 2 of the Uniform Commercial Code and differ from those for real property, services, and paper rights (stocks, bonds, insurance, etc.).

guarantee. The promise that a future commitment will be fulfilled, or to promise that a future contract will be carried out.

guaranty. The assurance that a duty or obligation will be carried out if the original party fails to carry it out.

I

implied warranty. A guarantee inferred from the actions and words of a seller.

independent contractor. A person hired to do work, but does so under his or her own business, using his or her own methods and equipment, and not as an employee of the one hiring.

intangible property. An asset that is not physical in nature, such as a good will, copyrights, and patents.

intellectual property. An abstract asset such as copyrights, trademarks, patents, trade secrets, and publicity.

L

liability. Legal obligation or responsibility.

limited liability company. A business that restricts the amount of money an investor risks to the amount that they contribute.

limited liability partnership. A partnership that restricts the amount of money a partner is liable for to the amount that he or she has in the business, and excludes personal assets of the partners.

limited partner. A partner who shares in the profits but whose losses are limited to his or her investment in the business. To keep this limited liability, a limited partner may not participate in managing the business.

limited partnership. A partnership with an active manager (general partner) and limited partners (investors). The general partner has personal liability. The limited partners can lose only their investment in the business.

limited warranty. A promise covering only limited labor, materials, and repairs. The terms "full" and "limited" warranty were created by the Magnuson-Moss Warranty Act of 1975.

M

merchant. One who deals regularly in the subject goods or is an expert in these goods. The Uniform Commercial Code sets higher standards for merchants than for those who only occasionally deal in the subject goods.

merchant's firm offer. A written and signed offer by a merchant, stating that it will remain open. The offer cannot be withdrawn (revoked), even though no consideration was given to keep it open. The offer remains open for the time stated, or a reasonable time if none is stated. Regardless of the stated time, the seller does not have to keep the offer open more than three months.

N

nonprofit corporation. A business not designed for making a profit and is afforded special tax treatment.

O

occupational license. A license required for certain occupations. There are two types. First is the license obtained by education, experience, and testing (doctor, lawyer, contractor, etc.). A contract with such a person who is unlicensed is an illegal contract and unenforceable. The second type is a revenue raising license. All that is really required is the payment of a fee to get the license. A contract made with an unlicensed person in this category is not illegal and is enforceable.

offer. The act of setting up the possibility for acceptance of a contract or agreement. There must be serious intent, communication, and definite terms.

P

partnership. Two or more people doing business as an entity for profit.

personal property. Any possession not classified as real property.

professional corporation. A business that requires its members to have a professional license, such as a doctor, lawyer, or certified public accountant.

R

real property. Land and all of its attachments, growths, and structures.

S

S corporation. A business that is taxed through the shareholders rather than through the entity itself.

sale on approval. Completion of a sale depends upon the buyer's approval and subsequent use. Title and risk of loss stay with the seller until approval.

sale or return. If goods are bought primarily for resale, then under sale or return terms, the unsold goods can be returned to the seller. Title and risk of loss pass to the buyer until returned.

security/securities. The goods given as a collateral guarantee that the contracted price will be paid.

sexual harassment. Employment discrimination of a verbal or physical nature centered on the sex of an individual, or on the topic of sex.

shares. A representation of a part ownership in a corporation.

sole proprietorship. A business owned by one person who does not share profits and is liable for all debts.

statute of frauds. The part of the law that requires certain transactions to be in writing to be valid.

stock. The certificate that represents ownership in a corporation.

sublease. A rental agreement where the first tenant remains liable to the landlord, and the second tenant is liable to the first tenant for rent and care of the premises.

T

tangible property. Moveable, nonabstract assets, such as equipment and automobiles.

trade secrets. Confidential information about the products, procedure, formula, method, etc. that a business uses to accomplish some goal.

trademark. The rights to the use of a symbol or words connected to a specific product or service to set one business apart from another.

U

unemployment compensation. State-funded pay to a person who has been laid off from a job.

Uniform Commercial Code. A set of laws used to unify business contracts from state to state. The code covers such things as goods (Article 2) and negotiable instruments, such as checks and notes (Article 3). The California version is simply called the Commercial Code.

usury. Charging illegally high interest rates on a loan.

W

warranty. The promise that something conforms to the legal specifications of a certain contract.

warranty of fitness for a particular purpose. A warranty that the goods are fit for the buyer's intended use rather than only for their ordinary use. The seller must know of the buyer's intended use and the buyer must rely on the seller's choice of the goods.

warranty of merchantability. The promise that the goods are fit for their ordinary use, are adequately packaged and labeled, must be of average quality, and pass without objection in the trade.

warranty of title. The promise that the seller has good title and transfers that title to the buyer in a rightful manner, free of liens unless disclosed to the buyer.

workers' compensation. Payments for those employees injured due to work-related activity.

Sample, Filled-In Forms

The following forms are selected filled-in forms for demonstration purposes. Most have a corresponding blank form in Appendix B. The form numbers in this appendix correspond to the form numbers in Appendix B. If there is no blank for a particular form, it is because you must obtain it from a government agency. If you need instructions for these forms as you follow how they are filled out, they can be found in Appendix B, or in the pages in the chapters that discuss those forms.

(Sample, filled-in forms A–D do not have an accompanying blank form in this appendix because you must use the original forms provided by the IRS.)

FICTITIOUS BUSINESS NAME STATEMENT

The following person (persons) is (are) doing business as

*____Joe's Diner_____

at **_1234 Main St. Anytown, CA 90000_____:

***_____

_____

_____

_____

This business is conducted by ****_____Joseph Frycook_____

The registrant commenced to transact business under the fictitious business name or names listed above on *****_____1/1/07_____

Signed _____*Joseph Frycook*_____

Statement filed with the County Clerk of _____Any_____ County on _____1/1/07_____

NOTICE

THIS FICTITIOUS BUSINESS NAME STATEMENT EXPIRES FIVE YEARS FROM THE DATE IT WAS FILED IN THE OFFICE OF THE COUNTY CLERK. A NEW FICTITIOUS BUSINESS NAME STATEMENT MUST BE FILED BEFORE THAT TIME. THE FILING OF THIS STATEMENT DOES NOT OF ITSELF AUTHORIZE THE USE IN THIS STATE OF A FICTITIOUS BUSINESS NAME IN VIOLATION OF THE RIGHTS OF ANOTHER UNDER FEDERAL, STATE, OR COMMON LAW (SEE SECTION 14411 ET SEQ., BUSINESS AND PROFESSIONAL CODE).

OMB No. 1615-0047; Expires 03/31/07

Department of Homeland Security
U.S. Citizenship and Immigration Services

Employment Eligibility Verification

Please read instructions carefully before completing this form. The instructions must be available during completion of this form. **ANTI-DISCRIMINATION NOTICE:** It is illegal to discriminate against work eligible individuals. Employers **CANNOT** specify which document(s) they will accept from an employee. The refusal to hire an individual because of a future expiration date may also constitute illegal discrimination.

Section 1. Employee Information and Verification. To be completed and signed by employee at the time employment begins.

Print Name: Last	First	Middle Initial	Maiden Name
REDDENBACHER	MARY	J.	HASSENFUSS

Address (Street Name and Number)	Apt. #	Date of Birth (month/day/year)
1234 LIBERTY LANE		1/26/69

City	State	Zip Code	Social Security #
Sacramento	CA	12345	123-45-6789

I am aware that federal law provides for imprisonment and/or fines for false statements or use of false documents in connection with the completion of this form.

I attest, under penalty of perjury, that I am (check one of the following):

[X] A citizen or national of the United States
[ ] A Lawful Permanent Resident (Alien #) A _____
[ ] An alien authorized to work until _____

(Alien # or Admission #) _____

Employee's Signature	Date (month/day/year)
Mary Reddenbacher	2/2/07

Preparer and/or Translator Certification. (To be completed and signed if Section 1 is prepared by a person other than the employee.) I attest, under penalty of perjury, that I have assisted in the completion of this form and that to the best of my knowledge the information is true and correct.

Preparer's/Translator's Signature	Print Name

Address (Street Name and Number, City, State, Zip Code)	Date (month/day/year)

Section 2. Employer Review and Verification. To be completed and signed by employer. Examine one document from List A OR examine one document from List B and one from List C, as listed on the reverse of this form, and record the title, number and expiration date, if any, of the document(s).

List A	OR	List B	AND	List C
Document title: PASSPORT		_____		_____
Issuing authority: PASSPORT AGENCY TPA		_____		_____
Document #: 123456789		_____		_____
Expiration Date (if any): 10 5 2010		_____		_____
Document #:				
Expiration Date (if any):				

CERTIFICATION - I attest, under penalty of perjury, that I have examined the document(s) presented by the above-named employee, that the above-listed document(s) appear to be genuine and to relate to the employee named, that the

employee began employment on (month/day/year) 02 0204 and that to the best of my knowledge the employee is eligible to work in the United States. (State employment agencies may omit the date the employee began employment.)

Signature of Employer or Authorized Representative	Print Name	Title
Darron Krebbs	Darron Krebbs	owner

Business or Organization Name	Address (Street Name and Number, City, State, Zip Code)	Date (month/day/year)
Krebbs Company	100 Maynard Dr., San Diego CA 54321	2/2/07

Section 3. Updating and Reverification. To be completed and signed by employer.

A. New Name (if applicable)	B. Date of rehire (month/day/year) (if applicable)

C. If employee's previous grant of work authorization has expired, provide the information below for the document that establishes current employment eligibility.

Document Title: _____ Document #: _____ Expiration Date (if any): _____

I attest, under penalty of perjury, that to the best of my knowledge, this employee is eligible to work in the United States, and if the employee presented document(s), the document(s) I have examined appear to be genuine and to relate to the individual.

Signature of Employer or Authorized Representative	Date (month/day/year)

NOTE: This is the 1991 edition of the Form I-9 that has been rebranded with a current printing date to reflect the recent transition from the INS to DHS and its components.

Form I-9 (Rev. 05/31/05)Y Page 2

Form **SS-4** (Rev. February 2006) Department of the Treasury Internal Revenue Service	**Application for Employer Identification Number** (For use by employers, corporations, partnerships, trusts, estates, churches, government agencies, Indian tribal entities, certain individuals, and others.) ▶ See separate instructions for each line. ▶ Keep a copy for your records.	OMB No. 1545-0003 EIN

Type or print clearly.

1 Legal name of entity (or individual) for whom the EIN is being requested
John Doe and James Doe

2 Trade name of business (if different from name on line 1)
Doe Company

3 Executor, administrator, trustee, "care of" name

4a Mailing address (room, apt., suite no. and street, or P.O. box)
123 Main Street

4b City, state, and ZIP code
Libertyville, CA 98765

5a Street address (if different) (Do not enter a P.O. box.)

5b City, state, and ZIP code

6 County and state where principal business is located
Libertyville, CA

7a Name of principal officer, general partner, grantor, owner, or trustor
John Doe

7b SSN, ITIN, or EIN
123-45-6789

8a Type of entity (check only one box)
☐ Sole proprietor (SSN) ____
☒ Partnership
☐ Corporation (enter form number to be filed) ▶ ____
☐ Personal service corporation
☐ Church or church-controlled organization
☐ Other nonprofit organization (specify) ▶ ____
☐ Other (specify) ▶
☐ Estate (SSN of decedent) ____
☐ Plan administrator (SSN) ____
☐ Trust (SSN of grantor) ____
☐ National Guard   ☐ State/local government
☐ Farmers' cooperative   ☐ Federal government/military
☐ REMIC   ☐ Indian tribal governments/enterprises
Group Exemption Number (GEN) ▶ ____

8b If a corporation, name the state or foreign country (if applicable) where incorporated   State ____   Foreign country ____

9 Reason for applying (check only one box)
☒ Started new business (specify type) ▶ clothing manufacturer
☐ Hired employees (Check the box and see line 12.)
☐ Compliance with IRS withholding regulations
☐ Other (specify) ▶
☐ Banking purpose (specify purpose) ▶ ____
☐ Changed type of organization (specify new type) ▶ ____
☐ Purchased going business
☐ Created a trust (specify type) ▶ ____
☐ Created a pension plan (specify type) ▶ ____

10 Date business started or acquired (month, day, year). See instructions.
10-15-2007

11 Closing month of accounting year
December

12 First date wages or annuities were paid (month, day, year). Note. If applicant is a withholding agent, enter date income will first be paid to nonresident alien. (month, day, year) ▶ 10-31-2007

13 Highest number of employees expected in the next 12 months (enter -0- if none).   Agricultural | Household | Other
Do you expect to have $1,000 or less in employment tax liability for the calendar year? ☐ Yes ☐ No. (If you expect to pay $4,000 or less in wages, you can mark yes.)

14 Check one box that best describes the principal activity of your business.
☐ Construction   ☐ Rental & leasing   ☐ Transportation & warehousing   ☐ Health care & social assistance   ☐ Wholesale–agent/broker
☐ Real estate   ☒ Manufacturing   ☐ Finance & insurance   ☐ Accommodation & food service   ☐ Wholesale–other   ☐ Retail
☐ Other (specify)

15 Indicate principal line of merchandise sold, specific construction work done, products produced, or services provided.
clothing

16a Has the applicant ever applied for an employer identification number for this or any other business? ☐ Yes ☒ No
Note. If "Yes," please complete lines 16b and 16c.

16b If you checked "Yes" on line 16a, give applicant's legal name and trade name shown on prior application if different from line 1 or 2 above.
Legal name ▶   Trade name ▶

16c Approximate date when, and city and state where, the application was filed. Enter previous employer identification number if known.
Approximate date when filed (mo., day, year) | City and state where filed | Previous EIN

Third Party Designee Complete this section only if you want to authorize the named individual to receive the entity's EIN and answer questions about the completion of this form.
Designee's name | Designee's telephone number (include area code) ( )
Address and ZIP code | Designee's fax number (include area code) ( )

Under penalties of perjury, I declare that I have examined this application, and to the best of my knowledge and belief, it is true, correct, and complete. | Applicant's telephone number (include area code) (123) 555-0000
Name and title (type or print clearly) ▶ John Doe, Partner | Applicant's fax number (include area code) ( )
Signature ▶ John Doe   Date ▶ 10/15/07

For Privacy Act and Paperwork Reduction Act Notice, see separate instructions.   Cat. No. 16055N   Form **SS-4** (Rev. 2-2006)

Form **SS-8**
(Rev. June 2003)
Department of the Treasury
Internal Revenue Service

Determination of Worker Status
for Purposes of Federal Employment Taxes
and Income Tax Withholding

OMB No. 1545-0004

Name of firm (or person) for whom the worker performed services	Worker's name
Doe Company	Mary Reddenbacher

Firm's address (include street address, apt. or suite no., city, state, and ZIP code)	Worker's address (include street address, apt. or suite no., city, state, and ZIP code)
123 Main St. Libertyville, CA 98765	1234 Liberty Lane Sacramento, CA 12345

Trade name	Telephone number (include area code)	Worker's social security number
	(813) 555-2000	123 45 6789

Telephone number (include area code)	Firm's employer identification number	Worker's employer identification number (if any)
(813) 555-0000	59 123 45678	

If the worker is paid by a firm other than the one listed on this form for these services, enter the name, address, and employer identification number of the payer.

Important Information Needed To Process Your Request

We must have your permission to disclose your name and the information on this form and any attachments to other parties involved with this request. **Do we have your permission to disclose this information?** . . . . ☐ **Yes** ☐ **No**
If you answered "No" or did not mark a box, we will not process your request and will not issue a determination.

You must answer ALL items OR mark them "Unknown" or "Does not apply." If you need more space, attach another sheet.

A This form is being completed by: ☒ Firm ☐ Worker; for services performed ___5/2/07___ to ___present___ .
(beginning date)   (ending date)

B Explain your reason(s) for filing this form (e.g., you received a bill from the IRS, you believe you received a Form 1099 or Form W-2 erroneously, you are unable to get worker's compensation benefits, you were audited or are being audited by the IRS). -----------------------------
----

C Total number of workers who performed or are performing the same or similar services _____ .

D How did the worker obtain the job? ☐ Application   ☐ Bid   ☐ Employment Agency   ☐ Other (specify) _____ .

E Attach copies of all supporting documentation (contracts, invoices, memos, Forms W-2, Forms 1099, IRS closing agreements, IRS rulings, etc.). In addition, please inform us of any current or past litigation concerning the worker's status. If no income reporting forms (Form 1099-MISC or W-2) were furnished to the worker, enter the amount of income earned for the year(s) at issue $ _____ .

F Describe the firm's business. clothing manufacturer ---

G Describe the work done by the worker and provide the worker's job title. personalized embroidering -----------------
----

H Explain why you believe the worker is an employee or an independent contractor. ----------------------------------
----

I Did the worker perform services for the firm before getting this position? . . . . ☐ **Yes** ☐ **No** ☐ **N/A**
If "Yes," what were the dates of the prior service? --
If "Yes," explain the differences, if any, between the current and prior service. ----------------------------
----

J If the work is done under a written agreement between the firm and the worker, attach a copy (preferably signed by both parties). Describe the terms and conditions of the work arrangement. ---
----

For Privacy Act and Paperwork Reduction Act Notice, see page 5.   Cat. No. 16106T   Form **SS-8** (Rev. 6-2003)

Part I   Behavioral Control

1 What specific training and/or instruction is the worker given by the firm? none

2 How does the worker receive work assignments?

3 Who determines the methods by which the assignments are performed?

4 Who is the worker required to contact if problems or complaints arise and who is responsible for their resolution?

5 What types of reports are required from the worker? Attach examples.

6 Describe the worker's daily routine (i.e., schedule, hours, etc.).

7 At what location(s) does the worker perform services (e.g., firm's premises, own shop or office, home, customer's location, etc.)?

8 Describe any meetings the worker is required to attend and any penalties for not attending (e.g., sales meetings, monthly meetings, staff meetings, etc.).

9 Is the worker required to provide the services personally?   ☒ Yes   ☐ No

10 If substitutes or helpers are needed, who hires them? the worker

11 If the worker hires the substitutes or helpers, is approval required?   ☐ Yes   ☒ No
If "Yes," by whom?

12 Who pays the substitutes or helpers? the worker

13 Is the worker reimbursed if the worker pays the substitutes or helpers?   ☐ Yes   ☒ No
If "Yes," by whom?

Part II   Financial Control

1 List the supplies, equipment, materials, and property provided by each party:
The firm none
The worker embroidery machine
Other party

2 Does the worker lease equipment?   ☐ Yes   ☐ No
If "Yes," what are the terms of the lease? (Attach a copy or explanatory statement.)

3 What expenses are incurred by the worker in the performance of services for the firm?

4 Specify which, if any, expenses are reimbursed by:
The firm
Other party

5 Type of pay the worker receives: ☐ Salary   ☐ Commission   ☐ Hourly Wage   ☒ Piece Work
☐ Lump Sum   ☐ Other (specify)
If type of pay is commission, and the firm guarantees a minimum amount of pay, specify amount $ _____ .

6 Is the worker allowed a drawing account for advances?   ☐ Yes   ☒ No
If "Yes," how often?
Specify any restrictions.

7 Whom does the customer pay?   ☐ Firm   ☐ Worker
If worker, does the worker pay the total amount to the firm?   ☐ Yes   ☐ No   If "No," explain.

8 Does the firm carry worker's compensation insurance on the worker?   ☐ Yes   ☒ No

9 What economic loss or financial risk, if any, can the worker incur beyond the normal loss of salary (e.g., loss or damage of equipment, material, etc.)?

Part III   **Relationship of the Worker and Firm**

1   List the benefits available to the worker (e.g., paid vacations, sick pay, pensions, bonuses). ....

2   Can the relationship be terminated by either party without incurring liability or penalty? . . . . ☒ **Yes**   ☐ **No**
      If "No," explain your answer. ....

3   Does the worker perform similar services for others?   . . . . ☐ **Yes**   ☐ **No**
      If "Yes," is the worker required to get approval from the firm? . . . . ☐ **Yes**   ☐ **No**

4   Describe any agreements prohibiting competition between the worker and the firm while the worker is performing services or during any later
      period. Attach any available documentation. ....
      ....

5   Is the worker a member of a union?   . . . . ☐ **Yes**   ☐ **No**

6   What type of advertising, if any, does the worker do (e.g., a business listing in a directory, business cards, etc.)? Provide copies, if applicable.
      ....

7   If the worker assembles or processes a product at home, who provides the materials and instructions or pattern? ....
      ....

8   What does the worker do with the finished product (e.g., return it to the firm, provide it to another party, or sell it)? ....
      ....

9   How does the firm represent the worker to its customers (e.g., employee, partner, representative, or contractor)? ....
      ....

10   If the worker no longer performs services for the firm, how did the relationship end? ....
      ....

Part IV   **For Service Providers or Salespersons**—Complete this part if the worker provided a service directly to
                customers or is a salesperson.

1   What are the worker's responsibilities in soliciting new customers? ....
      ....

2   Who provides the worker with leads to prospective customers? ....

3   Describe any reporting requirements pertaining to the leads. ....
      ....

4   What terms and conditions of sale, if any, are required by the firm? ....

5   Are orders submitted to and subject to approval by the firm? . . . . ☐ **Yes**   ☐ **No**

6   Who determines the worker's territory? ....

7   Did the worker pay for the privilege of serving customers on the route or in the territory? . . . . ☐ **Yes**   ☐ **No**
      If "Yes," whom did the worker pay? ....
      If "Yes," how much did the worker pay? . . . . $ _____ .

8   Where does the worker sell the product (e.g., in a home, retail establishment, etc.)? ....
      ....

9   List the product and/or services distributed by the worker (e.g., meat, vegetables, fruit, bakery products, beverages, or laundry or dry cleaning
      services). If more than one type of product and/or service is distributed, specify the principal one. ....
      ....

10   Does the worker sell life insurance full time? . . . . ☐ **Yes**   ☐ **No**

11   Does the worker sell other types of insurance for the firm? . . . . ☐ **Yes**   ☐ **No**
      If "Yes," enter the percentage of the worker's total working time spent in selling other types of insurance. . . . _____ %

12   If the worker solicits orders from wholesalers, retailers, contractors, or operators of hotels, restaurants, or other similar
      establishments, enter the percentage of the worker's time spent in the solicitation. . . . . _____ %

13   Is the merchandise purchased by the customers for resale or use in their business operations? . . . . ☐ **Yes**   ☐ **No**
      Describe the merchandise and state whether it is equipment installed on the customers' premises. ....
      ....

Part V   **Signature** (see page 4)

Under penalties of perjury, I declare that I have examined this request, including accompanying documents, and to the best of my knowledge and belief, the facts
presented are true, correct, and complete.

Signature ▶ _____*John Doe*_____   Title ▶ _____Partner_____   Date ▶ _*10/15/07*_
                (Type or print name below)

Form W-4 (2006)

Purpose. Complete Form W-4 so that your employer can withhold the correct federal income tax from your pay. Because your tax situation may change, you may want to refigure your withholding each year.

Exemption from withholding. If you are exempt, complete only lines 1, 2, 3, 4, and 7 and sign the form to validate it. Your exemption for 2006 expires February 16, 2007. See Pub. 505, Tax Withholding and Estimated Tax.

Note. You cannot claim exemption from withholding if (a) your income exceeds $850 and includes more than $300 of unearned income (for example, interest and dividends) and (b) another person can claim you as a dependent on their tax return.

Basic instructions. If you are not exempt, complete the **Personal Allowances Worksheet** below. The worksheets on page 2 adjust your withholding allowances based on itemized deductions, certain credits, adjustments to income, or two-

earner/two-job situations. Complete all worksheets that apply. However, you may claim fewer (or zero) allowances.

Head of household. Generally, you may claim head of household filing status on your tax return only if you are unmarried and pay more than 50% of the costs of keeping up a home for yourself and your dependent(s) or other qualifying individuals. See line **E** below.

Tax credits. You can take projected tax credits into account in figuring your allowable number of withholding allowances. Credits for child or dependent care expenses and the child tax credit may be claimed using the **Personal Allowances Worksheet** below. See Pub. 919, How Do I Adjust My Tax Withholding, for information on converting your other credits into withholding allowances.

Nonwage income. If you have a large amount of nonwage income, such as interest or dividends, consider making estimated tax payments using Form 1040-ES, Estimated Tax for Individuals. Otherwise, you may owe additional tax.

Two earners/two jobs. If you have a working spouse or more than one job, figure the total number of allowances you are entitled to claim on all jobs using worksheets from only one Form W-4. Your withholding usually will be most accurate when all allowances are claimed on the Form W-4 for the highest paying job and zero allowances are claimed on the others.

Nonresident alien. If you are a nonresident alien, see the Instructions for Form 8233 before completing this Form W-4.

Check your withholding. After your Form W-4 takes effect, use Pub. 919 to see how the dollar amount you are having withheld compares to your projected total tax for 2006. See Pub. 919, especially if your earnings exceed $130,000 (Single) or $180,000 (Married).

Recent name change? If your name on line 1 differs from that shown on your social security card, call 1-800-772-1213 to initiate a name change and obtain a social security card showing your correct name.

Personal Allowances Worksheet (Keep for your records.)

A	Enter "1" for **yourself** if no one else can claim you as a dependent	**A** _____
B	Enter "1" if: { • You are single and have only one job; or • You are married, have only one job, and your spouse does not work; or • Your wages from a second job or your spouse's wages (or the total of both) are $1,000 or less. } . .	**B** __1__
C	Enter "1" for your **spouse.** But, you may choose to enter "-0-" if you are married and have either a working spouse or more than one job. (Entering "-0-" may help you avoid having too little tax withheld.)	**C** _____
D	Enter number of **dependents** (other than your spouse or yourself) you will claim on your tax return	**D** _____
E	Enter "1" if you will file as **head of household** on your tax return (see conditions under **Head of household** above) .	**E** _____
F	Enter "1" if you have at least $1,500 of **child or dependent care expenses** for which you plan to claim a credit . .	**F** _____
	(**Note.** Do **not** include child support payments. See **Pub. 503,** Child and Dependent Care Expenses, for details.)	
G	**Child Tax Credit** (including additional child tax credit): • If your total income will be less than $55,000 ($82,000 if married), enter "2" for each eligible child. • If your total income will be between $55,000 and $84,000 ($82,000 and $119,000 if married), enter "1" for each eligible child plus "1" **additional** if you have four or more eligible children.	**G** __1__
H	Add lines A through G and enter total here. (**Note.** This may be different from the number of exemptions you claim on your tax return.) ▶	**H** _____

For accuracy, complete all worksheets that apply.	{	• If you plan to **itemize or claim adjustments to income** and want to reduce your withholding, see the **Deductions and Adjustments Worksheet** on page 2. • If you have **more than one job** or are **married and you and your spouse both work** and the combined earnings from all jobs exceed $35,000 ($25,000 if married) see the **Two-Earner/Two-Job Worksheet** on page 2 to avoid having too little tax withheld. • If **neither** of the above situations applies, **stop here** and enter the number from line H on line 5 of Form W-4 below.

- - - - - - - - - - - - - - - - - **Cut here and give Form W-4 to your employer. Keep the top part for your records.** - - - - - - - - - - - - - - - - -

Form **W-4** <small>Department of the Treasury Internal Revenue Service</small>	**Employee's Withholding Allowance Certificate** ▶ Whether you are entitled to claim a certain number of allowances or exemption from withholding is subject to review by the IRS. Your employer may be required to send a copy of this form to the IRS.	OMB No. 1545-0074 **2006**

1 Type or print your first name and middle initial. **John A.**	Last name **Smith**	2 Your social security number **123 45 6789**
Home address (number and street or rural route) **567 Wharf Boulevard**	**3** ☒ Single ☐ Married ☐ Married, but withhold at higher Single rate. **Note.** If married, but legally separated, or spouse is a nonresident alien, check the "Single" box.	
City or town, state, and ZIP code **San Diego, CA 54321**	**4 If your last name differs from that shown on your social security card, check here. You must call 1-800-772-1213 for a new card.** ▶ ☐	

5	Total number of allowances you are claiming (from line **H** above **or** from the applicable worksheet on page 2)	**5**	**1**
6	Additional amount, if any, you want withheld from each paycheck	**6**	$ **0**
7	I claim exemption from withholding for 2006, and I certify that I meet **both** of the following conditions for exemption. • Last year I had a right to a refund of **all** federal income tax withheld because I had **no** tax liability **and** • This year I expect a refund of **all** federal income tax withheld because I expect to have **no** tax liability. If you meet both conditions, write "Exempt" here . . . . ▶	**7**	

Under penalties of perjury, I declare that I have examined this certificate and to the best of my knowledge and belief, it is true, correct, and complete.

Employee's signature
(Form is not valid
unless you sign it.) ▶ *John A. Smith*   Date ▶ *June 6, 2007*

8 Employer's name and address (Employer: Complete lines 8 and 10 only if sending to the IRS.)	9 Office code (optional)	10 Employer identification number (EIN)

For Privacy Act and Paperwork Reduction Act Notice, see page 2.   Cat. No. 10220Q   Form **W-4** (2006)

Deductions and Adjustments Worksheet

Note. Use this worksheet *only* if you plan to itemize deductions, claim certain credits, or claim adjustments to income on your 2006 tax return.

1　Enter an estimate of your 2006 itemized deductions. These include qualifying home mortgage interest, charitable contributions, state and local taxes, medical expenses in excess of 7.5% of your income, and miscellaneous deductions. (For 2006, you may have to reduce your itemized deductions if your income is over $150,500 ($75,250 if married filing separately). See *Worksheet 3* in Pub. 919 for details.) . . .　**1**　$ _____

2　Enter:
$10,300 if married filing jointly or qualifying widow(er)
$ 7,550 if head of household
$ 5,150 if single or married filing separately
. . . .　**2**　$ _____

3　**Subtract** line 2 from line 1. If line 2 is greater than line 1, enter "-0-" . . . .　**3**　$ _____

4　Enter an estimate of your 2006 adjustments to income, including alimony, deductible IRA contributions, and student loan interest　**4**　$ _____

5　**Add** lines 3 and 4 and enter the total. (Include any amount for credits from *Worksheet 7* in Pub. 919) .　**5**　$ _____

6　Enter an estimate of your 2006 nonwage income (such as dividends or interest) . . . .　**6**　$ _____

7　**Subtract** line 6 from line 5. Enter the result, but not less than "-0-" . . . .　**7**　$ _____

8　**Divide** the amount on line 7 by $3,300 and enter the result here. Drop any fraction . . . .　**8**　_____

9　Enter the number from the **Personal Allowances Worksheet,** line H, page 1 . . . .　**9**　_____

10　**Add** lines 8 and 9 and enter the total here. If you plan to use the **Two-Earner/Two-Job Worksheet,** also enter this total on line 1 below. Otherwise, **stop here** and enter this total on Form W-4, line 5, page 1 .　**10**　_____

Two-Earner/Two-Job Worksheet (See *Two earners/two jobs* on page 1.)

Note. Use this worksheet *only* if the instructions under line H on page 1 direct you here.

1　Enter the number from line H, page 1 (or from line 10 above if you used the **Deductions and Adjustments Worksheet**)　**1**　_____

2　Find the number in **Table 1** below that applies to the **LOWEST** paying job and enter it here . . . .　**2**　_____

3　If line 1 is **more than or equal to** line 2, subtract line 2 from line 1. Enter the result here (if zero, enter "-0-") and on Form W-4, line 5, page 1. **Do not** use the rest of this worksheet . . . .　**3**　_____

Note. If line 1 is *less than* line 2, enter "-0-" on Form W-4, line 5, page 1. Complete lines 4–9 below to calculate the additional withholding amount necessary to avoid a year-end tax bill.

4　Enter the number from line 2 of this worksheet . . . .　**4**　_____

5　Enter the number from line 1 of this worksheet . . . .　**5**　_____

6　**Subtract** line 5 from line 4 . . . .　**6**　_____

7　Find the amount in **Table 2** below that applies to the **HIGHEST** paying job and enter it here . . . .　**7**　$ _____

8　**Multiply** line 7 by line 6 and enter the result here. This is the additional annual withholding needed . .　**8**　$ _____

9　Divide line 8 by the number of pay periods remaining in 2006. For example, divide by 26 if you are paid every two weeks and you complete this form in December 2005. Enter the result here and on Form W-4, line 6, page 1. This is the additional amount to be withheld from each paycheck . . . .　**9**　$ _____

Table 1: Two-Earner/Two-Job Worksheet

Married Filing Jointly						All Others	
If wages from **HIGHEST** paying job are—	AND, wages from **LOWEST** paying job are—	Enter on line 2 above	If wages from **HIGHEST** paying job are—	AND, wages from **LOWEST** paying job are—	Enter on line 2 above	If wages from **LOWEST** paying job are—	Enter on line 2 above
$0 - $42,000	$0 - $4,500	0	$42,001 and over	32,001 - 38,000	6	$0 - $6,000	0
	4,501 - 9,000	1		38,001 - 46,000	7	6,001 - 12,000	1
	9,001 - 18,000	2		46,001 - 55,000	8	12,001 - 19,000	2
	18,001 and over	3		55,001 - 60,000	9	19,001 - 26,000	3
				60,001 - 65,000	10	26,001 - 35,000	4
$42,001 and over	$0 - $4,500	0		65,001 - 75,000	11	35,001 - 50,000	5
	4,501 - 9,000	1		75,001 - 95,000	12	50,001 - 65,000	6
	9,001 - 18,000	2		95,001 - 105,000	13	65,001 - 80,000	7
	18,001 - 22,000	3		105,001 - 120,000	14	80,001 - 90,000	8
	22,001 - 26,000	4		120,001 and over	15	90,001 - 120,000	9
	26,001 - 32,000	5				120,001 and over	10

Table 2: Two-Earner/Two-Job Worksheet

Married Filing Jointly		All Others	
If wages from **HIGHEST** paying job are—	Enter on line 7 above	If wages from **HIGHEST** paying job are—	Enter on line 7 above
$0 - $60,000	$500	$0 - $30,000	$500
60,001 - 115,000	830	30,001 - 75,000	830
115,001 - 165,000	920	75,001 - 145,000	920
165,001 - 290,000	1,090	145,001 - 330,000	1,090
290,001 and over	1,160	330,001 and over	1,160

Printed on recycled paper

BOE-400-SPA REV. 1 (FRONT) (7-05)
APPLICATION FOR SELLER'S PERMIT

STATE OF CALIFORNIA
BOARD OF EQUALIZATION

| **1. PERMIT TYPE:** *(check one)* ☐ Regular ☐ Temporary | **FOR BOARD USE ONLY** | | | |

2. TYPE OF OWNERSHIP *(check one)*   * Must provide partnership agreement

☒ Sole Owner ☐ Husband/Wife Co-ownership
☐ Corporation ☐ Limited Liability Company (LLC)
☐ General Partnership ☐ Unincorporated Business Trust
☐ Limited Partnership (LP) * ☐ Limited Liability Partnership (LLP) *
(Registered to practice law, accounting or architecture)
☐ Registered Domestic Partnership
☐ Other *(describe)* _____

FOR BOARD USE ONLY

TAX	IND	OFFICE	PERMIT NUMBER
S			

NAICS CODE | BUS CODE | A.C.C. | REPORTING BASIS | TAX AREA CODE

RETURN TYPE
PROCESSED BY | PERMIT ISSUE DATE | ☐ (1) 401-A ☐ (2) 401-EZ
___/___/___ | VERIFICATION ☐ DL ☐ PA ☐ Other

3. NAME OF SOLE OWNER, CORPORATION, LLC, PARTNERSHIP, OR TRUST
Ralph Retailer

4. STATE OF INCORPORATION OR ORGANIZATION
California

5. BUSINESS TRADE NAME/"DOING BUSINESS AS" [DBA] *(if any)*
Ralph's Rugs

6. DATE YOU WILL BEGIN BUSINESS ACTIVITIES *(month, day, and year)*
04/01/07

7. CORPORATE, LLC, LLP OR LP NUMBER FROM CALIFORNIA SECRETARY OF STATE

8. FEDERAL EMPLOYER IDENTIFICATION NUMBER (FEIN)

CHECK ONE ☒ Owner/Co-Owners ☐ Partners ☐ Registered Domestic Partners ☐ Corp. Officers ☐ LLC Officers/Managers/Members ☐ Trustees/Beneficiaries
Use additional sheets to include information for more than three individuals.

9. FULL NAME *(first, middle, last)*
Ralph Retailer

10. TITLE

11. SOCIAL SECURITY NUMBER *(corporate officers excluded)*
123-45-6789

12. DRIVER LICENSE NUMBER *(attach copy)*
Cal 123456

13. HOME ADDRESS *(street, city, state, zip code)*
123 Main Street Anytown, CA 90000

14. HOME TELEPHONE NUMBER
(123)555-5555

15. NAME OF A PERSONAL REFERENCE NOT LIVING WITH YOU   **16. ADDRESS** *(street, city, state, zip code)*
Fred Friend 321 Main Street Anytown, CA 90000

17. REFERENCE TELEPHONE NUMBER
( )

18. FULL NAME OF ADDITIONAL PARTNER, OFFICER, OR MEMBER *(first, middle, last)*

19. TITLE

20. SOCIAL SECURITY NUMBER *(corporate officers excluded)*

21. DRIVER LICENSE NUMBER *(attach copy)*

22. HOME ADDRESS *(street, city, state, zip code)*

23. HOME TELEPHONE NUMBER
( )

24. NAME OF A PERSONAL REFERENCE NOT LIVING WITH YOU   **25. ADDRESS** *(street, city, state, zip code)*

26. REFERENCE TELEPHONE NUMBER
( )

27. FULL NAME OF ADDITIONAL PARTNER, OFFICER, OR MEMBER *(first, middle, last)*

28. TITLE

29. SOCIAL SECURITY NUMBER *(corporate officers excluded)*

30. DRIVER LICENSE NUMBER *(attach copy)*

31. HOME ADDRESS *(street, city, state, zip code)*

32. HOME TELEPHONE NUMBER
( )

33. NAME OF A PERSONAL REFERENCE NOT LIVING WITH YOU   **34. ADDRESS** *(street, city, state, zip code)*

35. REFERENCE TELEPHONE NUMBER
( )

36. TYPE OF BUSINESS *(check one that best describes your business)*
☒ Retail ☐ Wholesale ☐ Mfg. ☐ Repair ☐ Service ☐ Construction Contractor ☐ Leasing

37. NUMBER OF SELLING LOCATIONS *(if 2 or more, see Item No. 66)* one

38. WHAT ITEMS WILL YOU SELL?
rugs

39. CHECK ONE
☒ Full Time ☐ Part Time

40. BUSINESS ADDRESS *(street, city, state, zip code) [do not list P.O. Box or mailing service]*
123 Carpet Street Anytown, CA 90000

41. BUSINESS TELEPHONE NUMBER
(123)555-1234

42. MAILING ADDRESS *(street, city, state, zip code) [if different from business address]*
see above

43. BUSINESS FAX NUMBER
(123)555-4321

44. BUSINESS WEBSITE ADDRESS
www. ralphsrugs.com

45. BUSINESS EMAIL ADDRESS
ralph@ralphsrugs.com

46. DO YOU MAKE INTERNET SALES?
☒ Yes ☐ No

47. NAME OF BUSINESS LANDLORD
Arthur Asset

48. LANDLORD ADDRESS *(street, city, state, zip code)*
123 Number Street Anytown, CA 90000

49. LANDLORD TELEPHONE NUMBER
(123)555-0005

50. PROJECTED MONTHLY GROSS SALES
$ 10,000

51. PROJECTED MONTHLY TAXABLE SALES
$ 2,000

52. ALCOHOLIC BEVERAGE CONTROL LICENSE NUMBER *(if applicable)*
___ ___ - ___ ___ ___ ___ ___ ___

53. SELLING NEW TIRES?
☐ Yes ☒ No

54. SELLING COVERED ELECTRONIC DEVICES?
☐ Yes ☐ No

55. SELLING TOBACCO AT RETAIL?
☐ Yes ☒ No

(continued on reverse)

— *tear at perforation* —

59. NAME OF BANK OR OTHER FINANCIAL INSTITUTION *(note whether business or personal)*

Bank of Anytown

60. BANK BRANCH LOCATION

61. NAME OF MERCHANT CREDIT CARD PROCESSOR *(if you accept credit cards)*

ABC Credit Card Processor

62. MERCHANT CARD ACCOUNT NUMBER

9776543

63. NAMES OF MAJOR CALIFORNIA-BASED SUPPLIERS	**64. ADDRESSES** *(street, city, state, zip code)*	**65. PRODUCTS PURCHASED**
Rudy's Wholesale Rugs	123 Weaver Road, Anytown, CA 90000	rugs

ADDITIONAL SELLING LOCATIONS (List All Other Selling Locations)

66. PHYSICAL LOCATION OR STREET ADDRESS *(attach separate list, if required)*

OWNERSHIP AND ORGANIZATIONAL CHANGES (Do Not Complete for Temporary Permits)

67. ARE YOU BUYING AN EXISTING BUSINESS?

☐ Yes ☒ No   If yes, complete items 70 through 74.

68. ARE YOU CHANGING FROM ONE TYPE OF BUSINESS ORGANIZATION TO ANOTHER (FOR EXAMPLE, FROM A SOLE OWNER TO A CORPORATION OR FROM A PARTNERSHIP TO A LIMITED LIABILITY COMPANY, ETC.)?

☐ Yes ☒ No   If yes, complete items 70 and 71.

69. OTHER OWNERSHIP CHANGES *(please describe)*:

70. FORMER OWNER'S NAME	**71. SELLER'S PERMIT NUMBER**
72. PURCHASE PRICE $	**73. VALUE OF FIXTURES & EQUIPMENT** $

74. IF AN ESCROW COMPANY IS REQUESTING A TAX CLEARANCE ON YOUR BEHALF, PLEASE LIST THEIR NAME, ADDRESS, TELEPHONE NUMBER, AND THE ESCROW NUMBER

TEMPORARY PERMIT EVENT INFORMATION

75. PERIOD OF SALES FROM: ___ / ___ / ___ THROUGH: ___ / ___ / ___	**76. ESTIMATED EVENT SALES** $	**77. SPACE RENTAL COST** *(if any)* $	**78. ADMISSION CHARGED?** ☐ Yes ☐ No
79. ORGANIZER OR PROMOTER OF EVENT *(if any)*	**80. ADDRESS** *(street, city, state, zip code)*		**81. TELEPHONE NUMBER** ( )

82. ADDRESS OF EVENT *(If more than one, use line 66, above. Attach separate list, if required.)*

CERTIFICATION

All Corporate Officers, LLC Managing Members, Partners, or Owners must sign below.

I am duly authorized to sign the application and certify that the statements made are correct to the best of my knowledge and belief.

I also represent and acknowledge that the applicant will be engaged in or conduct business as a seller of tangible personal property.

NAME *(typed or printed)*	SIGNATURE	DATE
Ralph Retailer	*Ralph Retailer*	10/1/06
NAME *(typed or printed)*	SIGNATURE	DATE
NAME *(typed or printed)*	SIGNATURE	DATE

FOR BOARD USE ONLY

SECURITY REVIEW	FORMS	PUBLICATIONS
☐ BOE-598 ($_____) or ☐ BOE-1009 REQUIRED BY APPROVED BY	☐ BOE-8 ☐ BOE-400-Y ☐ BOE-162 ☐ BOE-519 ☐ BOE-467 ☐ BOE-1241-D	☐ PUB 73 ☐ PUB DE 44
	REGULATIONS ☐ REG. 1668 ☐ REG. 1698 ☐ REG. 1700 ☐ _____	**RETURNS**

Employment Development Department
State of California

This form will be the basic record of YOUR ACCOUNT. **DO NOT FILE THIS FORM UNTIL YOU HAVE PAID WAGES THAT EXCEED $100.00.** Please read the **INSTRUCTIONS** on page 2 before completing this form. **PLEASE PRINT OR TYPE..** Return this form to: ➤	EMPLOYMENT DEVELOPMENT DEPARTMENT ACCOUNT SERVICES GROUP MIC 28 PO BOX 826880 SACRAMENTO CA 94280-0001 **(916) 654-7041 FAX (916) 654-9211** **www.edd.ca.gov**

REGISTRATION FORM FOR COMMERCIAL EMPLOYERS, PACIFIC MARITIME, AND FISHING BOATS

ACCOUNT NUMBER	DEPT. USE	QUARTER	ON-LINE PROCESS DATE	TAS CODE

Industry specific registration forms are required relative to each type of employer. Please use the appropriate form to register.

Commercial/Pacific Maritime/Fishing Boat	DE 1	Household Workers	DE 1HW
Agricultural	DE 1AG	Non-profit	DE 1NP
Government/Public Schools/Indian Tribes	DE 1GS	Personal Income Tax Only	DE 1P

A. THIS IS A:
☒ New business ☐ Hired employees ☐ Change in form - (Individual to corporation; partnership to corporation; merger; corporation to LLC, etc.)
☐ Change of partner(s) ☐ Purchased on-going business ☐ All ☐ Part ☐ Other _____
IF THE BUSINESS WAS PURCHASED, PROVIDE THE FOLLOWING INFORMATION:

Previous Owner	Business Name	Purchase Price	Date of Transfer	EDD Account Number

B. HAVE YOU EVER REGISTERED A BUSINESS WITH THE DEPARTMENT?
☒ No ☐ Yes

IF YES, ENTER THE FOLLOWING:
ACCT NUMBER   BUSINESS NAME   ADDRESS

C. INDICATE FIRST QUARTER AND YEAR IN WHICH WAGES EXCEED $100. ☒ Jan.-Mar. 20 07 ☐ Apr.-June 20__ ☐ July-Sept. 20__ ☐ Oct.-Dec. 20__

D. BUSINESS NAME (DBA) Sam's Sporting Goods	**OWNERSHIP BEGAN OPERATING** MONTH: 03 DAY: 03 YEAR: 07	**FEDERAL I.D. NUMBER** 123-45-6788
E. INDIVIDUAL OWNER Sam Sport	**SOCIAL SECURITY NUMBER** 123-45-66789	**DRIVER'S LICENSE #** Cal 7654321
F. CORPORATION/LLC/LLP/LP NAME	**SECRETARY OF STATE CORP/LLC/LLP/LP I.D. NO.**	

G. List all partners*, corporate officers, or LLC/LLP members/managers/officers	**TITLE** (partner, officer title, LLC/LLP member/manager)	**SOCIAL SECURITY NUMBER**	**DRIVER'S LICENSE #**

*If entity is a **Limited Partnership**, indicate General Partner with an (*). List additional partners, LLC/LLP members/officers/managers on a separate sheet.

H. MAILING ADDRESS P.O. Box 11234	**CITY** Sportsville	**STATE** CA	**ZIP CODE** 90000	**PHONE NUMBER** (543)555-555
I. BUSINESS ADDRESS (if different from mailing address) 1234 Main Street	**CITY** Sportsville	**STATE** CA	**ZIP CODE** 90000	**PHONE NUMBER** (543)555-555

J. ORGANIZATION TYPE
☒ (IN) INDIVIDUAL OWNER   ☐ (AS) ASSOCIATION   ☐ (LQ) LIQUIDATION   ☐ (JV) JOINT VENTURE
☐ (HW) HUS/WIFE CO-OWNERSHIP ☐ (LC) LIMITED LIABILITY CO. ☐ (LP) LIMITED PARTNERSHIP ☐ (RC) RECEIVERSHIP
☐ (GP) GENERAL PARTNERSHIP ☐ (PL) LIMITED LIABILITY   ☐ (TR) TRUSTEESHIP   ☐ (BK) BANKRUPTCY
☐ (CP) CORPORATION   PARTNERSHIP   ☐ (EA) ESTATE ADMINISTRATION ☐ (OT) OTHER (Specify)

K. EMPLOYER TYPE   ☒ (01) COMMERCIAL   ☐ (22) PACIFIC MARITIME   ☐ (25) FISHING BOAT

L. INDUSTRY ACTIVITY: Identify the industry and specific product or service that represents the greatest portion of your sales receipts or revenue. Check one:
☐ SERVICES   ☒ RETAIL   ☐ WHOLESALE   ☐ MANUFACTURING   ☐ OTHER _____
Describe specific product and/or service in detail.

Sporting Goods

Number of CA Employees __3__   Are there multiple locations for this business? ☐ No ☒ Yes

M. CONTACT PERSON FOR BUSINESS Sam Sport	**TITLE/COMPANY NAME** owner, Sam's Sports	**ADDRESS** 1234 Main Street, Sportsville, CA, 90000	**PHONE** (543 555-1234

N. DECLARATION
These statements are hereby declared to be correct to the best knowledge and belief of the undersigned.

Signature *Sam Sport*   Title Owner   Date 04/01/07
(Owner, Partner, Officer, Member, Manager, etc.)

O. PAYROLL TAX EDUCATION: Attend a payroll tax seminar that will help you understand how, what, and when to report state payroll taxes. Visit our Web site at **www.edd.ca.gov/taxsem** or call us at (888) 745-3886 for more information.

Form 1040-ES
Department of the Treasury
Internal Revenue Service

2006 Payment Voucher **3**

OMB No. 1545-0074

File only if you are making a payment of estimated tax by check or money order. Mail this voucher with your check or money order payable to the **"United States Treasury."** Write your social security number and "2006 Form 1040-ES" on your check or money order. Do not send cash. Enclose, but do not staple or attach, your payment with this voucher.

Calendar year—Due Sept. 15, 2006

Amount of estimated tax you are paying by check or money order.

Dollars	Cents

Your first name and initial	Your last name	Your social security number
Rocky	Frankenfurter	123-45-6789

If joint payment, complete for spouse

Spouse's first name and initial	Spouse's last name	Spouse's social security number

Address (number, street, and apt. no.)
1234 Bayshore Blvd.

City, state, and ZIP code. (If a foreign address, enter city, province or state, postal code, and country.)
Sacramento, CA 12345

Print or type

For Privacy Act and Paperwork Reduction Act Notice, see instructions on page 5.

- **Tear off here** -

a Control number	22222	Void ☐	For Official Use Only ▶ OMB No. 1545-0008	

b Employer identification number (EIN) 33-4897044		**1** Wages, tips, other compensation 25,650.00	**2** Federal income tax withheld 5,050.00

c Employer's name, address, and ZIP code John Doe 123 Main Street Libertyville, CA 98765	**3** Social security wages 25,650.00	**4** Social security tax withheld 1,590.30
	5 Medicare wages and tips 25,650.00	**6** Medicare tax withheld 371.93
	7 Social security tips 0	**8** Allocated tips 0

d Employee's social security number 123-45-6789	**9** Advance EIC payment 0	**10** Dependent care benefits 0

e Employee's first name and initial Rocky	Last name Frankenfurter	Suff.	**11** Nonqualified plans 0	**12a** See instructions for box 12

13 Statutory employee ☐ Retirement plan ☐ Third-party sick pay ☐

12b

1234 Bayshore Boulevard
Sacramento, CA 12345

14 Other

12c

12d

f Employee's address and ZIP code

15 State Employer's state ID number CA 4448778	**16** State wages, tips, etc. 26,650.00	**17** State income tax 565.00	**18** Local wages, tips, etc.	**19** Local income tax	**20** Locality name

Form **W-2** Wage and Tax Statement   **2006**

Department of the Treasury—Internal Revenue Service

Copy A For Social Security Administration — Send this entire page with Form W-3 to the Social Security Administration; photocopies are **not** acceptable.

For Privacy Act and Paperwork Reduction Act Notice, see back of Copy D.

Cat. No. 10134D

Do Not Cut, Fold, or Staple Forms on This Page — Do Not Cut, Fold, or Staple Forms on This Page

9595   ☐ VOID   ☐ CORRECTED

PAYER'S name, street address, city, state, ZIP code, and telephone no.		1 Rents	OMB No. 1545-0115	
Jeremy Michaels XYZ Builders 123 Maple Avenue Oaktown, VA 22000 703-123-4567		$	**2006**	**Miscellaneous Income**
		2 Royalties $	Form **1099-MISC**	
		3 Other income $	4 Federal income tax withheld $	**Copy A**
PAYER'S federal identification number	RECIPIENT'S identification number	5 Fishing boat proceeds	6 Medical and health care payments	**For Internal Revenue Service Center**
10-9999999	123-45-6789	$	$	File with Form 1096.
RECIPIENT'S name Zachary Autin Rock Hill Drywall		7 Nonemployee compensation $ 5500.00	8 Substitute payments in lieu of dividends or interest $	For Privacy Act and Paperwork Reduction Act Notice, see the **2006 General Instructions for Forms 1099, 1098, 5498, and W-2G.**
Street address (including apt. no.) 456 Flower Lane		9 Payer made direct sales of $5,000 or more of consumer products to a buyer (recipient) for resale ▶ ☐	10 Crop insurance proceeds $	
City, state, and ZIP code Oaktown, VA 22000		11	12	
Account number (see instructions)	2nd TIN not. ☐	13 Excess golden parachute payments $	14 Gross proceeds paid to an attorney $	
15a Section 409A deferrals $	**15b** Section 409A income $	16 State tax withheld $ $	17 State/Payer's state no.	18 State income $ $

Form **1099-MISC**   Cat. No. 14425J   Department of the Treasury - Internal Revenue Service

Do Not Cut or Separate Forms on This Page   —   Do Not Cut or Separate Forms on This Page

Do Not Staple 6969

Form **1096**

Department of the Treasury
Internal Revenue Service

Annual Summary and Transmittal of
U.S. Information Returns

OMB No. 1545-0108

20**06**

FILER'S name
Doe Company

Street address (including room or suite number)
123 Main Street

City, state, and ZIP code
Libertyville, CA 98765

Name of person to contact
John Doe

Telephone number
(518) 555-0000

Email address
John@Doe.com

Fax number
(518) 555-0001

For Official Use Only

1 Employer identification number	2 Social security number	3 Total number of forms	4 Federal income tax withheld	5 Total amount reported with this Form 1096
59-123456	123-45-6789	3	$ 0	$ 63,000

Enter an "X" in only one box below to indicate the type of form being filed.　If this is your **final return**, enter an "X" here . . . ▶ ☒

W-2G 32	1098 81	1098-C 78	1098-E 84	1098-T 83	1099-A 80	1099-B 79	1099-C 85	1099-CAP 73	1099-DIV 91	1099-G 86	1099-H 71	1099-INT 92	1099-LTC 93
☐	☐	☐	☐	☐	☐	☐	☐	☐	☐	☐	☐	☐	☐

1099-MISC 95	1099-OID 96	1099-PATR 97	1099-Q 31	1099-R 98	1099-S 75	1099-SA 94	5498 28	5498-ESA 72	5498-SA 27
☐	☐	☐	☐	☐	☐	☐	☐	☐	☐

Return this entire page to the Internal Revenue Service. Photocopies are not acceptable.

Under penalties of perjury, I declare that I have examined this return and accompanying documents, and, to the best of my knowledge and belief, they are true, correct, and complete.

Signature ▶ *John Doe*　　Title ▶ Owner　　Date ▶ 3-11-2007

Blank Forms

The following forms may be photocopied or removed from this book and used immediately. It is recommended that you photocopy them and save the originals in case you make a mistake, or for future use. Some of the tax forms explained in this book are not included here because you should use original returns provided by the IRS (940, 941) or the California Department of Revenue (quarterly unemployment compensation form).

TAX TIMETABLE

		California					Federal			
	Sales	Unemployment	Tangible	Intangible	Corp. Income	Est. Payment	Annual Return	Form 941*	Misc.	
JAN	20th	31st				15th		31st	940 508	31st W-2 1099
FEB	20th			28th 4% disc.						28th W-3
MAR	20th		31st	31st 3% disc.			15th Corp. & Partnership			
APR	20th	30th	1st	30th 2% disc.	1st	15th	15th Personal	30th		30th 508
MAY	20th			31st 1% disc.						
JUN	20th			30th tax due		15th				
JUL	20th	31st						31st		31st 508
AUG	20th									
SEP	20th					15th				
OCT	20th	31st						31st		31st 508
NOV	20th									
DEC	20th									

* In addition to form 941, deposits must be made regularly if withholding exceeds $500 in any month

This page intentionally blank.

FICTITIOUS BUSINESS NAME STATEMENT

The following person (persons) is (are) doing business as

* _____

at ** _____ :

*** _____

_____

_____

_____

This business is conducted by **** _____

The registrant commenced to transact business under the fictitious business name or names listed above on ***** _____

Signed _____

Statement filed with the County Clerk of _____ County on

_____

NOTICE

THIS FICTITIOUS BUSINESS NAME STATEMENT EXPIRES FIVE YEARS FROM THE DATE IT WAS FILED IN THE OFFICE OF THE COUNTY CLERK. A NEW FICTITIOUS BUSINESS NAME STATEMENT MUST BE FILED BEFORE THAT TIME. THE FILING OF THIS STATEMENT DOES NOT OF ITSELF AUTHORIZE THE USE IN THIS STATE OF A FICTITIOUS BUSINESS NAME IN VIOLATION OF THE RIGHTS OF ANOTHER UNDER FEDERAL, STATE, OR COMMON LAW (SEE SECTION 14411 ET SEQ., BUSINESS AND PROFESSIONAL CODE).

INSTRUCTIONS

1. Where the asterisk (*) appears in the form, insert the fictitious business name or names. Only those businesses operated at the same address may be listed on one statement.

2. Where the two asterisks (**) appear on the form: If the registrant has a place of business in this state, insert the street address of his or her principal place of business in this state. If the registrant has no place of business in this state, insert the street address of his or her principal place of business outside this state.

3. Where the three asterisks (***) appear in the form: If the registrant is an individual, insert his or her full name and residence address. If the registrant is a partnership or other association of persons, insert the full name and residence address of each general partner. If the registrant is a limited liability company, insert the name of the limited liability company as set out in its articles of organization and the state of organization. If the registrant is a business trust, insert the full name and address of each trustee. If the registrant is a corporation, insert the name of the corporation as set out in its articles of incorporation and the state of incorporation.

4. Where four asterisks (****) appear in the form, insert whichever of the following best describes the nature of the business: (i) "an individual," (ii) "a general partnership," (iii) "a limited partnership," (iv) "a limited liability company," (v) "an unincorporated association other than a partnership," (vi) "a corporation," (vii) "a business trust," (viii) "copartners," (ix) "husband and wife," (x) "joint venture," or (xi) "other--please specify."

5. Where the five asterisks (*****) appear in the form, insert the date on which the registrant first commenced to transact business under the fictitious business name or names listed, if already transacting business under that name or names. If the registrant has not yet commenced to transact business under the fictitious business name or names listed, insert the statement, "Not applicable."

    If the registrant is an individual, the statement shall be signed by the individual; if a partnership or other association of persons, by a general partner; if a limited liability company, by a manager or officer; if a business trust, by a trustee; if a corporation, by an officer.

    Publication of notice pursuant to this section shall be once a week for four successive weeks. Four publications in a newspaper regularly published once a week or more often, with at least five days intervening between the respective publication dates not counting such publication dates, are sufficient. The period of notice commences with the first day of publication and terminates at the end of the twenty-eighth day, including therein the first day.

    The newspaper selected for the publication of the statement should be one that circulates in the area where the business is to be conducted. Where a new statement is required because the prior statement has expired, the new statement need not be published unless there has been a change in the information required in the expired statement.

APPLICATION FOR EMPLOYMENT

We consider applicants for all positions without regard to race, color, religion, sex, national origin, age, marital or veteran status, the presence of a non-job-related medical condition or handicap, or any other legally protected status. Proof of citizenship or immigration status will be required upon employment.

(PLEASE TYPE OR PRINT)

Position Applied For   Date of Application

Last Name	First Name	Middle Name or Initial

Is there any other information regarding your name that will be needed to check work or school records? ❑ Yes ❑ No

Address   Number Street   City   State   Zip Code

Telephone Number(s) [indicate home or work]	Social Security Number

Date Available:_____   Are you available: ❑ Full Time   ❑ Part Time   ❑ Weekends

Are you 18 years of age or older?   ❑ Yes   ❑ No

Have you been convicted of a felony within the past 7 years?   ❑ Yes   ❑ No

Conviction will not necessarily disqualify an applicant from employment.
If Yes, attach explanation.

Can you produce documents proving you are authorized to work in the United States? ❑ Yes   ❑ No

Education

	High School	Undergraduate	Graduate
School Name & Location			
Years Completed	1 2 3 4	1 2 3 4	1 2 3 4
Diploma / Degree			
Course of Study			

State any additional information you feel may be helpful to us in considering your application (such as any specialized training; skills; apprenticeships; honors received; professional, trade, business or civic organizations or activities; job-related military training or experience; foreign language abilities; etc.)

_____
_____
_____
_____

Employment Experience

Start with your present or last job. Include any job-related military service assignments and voluntary activities. You may exclude organizations which indicate race, color, religion, gender, national origin, handicap, or other protected status.

	Employer Name & Address	Dates Employed	Job Title/Duties
1.		Hourly Rate/Salary	
	May we contact this employer? ❑ Yes ❑ No	Hours Per Week	
	Employer Phone		
	Supervisor		
	Reason for Leaving		
2.	Employer Name & Address	Dates Employed	Job Title/Duties
		Hourly Rate/Salary	
	Employer Phone	Hours Per Week	
	Supervisor		
	Reason for Leaving		
3.	Employer Name & Address	Dates Employed	Job Title/Duties
		Hourly Rate/Salary	
	Employer Phone	Hours Per Week	
	Supervisor		
	Reason for Leaving		

References: Name   Occupation Address   Phone #   Relationship   Years known

1. _____
2. _____
3. _____

If you need additional space, continue on a separate sheet of paper.

Applicant's Statement

I certify that the information given on this application is true and complete to the best of my knowledge. I authorize investigation of all statements contained in this application, and understand that false or misleading information given in my application or interview(s) may result in discharge.

I understand and acknowledge that, unless otherwise defined by applicable law, any employment relationship with this organization is "at will," which means that I may resign at any time and the employer may discharge me at any time with or without cause. I further understand that this "at will" employment relationship may not be changed orally, by any written document, or by conduct, unless such change is specifically acknowledged in writing by an authorized executive of this organization.

_____   _____

Signature of Applicant   Date

Department of Homeland Security
U.S. Citizenship and Immigration Services

OMB No. 1615-0047; Expires 03/31/07

Employment Eligibility Verification

Please read instructions carefully before completing this form. The instructions must be available during completion of this form. ANTI-DISCRIMINATION NOTICE: It is illegal to discriminate against work eligible individuals. Employers CANNOT specify which document(s) they will accept from an employee. The refusal to hire an individual because of a future expiration date may also constitute illegal discrimination.

Section 1. Employee Information and Verification. To be completed and signed by employee at the time employment begins.

Print Name: Last	First	Middle Initial	Maiden Name
Address *(Street Name and Number)*		Apt. #	Date of Birth *(month/day/year)*
City	State	Zip Code	Social Security #

I am aware that federal law provides for imprisonment and/or fines for false statements or use of false documents in connection with the completion of this form.

I attest, under penalty of perjury, that I am (check one of the following):

☐ A citizen or national of the United States
☐ A Lawful Permanent Resident (Alien #) A _____
☐ An alien authorized to work until _____

(Alien # or Admission #) _____

Employee's Signature	Date *(month/day/year)*

Preparer and/or Translator Certification. *(To be completed and signed if Section 1 is prepared by a person other than the employee.) I attest, under penalty of perjury, that I have assisted in the completion of this form and that to the best of my knowledge the information is true and correct.*

Preparer's/Translator's Signature	Print Name
Address *(Street Name and Number, City, State, Zip Code)*	Date *(month/day/year)*

Section 2. Employer Review and Verification. To be completed and signed by employer. Examine one document from List A OR examine one document from List B and one from List C, as listed on the reverse of this form, and record the title, number and expiration date, if any, of the document(s).

List A	OR	List B	AND	List C
Document title: _____		_____		_____
Issuing authority: _____		_____		_____
Document #: _____		_____		_____
Expiration Date *(if any):* _____		_____		_____
Document #: _____				
Expiration Date *(if any):* _____				

CERTIFICATION - I attest, under penalty of perjury, that I have examined the document(s) presented by the above-named employee, that the above-listed document(s) appear to be genuine and to relate to the employee named, that the employee began employment on *(month/day/year)* _____ **and that to the best of my knowledge the employee is eligible to work in the United States. (State employment agencies may omit the date the employee began employment.)**

Signature of Employer or Authorized Representative	Print Name	Title
Business or Organization Name	Address *(Street Name and Number, City, State, Zip Code)*	Date *(month/day/year)*

Section 3. Updating and Reverification. To be completed and signed by employer.

A. New Name *(if applicable)*	B. Date of rehire *(month/day/year) (if applicable)*

C. If employee's previous grant of work authorization has expired, provide the information below for the document that establishes current employment eligibility.

Document Title: _____   Document #: _____   Expiration Date (if any): _____

I attest, under penalty of perjury, that to the best of my knowledge, this employee is eligible to work in the United States, and if the employee presented document(s), the document(s) I have examined appear to be genuine and to relate to the individual.

Signature of Employer or Authorized Representative	Date *(month/day/year)*

NOTE: This is the 1991 edition of the Form I-9 that has been rebranded with a current printing date to reflect the recent transition from the INS to DHS and its components.

Form I-9 (Rev. 05/31/05)Y Page 2

INSTRUCTIONS
PLEASE READ ALL INSTRUCTIONS CAREFULLY BEFORE COMPLETING THIS FORM.

Anti-Discrimination Notice. It is illegal to discriminate against any individual (other than an alien not authorized to work in the U.S.) in hiring, discharging, or recruiting or referring for a fee because of that individual's national origin or citizenship status. It is illegal to discriminate against work eligible individuals. Employers **CANNOT** specify which document(s) they will accept from an employee. The refusal to hire an individual because of a future expiration date may also constitute illegal discrimination.

Section 1- Employee.
All employees, citizens and noncitizens, hired after November 6, 1986, must complete Section 1 of this form at the time of hire, which is the actual beginning of employment. **The employer is responsible for ensuring that Section 1 is timely and properly completed.**

Preparer/Translator Certification. The Preparer/Translator Certification must be completed if Section 1 is prepared by a person other than the employee. A preparer/translator may be used only when the employee is unable to complete Section 1 on his/her own. However, the employee must still sign Section 1 personally.

Section 2 - Employer.
For the purpose of completing this form, the term "employer" includes those recruiters and referrers for a fee who are agricultural associations, agricultural employers or farm labor contractors.

Employers must complete Section 2 by examining evidence of identity and employment eligibility within three (3) business days of the date employment begins. If employees are authorized to work, but are unable to present the required document(s) within three business days, they must present a receipt for the application of the document(s) within three business days and the actual document(s) within ninety (90) days. However, if employers hire individuals for a duration of less than three business days, Section 2 must be completed at the time employment begins. **Employers must record: 1)** document title; **2)** issuing authority; **3)** document number, **4)** expiration date, if any; and **5)** the date employment begins. Employers must sign and date the certification. Employees must present original documents. Employers may, but are not required to, photocopy the document(s) presented. These photocopies may only be used for the verification process and must be retained with the I-9. **However, employers are still responsible for completing the I-9.**

Section 3 - Updating and Reverification.
Employers must complete Section 3 when updating and/or reverifying the I-9. Employers must reverify employment eligibility of their employees on or before the expiration date recorded in Section 1. Employers **CANNOT** specify which document(s) they will accept from an employee.

- If an employee's name has changed at the time this form is being updated/reverified, complete Block A.

- If an employee is rehired within three (3) years of the date this form was originally completed and the employee is still eligible to be employed on the same basis as previously indicated on this form (updating), complete Block B and the signature block.

- If an employee is rehired within three (3) years of the date this form was originally completed and the employee's work authorization has expired **or** if a current employee's work authorization is about to expire (reverification), complete Block B and:

- examine any document that reflects that the employee is authorized to work in the U.S. (see List A **or** C),

- record the document title, document number and expiration date (if any) in Block C, and

- complete the signature block.

Photocopying and Retaining Form I-9. A blank I-9 may be reproduced, provided both sides are copied. The Instructions must be available to all employees completing this form. Employers must retain completed I-9s for three (3) years after the date of hire or one (1) year after the date employment ends, whichever is later.

For more detailed information, you may refer to the Department of Homeland Security (DHS) Handbook for Employers, (Form M-274). You may obtain the handbook at your local U.S. Citizenship and Immigration Services (USCIS) office.

Privacy Act Notice. The authority for collecting this information is the Immigration Reform and Control Act of 1986, Pub. L. 99-603 (8 USC 1324a).

This information is for employers to verify the eligibility of individuals for employment to preclude the unlawful hiring, or recruiting or referring for a fee, of aliens who are not authorized to work in the United States.

This information will be used by employers as a record of their basis for determining eligibility of an employee to work in the United States. The form will be kept by the employer and made available for inspection by officials of the U.S. Immigration and Customs Enforcement, Department of Labor and Office of Special Counsel for Immigration Related Unfair Employment Practices.

Submission of the information required in this form is voluntary. However, an individual may not begin employment unless this form is completed, since employers are subject to civil or criminal penalties if they do not comply with the Immigration Reform and Control Act of 1986.

Reporting Burden. We try to create forms and instructions that are accurate, can be easily understood and which impose the least possible burden on you to provide us with information. Often this is difficult because some immigration laws are very complex. Accordingly, the reporting burden for this collection of information is computed as follows: **1)** learning about this form, 5 minutes; **2)** completing the form, 5 minutes; and **3)** assembling and filing (recordkeeping) the form, 5 minutes, for an average of 15 minutes per response. If you have comments regarding the accuracy of this burden estimate, or suggestions for making this form simpler, you can write to U.S. Citizenship and Immigration Services, Regulatory Management Division, 111 Massachusetts Avenue, N.W., Washington, DC 20529. OMB No. 1615-0047.

NOTE: This is the 1991 edition of the Form I-9 that has been rebranded with a current printing date to reflect the recent transition from the INS to DHS and its components.

This page intentionally blank.

LISTS OF ACCEPTAE

LIST A		LIST B

LIST A

Documents that Establish Both Identity and Employment Eligibility

1. U.S. Passport (unexpired or expired)

2. Certificate of U.S. Citizenship *(Form N-560 or N-561)*

3. Certificate of Naturalization *(Form N-550 or N-570)*

4. Unexpired foreign passport, with *I-551 stamp or* attached *Form I-94* indicating unexpired employment authorization

5. Permanent Resident Card or Alien Registration Receipt Card with photograph *(Form I-151 or I-551)*

6. Unexpired Temporary Resident Card *(Form I-688)*

7. Unexpired Employment Authorization Card *(Form I-688A)*

8. Unexpired Reentry Permit *(Form I-327)*

9. Unexpired Refugee Travel Document *(Form I-571)*

10. Unexpired Employment Authorization Document issued by DHS that contains a photograph *(Form I-688B)*

OR

LIST B

Documents that Esta Identity

1. Driver's license or ID card issued by a state or outlyi possession of the United S provided it contains a photograph or information s name, date of birth, gender, eye color and address

2. ID card issued by federal, state or local government agencies o entities, provided it contains a photograph or information such a name, date of birth, gender, heigh eye color and address

3. School ID card with a photograph

4. Voter's registration card

5. U.S. Military card or draft record

6. Military dependent's ID card

7. U.S. Coast Guard Merchant Mariner Card

8. Native American tribal document

9. Driver's license issued by a Canadian government authority

For persons under age 18 who are unable to present a document listed above:

10. School record or report card

11. Clinic, doctor or hospital record

12. Day-care or nursery school record

4.

5. l I

6. ID (Citiz *(Forn*

7. Unexpir authoriza DHS *(oth under List*

Illustrations of many of these documents appear in Part 8 of the Handbook for Employers (

Form **SS-4**

(Rev. February 2006)

Department of the Treasury
Internal Revenue Service

Application for Employer Identification Number

(For use by employers, corporations, partnerships, trusts, estates, churches, government agencies, Indian tribal entities, certain individuals, and others.)

▶ See separate instructions for each line.   ▶ Keep a copy for your records.

OMB No. 1545-0003

EIN

Type or print clearly.

1 Legal name of entity (or individual) for whom the EIN is being requested	

2 Trade name of business (if different from name on line 1)	**3** Executor, administrator, trustee, "care of" name

4a Mailing address (room, apt., suite no. and street, or P.O. box)	**5a** Street address (if different) (Do not enter a P.O. box.)
4b City, state, and ZIP code	**5b** City, state, and ZIP code

6 County and state where principal business is located

7a Name of principal officer, general partner, grantor, owner, or trustor	**7b** SSN, ITIN, or EIN

8a **Type of entity** (check only one box)

☐ Sole proprietor (SSN) _____
☐ Partnership
☐ Corporation (enter form number to be filed) ▶ _____
☐ Personal service corporation
☐ Church or church-controlled organization
☐ Other nonprofit organization (specify) ▶ _____
☐ Other (specify) ▶

☐ Estate (SSN of decedent) _____
☐ Plan administrator (SSN) _____
☐ Trust (SSN of grantor) _____
☐ National Guard   ☐ State/local government
☐ Farmers' cooperative   ☐ Federal government/military
☐ REMIC   ☐ Indian tribal governments/enterprises
Group Exemption Number (GEN) ▶ _____

8b If a corporation, name the state or foreign country (if applicable) where incorporated

State	Foreign country

9 **Reason for applying** (check only one box)

☐ Started new business (specify type) ▶_____
_____
☐ Hired employees (Check the box and see line 12.)
☐ Compliance with IRS withholding regulations
☐ Other (specify) ▶

☐ Banking purpose (specify purpose) ▶ _____
☐ Changed type of organization (specify new type) ▶ _____
☐ Purchased going business
☐ Created a trust (specify type) ▶ _____
☐ Created a pension plan (specify type) ▶ _____

10 Date business started or acquired (month, day, year). See instructions.	**11** Closing month of accounting year

12 First date wages or annuities were paid (month, day, year). **Note.** If applicant is a withholding agent, enter date income will first be paid to nonresident alien. (month, day, year)   . . . . ▶

13 Highest number of employees expected in the next 12 months (enter -0- if none).

Do you expect to have $1,000 or less in employment tax liability for the calendar year? ☐ **Yes** ☐ **No.** (If you expect to pay $4,000 or less in wages, you can mark yes.)

Agricultural	Household	Other

14 Check **one** box that best describes the principal activity of your business.
☐ Construction   ☐ Rental & leasing   ☐ Transportation & warehousing
☐ Real estate   ☐ Manufacturing   ☐ Finance & insurance
☐ Health care & social assistance   ☐ Wholesale–agent/broker
☐ Accommodation & food service   ☐ Wholesale–other   ☐ Retail
☐ Other (specify)

15 Indicate principal line of merchandise sold, specific construction work done, products produced, or services provided.

16a Has the applicant ever applied for an employer identification number for this or any other business? . . . . ☐ **Yes** ☐ **No**
Note. If "Yes," please complete lines 16b and 16c.

16b If you checked "Yes" on line 16a, give applicant's legal name and trade name shown on prior application if different from line 1 or 2 above.
Legal name ▶   Trade name ▶

16c Approximate date when, and city and state where, the application was filed. Enter previous employer identification number if known.

Approximate date when filed (mo., day, year)	City and state where filed	Previous EIN

Third Party Designee	Complete this section **only** if you want to authorize the named individual to receive the entity's EIN and answer questions about the completion of this form.	
	Designee's name	Designee's telephone number (include area code) ( )
	Address and ZIP code	Designee's fax number (include area code) ( )

Under penalties of perjury, I declare that I have examined this application, and to the best of my knowledge and belief, it is true, correct, and complete.

Name and title (type or print clearly) ▶

Applicant's telephone number (include area code) ( )

Signature ▶   Date ▶

Applicant's fax number (include area code) ( )

For Privacy Act and Paperwork Reduction Act Notice, see separate instructions.   Cat. No. 16055N   Form **SS-4** (Rev. 2-2006)

Do I Need an EIN?

File Form SS-4 if the applicant entity does not already have an EIN but is required to show an EIN on any return, statement, or other document.[1] See also the separate instructions for each line on Form SS-4.

IF the applicant...	AND...	THEN...
Started a new business	Does not currently have (nor expect to have) employees	Complete lines 1, 2, 4a–8a, 8b (if applicable), and 9–16c.
Hired (or will hire) employees, including household employees	Does not already have an EIN	Complete lines 1, 2, 4a–6, 7a–b (if applicable), 8a, 8b (if applicable), and 9–16c.
Opened a bank account	Needs an EIN for banking purposes only	Complete lines 1–5b, 7a–b (if applicable), 8a, 9, and 16a–c.
Changed type of organization	Either the legal character of the organization or its ownership changed (for example, you incorporate a sole proprietorship or form a partnership)[2]	Complete lines 1–16c (as applicable).
Purchased a going business[3]	Does not already have an EIN	Complete lines 1–16c (as applicable).
Created a trust	The trust is other than a grantor trust or an IRA trust[4]	Complete lines 1–16c (as applicable).
Created a pension plan as a plan administrator[5]	Needs an EIN for reporting purposes	Complete lines 1, 3, 4a–b, 8a, 9, and 16a–c.
Is a foreign person needing an EIN to comply with IRS withholding regulations	Needs an EIN to complete a Form W-8 (other than Form W-8ECI), avoid withholding on portfolio assets, or claim tax treaty benefits[6]	Complete lines 1–5b, 7a–b (SSN or ITIN optional), 8a–9, and 16a–c.
Is administering an estate	Needs an EIN to report estate income on Form 1041	Complete lines 1, 2, 3, 4a–6, 8a, 9-11, 12-15 (if applicable), and 16a–c.
Is a withholding agent for taxes on non-wage income paid to an alien (i.e., individual, corporation, or partnership, etc.)	Is an agent, broker, fiduciary, manager, tenant, or spouse who is required to file Form 1042, Annual Withholding Tax Return for U.S. Source Income of Foreign Persons	Complete lines 1, 2, 3 (if applicable), 4a–5b, 7a–b (if applicable), 8a, 9, and 16a–c.
Is a state or local agency	Serves as a tax reporting agent for public assistance recipients under Rev. Proc. 80-4, 1980-1 C.B. 581[7]	Complete lines 1, 2, 4a–5b, 8a, 9, and 16a–c.
Is a single-member LLC	Needs an EIN to file Form 8832, Entity Classification Election, for filing employment tax returns, **or** for state reporting purposes[8]	Complete lines 1–16c (as applicable).
Is an S corporation	Needs an EIN to file Form 2553, Election by a Small Business Corporation[9]	Complete lines 1–16c (as applicable).

[1] For example, a sole proprietorship or self-employed farmer who establishes a qualified retirement plan, or is required to file excise, employment, alcohol, tobacco, or firearms returns, must have an EIN. A partnership, corporation, REMIC (real estate mortgage investment conduit), nonprofit organization (church, club, etc.), or farmers' cooperative must use an EIN for any tax-related purpose even if the entity does not have employees.

[2] However, do not apply for a new EIN if the existing entity only (a) changed its business name, (b) elected on Form 8832 to change the way it is taxed (or is covered by the default rules), or (c) terminated its partnership status because at least 50% of the total interests in partnership capital and profits were sold or exchanged within a 12-month period. The EIN of the terminated partnership should continue to be used. See Regulations section 301.6109-1(d)(2)(iii).

[3] Do not use the EIN of the prior business unless you became the "owner" of a corporation by acquiring its stock.

[4] However, grantor trusts that do not file using Optional Method 1 and IRA trusts that are required to file Form 990-T, Exempt Organization Business Income Tax Return, must have an EIN. For more information on grantor trusts, see the Instructions for Form 1041.

[5] A plan administrator is the person or group of persons specified as the administrator by the instrument under which the plan is operated.

[6] Entities applying to be a Qualified Intermediary (QI) need a QI-EIN even if they already have an EIN. See Rev. Proc. 2000-12.

[7] See also *Household employer* on page 3. **Note.** State or local agencies may need an EIN for other reasons, for example, hired employees.

[8] Most LLCs do not need to file Form 8832. See *Limited liability company (LLC)* on page 4 for details on completing Form SS-4 for an LLC.

[9] An existing corporation that is electing or revoking S corporation status should use its previously-assigned EIN.

Instructions for Form SS-4

Department of the Treasury
Internal Revenue Service

(Rev. February 2006)

Application for Employer Identification Number

Section references are to the Internal Revenue Code unless otherwise noted.

General Instructions

Use these instructions to complete Form SS-4, Application for Employer Identification Number. Also see *Do I Need an EIN?* on page 2 of Form SS-4.

Purpose of Form

Use Form SS-4 to apply for an employer identification number (EIN). An EIN is a nine-digit number (for example, 12-3456789) assigned to sole proprietors, corporations, partnerships, estates, trusts, and other entities for tax filing and reporting purposes. The information you provide on this form will establish your business tax account.

 An EIN is for use in connection with your business activities only. Do not use your EIN in place of your social security number (SSN).

Reminders

Apply online. Generally, you can apply for and receive an EIN online using the Internet. See *How To Apply* below.

File only one Form SS-4. Generally, a sole proprietor should file only one Form SS-4 and needs only one EIN, regardless of the number of businesses operated as a sole proprietorship or trade names under which a business operates. However, if the proprietorship incorporates or enters into a partnership, a new EIN is required. Also, each corporation in an affiliated group must have its own EIN.

EIN applied for, but not received. If you do not have an EIN by the time a return is due, write "Applied For" and the date you applied in the space shown for the number. Do not show your SSN as an EIN on returns.

If you do not have an EIN by the time a tax deposit is due, send your payment to the Internal Revenue Service Center for your filing area as shown in the instructions for the form that you are filing. Make your check or money order payable to the "United States Treasury" and show your name (as shown on Form SS-4), address, type of tax, period covered, and date you applied for an EIN.

Federal tax deposits. New employers that have a federal tax obligation will be pre-enrolled in the Electronic Federal Tax Payment System (EFTPS). EFTPS allows you to make all of your federal tax payments online at *www.eftps.gov* or by telephone. Shortly after we have assigned you your EIN, you will receive instructions by mail for activating your EFTPS enrollment. You will also receive an EFTPS Personal Identification Number (PIN) that you will use to make your payments, as well as instructions for obtaining an Internet password you will need to make payments online.

If you are not required to make deposits by EFTPS, you can use Form 8109, Federal Tax Deposit (FTD) Coupon, to make deposits at an authorized depositary. If

you would like to receive Form 8109, call 1-800-829-4933. Allow 5 to 6 weeks for delivery. For more information on federal tax deposits, see Pub. 15 (Circular E).

How To Apply

You can apply for an EIN online, by telephone, by fax, or by mail depending on how soon you need to use the EIN. Use only one method for each entity so you do not receive more than one EIN for an entity.

Online. Generally, you can receive your EIN by Internet and use it immediately to file a return or make a payment. Go to the IRS website at *www.irs.gov/businesses* and click on Employer ID Numbers.

Applicants that may not apply online. The online application process is not yet available to:
- Applicants with foreign addresses (including Puerto Rico),
- Limited Liability Companies (LLCs) that have not yet determined their entity classification for federal tax purposes (see *Limited liability company (LLC)* on page 4),
- Real Estate Investment Conduits (REMICs),
- State and local governments,
- Federal Government/Military, and
- Indian Tribal Governments/Enterprises.

Telephone. You can receive your EIN by telephone and use it immediately to file a return or make a payment. Call the IRS at 1-800-829-4933. (International applicants must call 215-516-6999.) The hours of operation are 7:00 a.m. to 10:00 p.m. local time (Pacific time for Alaska and Hawaii). The person making the call must be authorized to sign the form or be an authorized designee. See *Signature* and *Third Party Designee* on page 6. Also see the *TIP* below.

If you are applying by telephone, it will be helpful to complete Form SS-4 before contacting the IRS. An IRS representative will use the information from the Form SS-4 to establish your account and assign you an EIN. Write the number you are given on the upper right corner of the form and sign and date it. Keep this copy for your records.

If requested by an IRS representative, mail or fax (facsimile) the signed Form SS-4 (including any Third Party Designee authorization) within 24 hours to the IRS address provided by the IRS representative.

 Taxpayer representatives can apply for an EIN on behalf of their client and request that the EIN be faxed to their client on the same day. **Note.** *By using this procedure, you are authorizing the IRS to fax the EIN without a cover sheet.*

Fax. Under the Fax-TIN program, you can receive your EIN by fax within 4 business days. Complete and fax Form SS-4 to the IRS using the Fax-TIN number listed on page 2 for your state. A long-distance charge to callers outside of the local calling area will apply. Fax-TIN numbers can only be used to apply for an EIN. The numbers may change without notice. Fax-TIN is available 24 hours a day, 7 days a week.

Be sure to provide your fax number so the IRS can fax the EIN back to you.

Note. By using this procedure, you are authorizing the IRS to fax the EIN without a cover sheet.

Mail. Complete Form SS-4 at least 4 to 5 weeks before you will need an EIN. Sign and date the application and mail it to the service center address for your state. You will receive your EIN in the mail in approximately 4 weeks. See also *Third Party Designee* on page 6.

Call 1-800-829-4933 to verify a number or to ask about the status of an application by mail.

Where to Fax or File

If your principal business, office or agency, or legal residence in the case of an individual, is located in:	Fax or file with the "Internal Revenue Service Center" at:
Connecticut, Delaware, District of Columbia, Florida, Georgia, Maine, Maryland, Massachusetts, New Hampshire, New Jersey, New York, North Carolina, Ohio, Pennsylvania, Rhode Island, South Carolina, Vermont, Virginia, West Virginia	Attn: EIN Operation Holtsville, NY 11742 Fax-TIN: 631-447-8960
Illinois, Indiana, Kentucky, Michigan	Attn: EIN Operation Cincinnati, OH 45999 Fax-TIN: 859-669-5760
Alabama, Alaska, Arizona, Arkansas, California, Colorado, Hawaii, Idaho, Iowa, Kansas, Louisiana, Minnesota, Mississippi, Missouri, Montana, Nebraska, Nevada, New Mexico, North Dakota, Oklahoma, Oregon, South Dakota, Tennessee, Texas, Utah, Washington, Wisconsin, Wyoming	Attn: EIN Operation Philadelphia, PA 19255 Fax-TIN: 859-669-5760
If you have no legal residence, principal place of business, or principal office or agency in any state:	Attn: EIN Operation Philadelphia, PA 19255 Fax-TIN: 215-516-1040

How To Get Forms and Publications

Phone. Call 1-800-TAX-FORM (1-800-829-3676) to order forms, instructions, and publications. You should receive your order or notification of its status within 10 workdays.

Internet. You can access the IRS website 24 hours a day, 7 days a week at *www.irs.gov* to download forms, instructions, and publications.

CD-ROM. For small businesses, return preparers, or others who may frequently need tax forms or publications, a CD-ROM containing over 2,000 tax products (including many prior year forms) can be

purchased from the National Technical Information Service (NTIS).

To order Pub. 1796, IRS Tax Products CD, call 1-877-CDFORMS (1-877-233-6767) toll free or connect to *www.irs.gov/cdorders*.

Tax Help for Your Business

IRS-sponsored Small Business Workshops provide information about your federal and state tax obligations. For information about workshops in your area, call 1-800-829-4933.

Related Forms and Publications

The following forms and instructions may be useful to filers of Form SS-4.
- Form 990-T, Exempt Organization Business Income Tax Return.
- Instructions for Form 990-T.
- Schedule C (Form 1040), Profit or Loss From Business.
- Schedule F (Form 1040), Profit or Loss From Farming.
- Instructions for Form 1041 and Schedules A, B, D, G, I, J, and K-1, U.S. Income Tax Return for Estates and Trusts.
- Form 1042, Annual Withholding Tax Return for U.S. Source Income of Foreign Persons.
- Instructions for Form 1065, U.S. Return of Partnership Income.
- Instructions for Form 1066, U.S. Real Estate Mortgage Investment Conduit (REMIC) Income Tax Return.
- Instructions for Forms 1120 and 1120-A.
- Form 2553, Election by a Small Business Corporation.
- Form 2848, Power of Attorney and Declaration of Representative.
- Form 8821, Tax Information Authorization.
- Form 8832, Entity Classification Election.

For more information about filing Form SS-4 and related issues, see:
- Pub. 51 (Circular A), Agricultural Employer's Tax Guide;
- Pub. 15 (Circular E), Employer's Tax Guide;
- Pub. 538, Accounting Periods and Methods;
- Pub. 542, Corporations;
- Pub. 557, Tax-Exempt Status for Your Organization;
- Pub. 583, Starting a Business and Keeping Records;
- Pub. 966, The Secure Way to Pay Your Federal Taxes for Business and Individual Taxpayers;
- Pub. 1635, Understanding Your EIN;
- Package 1023, Application for Recognition of Exemption Under Section 501(c)(3) of the Internal Revenue Code; and
- Package 1024, Application for Recognition of Exemption Under Section 501(a).

Specific Instructions

Print or type all entries on Form SS-4. Follow the instructions for each line to expedite processing and to avoid unnecessary IRS requests for additional information. Enter "N/A" (nonapplicable) on the lines that do not apply.

Line 1 — Legal name of entity (or individual) for whom the EIN is being requested. Enter the legal name of the entity (or individual) applying for the EIN exactly as it appears on the social security card, charter, or other applicable legal document. An entry is required.

Individuals. Enter your first name, middle initial, and last name. If you are a sole proprietor, enter your individual name, not your business name. Enter your business name on line 2. Do not use abbreviations or nicknames on line 1.

Trusts. Enter the name of the trust.

Estate of a decedent. Enter the name of the estate. For an estate that has no legal name, enter the name of the decedent followed by "Estate."

Partnerships. Enter the legal name of the partnership as it appears in the partnership agreement.

Corporations. Enter the corporate name as it appears in the corporate charter or other legal document creating it.

Plan administrators. Enter the name of the plan administrator. A plan administrator who already has an EIN should use that number.

Line 2 — Trade name of business. Enter the trade name of the business if different from the legal name. The trade name is the "doing business as " (DBA) name.

 Use the full legal name shown on line 1 on all tax returns filed for the entity. (However, if you enter a trade name on line 2 and choose to use the trade name instead of the legal name, enter the trade name on all returns you file.) To prevent processing delays and errors, always use the legal name only (or the trade name only) on all tax returns.

Line 3 — Executor, administrator, trustee, "care of" name. Trusts enter the name of the trustee. Estates enter the name of the executor, administrator, or other fiduciary. If the entity applying has a designated person to receive tax information, enter that person's name as the "care of" person. Enter the individual's first name, middle initial, and last name.

Lines 4a-b — Mailing address. Enter the mailing address for the entity's correspondence. If line 3 is completed, enter the address for the executor, trustee or "care of" person. Generally, this address will be used on all tax returns.

 File Form 8822, Change of Address, to report any subsequent changes to the entity's mailing address.

Lines 5a-b — Street address. Provide the entity's physical address only if different from its mailing address shown in lines 4a-b. Do not enter a P.O. box number here.

Line 6 — County and state where principal business is located. Enter the entity's primary physical location.

Lines 7a-b — Name of principal officer, general partner, grantor, owner, or trustor. Enter the first name, middle initial, last name, and SSN of (a) the principal officer if the business is a corporation, (b) a general partner if a partnership, (c) the owner of an entity that is disregarded as separate from its owner (disregarded entities owned by a corporation enter the corporation's name and EIN), or (d) a grantor, owner, or trustor if a trust.

If the person in question is an alien individual with a previously assigned individual taxpayer identification number (ITIN), enter the ITIN in the space provided and submit a copy of an official identifying document. If necessary, complete Form W-7, Application for IRS Individual Taxpayer Identification Number, to obtain an ITIN.

You must enter an SSN, ITIN, or EIN unless the only reason you are applying for an EIN is to make an entity classification election (see Regulations sections 301.7701-1 through 301.7701-3) and you are a nonresident alien or other foreign entity with no effectively connected income from sources within the United States.

Line 8a — Type of entity. Check the box that best describes the type of entity applying for the EIN. If you are an alien individual with an ITIN previously assigned to you, enter the ITIN in place of a requested SSN.

 This is not an election for a tax classification of an entity. See Limited liability company (LLC) *on page 4.*

Other. If not specifically listed, check the "Other" box, enter the type of entity and the type of return, if any, that will be filed (for example, "Common Trust Fund, Form 1065" or "Created a Pension Plan"). Do not enter "N/A." If you are an alien individual applying for an EIN, see the *Lines 7a-b* instructions above.

● **Household employer.** If you are an individual, check the "Other" box and enter "Household Employer" and your SSN. If you are a state or local agency serving as a tax reporting agent for public assistance recipients who become household employers, check the "Other" box and enter "Household Employer Agent." If you are a trust that qualifies as a household employer, you do not need a separate EIN for reporting tax information relating to household employees; use the EIN of the trust.
● **QSub.** For a qualified subchapter S subsidiary (QSub) check the "Other" box and specify "QSub."
● **Withholding agent.** If you are a withholding agent required to file Form 1042, check the "Other" box and enter "Withholding Agent."

Sole proprietor. Check this box if you file Schedule C, C-EZ, or F (Form 1040) and have a qualified plan, or are required to file excise, employment, alcohol, tobacco, or firearms returns, or are a payer of gambling winnings. Enter your SSN (or ITIN) in the space provided. If you are a nonresident alien with no effectively connected income from sources within the United States, you do not need to enter an SSN or ITIN.

Corporation. This box is for any corporation other than a personal service corporation. If you check this box, enter the income tax form number to be filed by the entity in the space provided.

 If you entered "1120S" after the "Corporation" checkbox, the corporation must file Form 2553 no later than the 15th day of the 3rd month of the tax year the election is to take effect. Until Form 2553 has been received and approved, you will be considered a Form 1120 filer. See the Instructions for Form 2553.

Personal service corporation. Check this box if the entity is a personal service corporation. An entity is a personal service corporation for a tax year only if:
● The principal activity of the entity during the testing period (prior tax year) for the tax year is the performance of personal services substantially by employee-owners, and
● The employee-owners own at least 10% of the fair market value of the outstanding stock in the entity on the last day of the testing period.

Personal services include performance of services in such fields as health, law, accounting, or consulting. For more information about personal service corporations, see the Instructions for Forms 1120 and 1120-A and Pub. 542.

Other nonprofit organization. Check this box if the nonprofit organization is other than a church or church-controlled organization and specify the type of nonprofit organization (for example, an educational organization).

 If the organization also seeks tax-exempt status, you must file either Package 1023 or Package 1024. See Pub. 557 for more information.

If the organization is covered by a group exemption letter, enter the four-digit group exemption number (GEN). (Do not confuse the GEN with the nine-digit EIN.) If you do not know the GEN, contact the parent organization. Get Pub. 557 for more information about group exemption numbers.

If the organization is a section 527 political organization, check the box for *Other nonprofit organization* and specify "section 527 organization" in the space to the right. To be recognized as exempt from tax, a section 527 political organization must electronically file Form 8871, Political Organization Notice of Section 527 Status, within 24 hours of the date on which the organization was established. The organization may also have to file Form 8872, Political Organization Report of Contributions and Expenditures. See *www.irs.gov/polorgs* for more information.

Plan administrator. If the plan administrator is an individual, enter the plan administrator's SSN in the space provided.

REMIC. Check this box if the entity has elected to be treated as a real estate mortgage investment conduit (REMIC). See the Instructions for Form 1066 for more information.

State/local government. If you are a government employer and you are not sure of your social security and Medicare coverage options, go to *www.ncsssa.org/ssaframes.html* to obtain the contact information for your state's Social Security Administrator.

Limited liability company (LLC). An LLC is an entity organized under the laws of a state or foreign country as a limited liability company. For federal tax purposes, an LLC may be treated as a partnership or corporation or be disregarded as an entity separate from its owner.

By default, a domestic LLC with only one member is disregarded as an entity separate from its owner and must include all of its income and expenses on the owner's tax return (for example, Schedule C (Form 1040)). Also by default, a domestic LLC with two or more members is treated as a partnership. A domestic LLC may file Form 8832 to avoid either default classification and elect to be classified as an association taxable as a corporation. For more information on entity classifications (including the rules for foreign entities), see the instructions for Form 8832.

 Do not file Form 8832 if the LLC accepts the default classifications above. If the LLC is eligible to be treated as a corporation that meets certain tests and it will be electing S corporation status, it must timely file Form 2553. The LLC will be treated as a corporation as of the effective date of the S corporation election and does not need to file Form 8832. See the Instructions for Form 2553.

Complete Form SS-4 for LLCs as follows.

• A single-member domestic LLC that accepts the default classification (above) does not need an EIN and generally should not file Form SS-4. Generally, the LLC should use the name and EIN of its owner for all federal tax purposes. However, the reporting and payment of employment taxes for employees of the LLC may be made using the name and EIN of either the owner or the LLC as explained in Notice 99-6. You can find Notice 99-6 on page 12 of Internal Revenue Bulletin 1999-3 at *www.irs.gov/pub/irs-irbs/irb99-03.pdf.* (**Note.** If the LLC applicant indicates in box 13 that it has employees or expects to have employees, the owner (whether an individual or other entity) of a single-member domestic LLC will also be assigned its own EIN (if it does not already have one) even if the LLC will be filing the employment tax returns.)

• A single-member, domestic LLC that accepts the default classification (above) and wants an EIN for filing employment tax returns (see above) or non-federal purposes, such as a state requirement, must check the "Other" box and write "Disregarded Entity" or, when applicable, "Disregarded Entity — Sole Proprietorship" in the space provided.

• A multi-member, domestic LLC that accepts the default classification (above) must check the "Partnership" box.

• A domestic LLC that will be filing Form 8832 to elect corporate status must check the "Corporation" box and write in "Single-Member" or "Multi-Member" immediately below the "form number" entry line.

Line 9 — Reason for applying. Check only one box. Do not enter "N/A."

Started new business. Check this box if you are starting a new business that requires an EIN. If you check this box, enter the type of business being started. Do not apply if you already have an EIN and are only adding another place of business.

Hired employees. Check this box if the existing business is requesting an EIN because it has hired or is hiring employees and is therefore required to file employment tax returns. Do not apply if you already have an EIN and are only hiring employees. For information on employment taxes (for example, for family members), see Pub. 15 (Circular E).

 You may have to make electronic deposits of all depository taxes (such as employment tax, excise tax, and corporate income tax) using the Electronic Federal Tax Payment System (EFTPS). See Federal tax deposits *on page 1; section 11,* Depositing Taxes, *of Pub. 15 (Circular E); and Pub. 966.*

Created a pension plan. Check this box if you have created a pension plan and need an EIN for reporting purposes. Also, enter the type of plan in the space provided.

 Check this box if you are applying for a trust EIN when a new pension plan is established. In addition, check the "Other" box in line 8a and write "Created a Pension Plan" in the space provided.

Banking purpose. Check this box if you are requesting an EIN for banking purposes only, and enter the banking purpose (for example, a bowling league for depositing dues or an investment club for dividend and interest reporting).

Changed type of organization. Check this box if the business is changing its type of organization. For example, the business was a sole proprietorship and has been incorporated or has become a partnership. If you check this box, specify in the space provided (including available space immediately below) the type of change made. For example, "From Sole Proprietorship to Partnership."

Purchased going business. Check this box if you purchased an existing business. Do not use the former owner's EIN unless you became the "owner" of a corporation by acquiring its stock.

Created a trust. Check this box if you created a trust, and enter the type of trust created. For example, indicate if the trust is a nonexempt charitable trust or a split-interest trust.

Exception. Do not file this form for certain grantor-type trusts. The trustee does not need an EIN for the trust if the trustee furnishes the name and TIN of the grantor/owner and the address of the trust to all payors. However, grantor trusts that do not file using Optional Method 1 and IRA trusts that are required to file Form 990-T, Exempt Organization Business Income Tax Return, must have an EIN. For more information on grantor trusts, see the Instructions for Form 1041.

 Do not check this box if you are applying for a trust EIN when a new pension plan is established. Check "Created a pension plan."

Other. Check this box if you are requesting an EIN for any other reason; and enter the reason. For example, a newly-formed state government entity should enter "Newly-Formed State Government Entity" in the space provided.

Line 10 — Date business started or acquired. If you are starting a new business, enter the starting date of the business. If the business you acquired is already operating, enter the date you acquired the business. If you are changing the form of ownership of your business, enter the date the new ownership entity began. Trusts should enter the date the trust was funded. Estates should enter the date of death of the decedent whose name appears on line 1 or the date when the estate was legally funded.

Line 11 — Closing month of accounting year. Enter the last month of your accounting year or tax year. An accounting or tax year is usually 12 consecutive months, either a calendar year or a fiscal year (including a period of 52 or 53 weeks). A calendar year is 12 consecutive months ending on December 31. A fiscal year is either 12 consecutive months ending on the last day of any month other than December or a 52-53 week year. For more information on accounting periods, see Pub. 538.

Individuals. Your tax year generally will be a calendar year.

Partnerships. Partnerships must adopt one of the following tax years.
● The tax year of the majority of its partners.
● The tax year common to all of its principal partners.
● The tax year that results in the least aggregate deferral of income.
● In certain cases, some other tax year.

See the Instructions for Form 1065 for more information.

REMICs. REMICs must have a calendar year as their tax year.

Personal service corporations. A personal service corporation generally must adopt a calendar year unless it meets one of the following requirements.
● It can establish a business purpose for having a different tax year.
● It elects under section 444 to have a tax year other than a calendar year.

Trusts. Generally, a trust must adopt a calendar year except for the following trusts.
● Tax-exempt trusts.
● Charitable trusts.
● Grantor-owned trusts.

Line 12 — First date wages or annuities were paid. If the business has employees, enter the date on which the business began to pay wages. If the business does not plan to have employees, enter "N/A."

Withholding agent. Enter the date you began or will begin to pay income (including annuities) to a nonresident alien. This also applies to individuals who are required to file Form 1042 to report alimony paid to a nonresident alien.

Line 13 — Highest number of employees expected in the next 12 months. Complete each box by entering the number (including zero ("-0-")) of "Agricultural," "Household," or "Other" employees expected by the applicant in the next 12 months. Check the appropriate box to indicate if you expect your annual employment tax liability to be $1,000 or less. Generally, if you pay $4,000 or less in wages subject to social security and Medicare taxes and federal income tax withholding, you are likely to pay $1,000 or less in employment taxes.

For more information on employment taxes, see Pub. 15 (Circular E); or Pub. 51 (Circular A) if you have agricultural employees (farmworkers).

Lines 14 and 15. Check the one box in line 14 that best describes the principal activity of the applicant's business. Check the "Other" box (and specify the applicant's principal activity) if none of the listed boxes applies. You must check a box.

Use line 15 to describe the applicant's principal line of business in more detail. For example, if you checked the "Construction" box in line 14, enter additional detail such as "General contractor for residential buildings" in line 15. An entry is required.

Construction. Check this box if the applicant is engaged in erecting buildings or engineering projects, (for example, streets, highways, bridges, tunnels). The term "Construction" also includes special trade contractors, (for example, plumbing, HVAC, electrical, carpentry, concrete, excavation, etc. contractors).

Real estate. Check this box if the applicant is engaged in renting or leasing real estate to others; managing, selling, buying or renting real estate for others; or providing related real estate services (for example, appraisal services).

Rental and leasing. Check this box if the applicant is engaged in providing tangible goods such as autos, computers, consumer goods, or industrial machinery and equipment to customers in return for a periodic rental or lease payment.

Manufacturing. Check this box if the applicant is engaged in the mechanical, physical, or chemical transformation of materials, substances, or components into new products. The assembling of component parts of manufactured products is also considered to be manufacturing.

Transportation & warehousing. Check this box if the applicant provides transportation of passengers or cargo; warehousing or storage of goods; scenic or sight-seeing transportation; or support activities related to transportation.

Finance & insurance. Check this box if the applicant is engaged in transactions involving the creation, liquidation, or change of ownership of financial assets and/or facilitating such financial transactions; underwriting annuities/insurance policies; facilitating such underwriting by selling insurance policies; or by providing other insurance or employee-benefit related services.

Health care and social assistance. Check this box if the applicant is engaged in providing physical, medical, or psychiatric care or providing social assistance activities such as youth centers, adoption agencies, individual/family services, temporary shelters, daycare, etc.

Accommodation & food services. Check this box if the applicant is engaged in providing customers with lodging, meal preparation, snacks, or beverages for immediate consumption.

Wholesale–agent/broker. Check this box if the applicant is engaged in arranging for the purchase or sale of goods owned by others or purchasing goods on a commission basis for goods traded in the wholesale market, usually between businesses.

Wholesale–other. Check this box if the applicant is engaged in selling goods in the wholesale market generally to other businesses for resale on their own account, goods used in production, or capital or durable nonconsumer goods.

Retail. Check this box if the applicant is engaged in selling merchandise to the general public from a fixed store; by direct, mail-order, or electronic sales; or by using vending machines.

Other. Check this box if the applicant is engaged in an activity not described above. Describe the applicant's principal business activity in the space provided.

Lines 16a-c. Check the applicable box in line 16a to indicate whether or not the entity (or individual) applying for an EIN was issued one previously. Complete lines 16b and 16c only if the "Yes" box in line 16a is checked. If the applicant previously applied for more than one EIN, write "See Attached" in the empty space in line 16a and attach a separate sheet providing the line 16b and 16c information for each EIN previously requested.

Third Party Designee. Complete this section only if you want to authorize the named individual to receive the entity's EIN and answer questions about the completion of Form SS-4. The designee's authority terminates at the time the EIN is assigned and released to the designee. You must complete the signature area for the authorization to be valid.

Signature. When required, the application must be signed by (a) the individual, if the applicant is an individual, (b) the president, vice president, or other principal officer, if the applicant is a corporation, (c) a responsible and duly authorized member or officer having knowledge of its affairs, if the applicant is a partnership, government entity, or other unincorporated organization, or (d) the fiduciary, if the applicant is a trust or an estate. Foreign applicants may have any duly-authorized person, (for example, division manager), sign Form SS-4.

Privacy Act and Paperwork Reduction Act Notice. We ask for the information on this form to carry out the Internal Revenue laws of the United States. We need it to comply with section 6109 and the regulations thereunder, which generally require the inclusion of an employer identification number (EIN) on certain returns, statements, or other documents filed with the Internal Revenue Service. If your entity is required to obtain an EIN, you are required to provide all of the information requested on this form. Information on this form may be used to determine which federal tax returns you are required to file and to provide you with related forms and publications.

We disclose this form to the Social Security Administration (SSA) for their use in determining compliance with applicable laws. We may give this information to the Department of Justice for use in civil and criminal litigation, and to the cities, states, and the District of Columbia for use in administering their tax laws. We may also disclose this information to other countries under a tax treaty, to federal and state agencies to enforce federal nontax criminal laws, and to federal law enforcement and intelligence agencies to combat terrorism.

We will be unable to issue an EIN to you unless you provide all of the requested information that applies to your entity. Providing false information could subject you to penalties.

You are not required to provide the information requested on a form that is subject to the Paperwork Reduction Act unless the form displays a valid OMB control number. Books or records relating to a form or its instructions must be retained as long as their contents may become material in the administration of any Internal Revenue law. Generally, tax returns and return information are confidential, as required by section 6103.

The time needed to complete and file this form will vary depending on individual circumstances. The estimated average time is:

Recordkeeping	8 hrs., 22 min.
Learning about the law or the form	42 min.
Preparing the form	52 min.
Copying, assembling, and sending the form to the IRS	- - - - -

If you have comments concerning the accuracy of these time estimates or suggestions for making this form simpler, we would be happy to hear from you. You can write to Internal Revenue Service, Tax Products Coordinating Committee, SE:W:CAR:MP:T:T:SP, IR-6406, 1111 Constitution Avenue, NW, Washington, DC 20224. Do not send the form to this address. Instead, see *Where to Fax or File* on page 2.

Form SS-8
(Rev. June 2003)
Department of the Treasury
Internal Revenue Service

Determination of Worker Status
for Purposes of Federal Employment Taxes
and Income Tax Withholding

OMB No. 1545-0004

Name of firm (or person) for whom the worker performed services	Worker's name

Firm's address (include street address, apt. or suite no., city, state, and ZIP code)	Worker's address (include street address, apt. or suite no., city, state, and ZIP code)

Trade name	Telephone number (include area code) ( )	Worker's social security number

Telephone number (include area code) ( )	Firm's employer identification number	Worker's employer identification number (if any)

If the worker is paid by a firm other than the one listed on this form for these services, enter the name, address, and employer identification number of the payer.

Important Information Needed To Process Your Request

We must have your permission to disclose your name and the information on this form and any attachments to other parties involved with this request. **Do we have your permission to disclose this information?** . . . . ☐ **Yes** ☐ **No**
If you answered "No" or did not mark a box, we will not process your request and will not issue a determination.

You must answer ALL items OR mark them "Unknown" or "Does not apply." If you need more space, attach another sheet.

A This form is being completed by: ☐ Firm ☐ Worker; for services performed _____ to _____ .
(beginning date)   (ending date)

B Explain your reason(s) for filing this form (e.g., you received a bill from the IRS, you believe you received a Form 1099 or Form W-2 erroneously, you are unable to get worker's compensation benefits, you were audited or are being audited by the IRS). ------------------------------
----

C Total number of workers who performed or are performing the same or similar services _____ .

D How did the worker obtain the job? ☐ Application ☐ Bid ☐ Employment Agency ☐ Other (specify) _____ .

E Attach copies of all supporting documentation (contracts, invoices, memos, Forms W-2, Forms 1099, IRS closing agreements, IRS rulings, etc.). In addition, please inform us of any current or past litigation concerning the worker's status. If no income reporting forms (Form 1099-MISC or W-2) were furnished to the worker, enter the amount of income earned for the year(s) at issue $ _____ .

F Describe the firm's business. --

G Describe the work done by the worker and provide the worker's job title. --------------------------------
----

H Explain why you believe the worker is an employee or an independent contractor. --------------------------
----

I Did the worker perform services for the firm before getting this position? . . . . ☐ **Yes** ☐ **No** ☐ **N/A**
If "Yes," what were the dates of the prior service? ---
If "Yes," explain the differences, if any, between the current and prior service. -----------------------------
----

J If the work is done under a written agreement between the firm and the worker, attach a copy (preferably signed by both parties). Describe the terms and conditions of the work arrangement. ---
----

For Privacy Act and Paperwork Reduction Act Notice, see page 5.   Cat. No. 16106T   Form **SS-8** (Rev. 6-2003)

Form SS-8 (Rev. 6-2003)

Part I   Behavioral Control

1   What specific training and/or instruction is the worker given by the firm? ....

....

2   How does the worker receive work assignments? ....

....

3   Who determines the methods by which the assignments are performed? ....

4   Who is the worker required to contact if problems or complaints arise and who is responsible for their resolution? ....

....

5   What types of reports are required from the worker? Attach examples. ....

....

6   Describe the worker's daily routine (i.e., schedule, hours, etc.). ....

....

....

7   At what location(s) does the worker perform services (e.g., firm's premises, own shop or office, home, customer's location, etc.)? ....

....

8   Describe any meetings the worker is required to attend and any penalties for not attending (e.g., sales meetings, monthly meetings, staff

meetings, etc.). ....

9   Is the worker required to provide the services personally?   .   .   .   .   ☐ **Yes**   ☐ **No**

10 If substitutes or helpers are needed, who hires them? ....

11 If the worker hires the substitutes or helpers, is approval required?   .   .   .   .   ☐ **Yes**   ☐ **No**

If "Yes," by whom? ....

12 Who pays the substitutes or helpers? ....

13 Is the worker reimbursed if the worker pays the substitutes or helpers?   .   .   .   .   ☐ **Yes**   ☐ **No**

If "Yes," by whom?

Part II   Financial Control

1   List the supplies, equipment, materials, and property provided by each party:

The firm ....

The worker ....

Other party ....

2   Does the worker lease equipment?   .   .   .   .   ☐ **Yes**   ☐ **No**

If "Yes," what are the terms of the lease? (Attach a copy or explanatory statement.) ....

....

3   What expenses are incurred by the worker in the performance of services for the firm? ....

....

4   Specify which, if any, expenses are reimbursed by:

The firm ....

Other party ....

5   Type of pay the worker receives: ☐ Salary   ☐ Commission   ☐ Hourly Wage   ☐ Piece Work

☐ Lump Sum   ☐ Other (specify) ....

If type of pay is commission, and the firm guarantees a minimum amount of pay, specify amount $ _____ .

6   Is the worker allowed a drawing account for advances?   .   .   .   .   ☐ **Yes**   ☐ **No**

If "Yes," how often? ....

Specify any restrictions. ....

....

7   Whom does the customer pay?   .   .   .   .   ☐ Firm   ☐ Worker

If worker, does the worker pay the total amount to the firm?   ☐ **Yes**   ☐ **No**   If "No," explain. ....

....

8   Does the firm carry worker's compensation insurance on the worker?   .   .   .   .   ☐ **Yes**   ☐ **No**

9   What economic loss or financial risk, if any, can the worker incur beyond the normal loss of salary (e.g., loss or damage of equipment,

material, etc.)? ....

....

Part III   Relationship of the Worker and Firm

1   List the benefits available to the worker (e.g., paid vacations, sick pay, pensions, bonuses). ------------------------------------

----

2   Can the relationship be terminated by either party without incurring liability or penalty? . . . .   ☐ **Yes**   ☐ **No**
         If "No," explain your answer. --

----

3   Does the worker perform similar services for others? . . . .   ☐ **Yes**   ☐ **No**
         If "Yes," is the worker required to get approval from the firm? . . . .   ☐ **Yes**   ☐ **No**

4   Describe any agreements prohibiting competition between the worker and the firm while the worker is performing services or during any later
         period. Attach any available documentation. --

----

5   Is the worker a member of a union? . . . .   ☐ **Yes**   ☐ **No**

6   What type of advertising, if any, does the worker do (e.g., a business listing in a directory, business cards, etc.)? Provide copies, if applicable.

----

7   If the worker assembles or processes a product at home, who provides the materials and instructions or pattern? ----------------------

----

8   What does the worker do with the finished product (e.g., return it to the firm, provide it to another party, or sell it)? ----------------

----

9   How does the firm represent the worker to its customers (e.g., employee, partner, representative, or contractor)? ------------------

----

10   If the worker no longer performs services for the firm, how did the relationship end? ------------------------------------

----

Part IV   For Service Providers or Salespersons—Complete this part if the worker provided a service directly to customers or is a salesperson.

1   What are the worker's responsibilities in soliciting new customers? --

----

2   Who provides the worker with leads to prospective customers? --

3   Describe any reporting requirements pertaining to the leads. --

----

4   What terms and conditions of sale, if any, are required by the firm? --

5   Are orders submitted to and subject to approval by the firm? . . . .   ☐ **Yes**   ☐ **No**

6   Who determines the worker's territory? --

7   Did the worker pay for the privilege of serving customers on the route or in the territory? . . . .   ☐ **Yes**   ☐ **No**
         If "Yes," whom did the worker pay? --
         If "Yes," how much did the worker pay? . . . . $ _____ .

8   Where does the worker sell the product (e.g., in a home, retail establishment, etc.)? ----------------------------------

----

9   List the product and/or services distributed by the worker (e.g., meat, vegetables, fruit, bakery products, beverages, or laundry or dry cleaning
         services). If more than one type of product and/or service is distributed, specify the principal one. ------------------------

----

10   Does the worker sell life insurance full time? . . . .   ☐ **Yes**   ☐ **No**

11   Does the worker sell other types of insurance for the firm? . . . .   ☐ **Yes**   ☐ **No**
         If "Yes," enter the percentage of the worker's total working time spent in selling other types of insurance. . . .   _____ %

12   If the worker solicits orders from wholesalers, retailers, contractors, or operators of hotels, restaurants, or other similar
         establishments, enter the percentage of the worker's time spent in the solicitation. . . . .   _____ %

13   Is the merchandise purchased by the customers for resale or use in their business operations? . . . .   ☐ **Yes**   ☐ **No**
         Describe the merchandise and state whether it is equipment installed on the customers' premises. ------------------

----

Part V   Signature (see page 4)

Under penalties of perjury, I declare that I have examined this request, including accompanying documents, and to the best of my knowledge and belief, the facts
presented are true, correct, and complete.

Signature ▶ _____   Title ▶ _____   Date ▶ _____
                    (Type or print name below)

General Instructions

Section references are to the Internal Revenue Code unless otherwise noted.

Purpose

Firms and workers file Form SS-8 to request a determination of the status of a worker for purposes of Federal employment taxes and income tax withholding.

A Form SS-8 determination may be requested only in order to resolve Federal tax matters. If Form SS-8 is submitted for a tax year for which the statute of limitations on the tax return has expired, a determination letter will not be issued. The statute of limitations expires 3 years from the due date of the tax return or the date filed, whichever is later.

The IRS does not issue a determination letter for proposed transactions or on hypothetical situations. We may, however, issue an information letter when it is considered appropriate.

Definition

Firm. For the purposes of this form, the term "firm" means any individual, business enterprise, organization, state, or other entity for which a worker has performed services. The firm may or may not have paid the worker directly for these services. **If the firm was not responsible for payment for services, be sure to enter the name, address, and employer identification number of the payer on the first page of Form SS-8 below the identifying information for the firm and the worker.**

The SS-8 Determination Process

The IRS will acknowledge the receipt of your Form SS-8. Because there are usually two (or more) parties who could be affected by a determination of employment status, the IRS attempts to get information from all parties involved by sending those parties blank Forms SS-8 for completion. The case will be assigned to a technician who will review the facts, apply the law, and render a decision. The technician may ask for additional information from the requestor, from other involved parties, or from third parties that could help clarify the work relationship before rendering a decision. The IRS will generally issue a formal determination to the firm or payer (if that is a different entity), and will send a copy to the worker. A determination letter applies only to a worker (or a class of workers) requesting it, and the decision is binding on the IRS. In certain cases, a formal determination will not be issued. Instead, an information letter may be issued. Although an information letter is advisory only and is not binding on the IRS, it may be used to assist the worker to fulfill his or her Federal tax obligations.

Neither the SS-8 determination process nor the review of any records in connection with the determination constitutes an examination (audit) of any Federal tax return. If the periods under consideration have previously been examined, the SS-8 determination process will not constitute a reexamination under IRS reopening procedures. Because this is not an examination of any Federal tax return, the appeal rights available in connection with an examination do not apply to an SS-8 determination. However, if you disagree with a determination and you have additional information concerning the work relationship that you believe was not previously considered, you may request that the determining office reconsider the determination.

Completing Form SS-8

Answer all questions as completely as possible. Attach additional sheets if you need more space. Provide information for all years the worker provided services for the firm. Determinations are based on the entire relationship between the firm and the worker.

Additional copies of this form may be obtained by calling 1-800-829-4933 or from the IRS website at **www.irs.gov.**

Fee

There is no fee for requesting an SS-8 determination letter.

Signature

Form SS-8 must be signed and dated by the taxpayer. A stamped signature will not be accepted.

The person who signs for a corporation must be an officer of the corporation who has personal knowledge of the facts. If the corporation is a member of an affiliated group filing a consolidated return, it must be signed by an officer of the common parent of the group.

The person signing for a trust, partnership, or limited liability company must be, respectively, a trustee, general partner, or member-manager who has personal knowledge of the facts.

Where To File

Send the completed Form SS-8 to the address listed below for the firm's location. However, for cases involving Federal agencies, send Form SS-8 to the Internal Revenue Service, Attn: CC:CORP:T:C, Ben Franklin Station, P.O. Box 7604, Washington, DC 20044.

Firm's location:	Send to:
Alaska, Arizona, Arkansas, California, Colorado, Hawaii, Idaho, Illinois, Iowa, Kansas, Minnesota, Missouri, Montana, Nebraska, Nevada, New Mexico, North Dakota, Oklahoma, Oregon, South Dakota, Texas, Utah, Washington, Wisconsin, Wyoming, American Samoa, Guam, Puerto Rico, U.S. Virgin Islands	Internal Revenue Service SS-8 Determinations P.O. Box 630 Stop 631 Holtsville, NY 11742-0630
Alabama, Connecticut, Delaware, District of Columbia, Florida, Georgia, Indiana, Kentucky, Louisiana, Maine, Maryland, Massachusetts, Michigan, Mississippi, New Hampshire, New Jersey, New York, North Carolina, Ohio, Pennsylvania, Rhode Island, South Carolina, Tennessee, Vermont, Virginia, West Virginia, all other locations not listed	Internal Revenue Service SS-8 Determinations 40 Lakemont Road Newport, VT 05855-1555

Instructions for Workers

If you are requesting a determination for more than one firm, complete a separate Form SS-8 for each firm.

 Form SS-8 is not a claim for refund of social security and Medicare taxes or Federal income tax withholding.

If the IRS determines that you are an employee, you are responsible for filing an amended return for any corrections related to this decision. A determination that a worker is an employee does not necessarily reduce any current or prior tax liability. For more information, call 1-800-829-1040.

Time for filing a claim for refund. Generally, you must file your claim for a credit or refund within 3 years from the date your original return was filed or within 2 years from the date the tax was paid, whichever is later.

Filing Form SS-8 does not prevent the expiration of the time in which a claim for a refund must be filed. If you are concerned about a refund, and the statute of limitations for filing a claim for refund for the year(s) at issue has not yet expired, you should file **Form 1040X,** Amended U.S. Individual Income Tax Return, to protect your statute of limitations. File a separate Form 1040X for each year.

On the Form 1040X you file, do not complete lines 1 through 24 on the form. Write "Protective Claim" at the top of the form, sign and date it. In addition, you should enter the following statement in Part II, Explanation of Changes to Income, Deductions, and Credits: "Filed Form SS-8 with the Internal Revenue Service Office in (Holtsville, NY; Newport, VT; or Washington, DC; as appropriate). By filing this protective claim, I reserve the right to file a claim for any refund that may be due after a determination of my employment tax status has been completed."

Filing Form SS-8 does not alter the requirement to timely file an income tax return. Do not delay filing your tax return in anticipation of an answer to your SS-8 request. In addition, if applicable, do not delay in responding to a request for payment while waiting for a determination of your worker status.

Instructions for Firms

If a **worker** has requested a determination of his or her status while working for you, you will receive a request from the IRS to complete a Form SS-8. In cases of this type, the IRS usually gives each party an opportunity to present a statement of the facts because any decision will affect the employment tax status of the parties. Failure to respond to this request will not prevent the IRS from issuing a determination letter based on the information he or she has made available so that the worker may fulfill his or her Federal tax obligations. However, the information that you provide is extremely valuable in determining the status of the worker.

If **you** are requesting a determination for a particular class of worker, complete the form for **one** individual who is representative of the class of workers whose status is in question. If you want a written determination for more than one class of workers, complete a separate Form SS-8 for one worker from each class whose status is typical of that class. A written determination for any worker will apply to other workers of the same class if the facts are not materially different for these workers. Please provide a list of names and addresses of all workers potentially affected by this determination.

If you have a reasonable basis for not treating a worker as an employee, you may be relieved from having to pay employment taxes for that worker under section 530 of the 1978 Revenue Act. However, this relief provision cannot be

considered in conjunction with a Form SS-8 determination because the determination does not constitute an examination of any tax return. For more information regarding section 530 of the 1978 Revenue Act and to determine if you qualify for relief under this section, you may visit the IRS website at **www.irs.gov.**

Privacy Act and Paperwork Reduction Act Notice. We ask for the information on this form to carry out the Internal Revenue laws of the United States. This information will be used to determine the employment status of the worker(s) described on the form. Subtitle C, Employment Taxes, of the Internal Revenue Code imposes employment taxes on wages. Sections 3121(d), 3306(a), and 3401(c) and (d) and the related regulations define employee and employer for purposes of employment taxes imposed under Subtitle C. Section 6001 authorizes the IRS to request information needed to determine if a worker(s) or firm is subject to these taxes. Section 6109 requires you to provide your taxpayer identification number. Neither workers nor firms are required to request a status determination, but if you choose to do so, you must provide the information requested on this form. Failure to provide the requested information may prevent us from making a status determination. If any worker or the firm has requested a status determination and you are being asked to provide information for use in that determination, you are not required to provide the requested information. However, failure to provide such information will prevent the IRS from considering it in making the status determination. Providing false or fraudulent information may subject you to penalties. Routine uses of this information include providing it to the Department of Justice for use in civil and criminal litigation, to the Social Security Administration for the administration of social security programs, and to cities, states, and the District of Columbia for the administration of their tax laws. We may also disclose this information to Federal and state agencies to enforce Federal nontax criminal laws and to combat terrorism. We may provide this information to the affected worker(s) or the firm as part of the status determination process.

You are not required to provide the information requested on a form that is subject to the Paperwork Reduction Act unless the form displays a valid OMB control number. Books or records relating to a form or its instructions must be retained as long as their contents may become material in the administration of any Internal Revenue law. Generally, tax returns and return information are confidential, as required by section 6103.

The time needed to complete and file this form will vary depending on individual circumstances. The estimated average time is: **Recordkeeping,** 22 hrs.; **Learning about the law or the form,** 47 min.; and **Preparing and sending the form to the IRS,** 1 hr., 11 min. If you have comments concerning the accuracy of these time estimates or suggestions for making this form simpler, we would be happy to hear from you. You can write to the Tax Products Coordinating Committee, Western Area Distribution Center, Rancho Cordova, CA 95743-0001. **Do not** send the tax form to this address. Instead, see **Where To File** on page 4.

This page intentionally blank.

Form W-4 (2006)

Purpose. Complete Form W-4 so that your employer can withhold the correct federal income tax from your pay. Because your tax situation may change, you may want to refigure your withholding each year.

Exemption from withholding. If you are exempt, complete only lines 1, 2, 3, 4, and 7 and sign the form to validate it. Your exemption for 2006 expires February 16, 2007. See Pub. 505, Tax Withholding and Estimated Tax.

Note. You cannot claim exemption from withholding if (a) your income exceeds $850 and includes more than $300 of unearned income (for example, interest and dividends) and (b) another person can claim you as a dependent on their tax return.

Basic instructions. If you are not exempt, complete the **Personal Allowances Worksheet** below. The worksheets on page 2 adjust your withholding allowances based on itemized deductions, certain credits, adjustments to income, or two-

earner/two-job situations. Complete all worksheets that apply. However, you may claim fewer (or zero) allowances.

Head of household. Generally, you may claim head of household filing status on your tax return only if you are unmarried and pay more than 50% of the costs of keeping up a home for yourself and your dependent(s) or other qualifying individuals. See line **E** below.

Tax credits. You can take projected tax credits into account in figuring your allowable number of withholding allowances. Credits for child or dependent care expenses and the child tax credit may be claimed using the **Personal Allowances Worksheet** below. See Pub. 919, How Do I Adjust My Tax Withholding, for information on converting your other credits into withholding allowances.

Nonwage income. If you have a large amount of nonwage income, such as interest or dividends, consider making estimated tax payments using Form 1040-ES, Estimated Tax for Individuals. Otherwise, you may owe additional tax.

Two earners/two jobs. If you have a working spouse or more than one job, figure the total number of allowances you are entitled to claim on all jobs using worksheets from only one Form W-4. Your withholding usually will be most accurate when all allowances are claimed on the Form W-4 for the highest paying job and zero allowances are claimed on the others.

Nonresident alien. If you are a nonresident alien, see the Instructions for Form 8233 before completing this Form W-4.

Check your withholding. After your Form W-4 takes effect, use Pub. 919 to see how the dollar amount you are having withheld compares to your projected total tax for 2006. See Pub. 919, especially if your earnings exceed $130,000 (Single) or $180,000 (Married).

Recent name change? If your name on line 1 differs from that shown on your social security card, call 1-800-772-1213 to initiate a name change and obtain a social security card showing your correct name.

Personal Allowances Worksheet (Keep for your records.)

A Enter "1" for **yourself** if no one else can claim you as a dependent . . . . **A** _____

B Enter "1" if:
- You are single and have only one job; or
- You are married, have only one job, and your spouse does not work; or
- Your wages from a second job or your spouse's wages (or the total of both) are $1,000 or less.

} . . **B** _____

C Enter "1" for your **spouse**. But, you may choose to enter "-0-" if you are married and have either a working spouse or more than one job. (Entering "-0-" may help you avoid having too little tax withheld.) . . . . . . **C** _____

D Enter number of **dependents** (other than your spouse or yourself) you will claim on your tax return . . . . . . **D** _____

E Enter "1" if you will file as **head of household** on your tax return (see conditions under **Head of household** above) . **E** _____

F Enter "1" if you have at least $1,500 of **child or dependent care expenses** for which you plan to claim a credit . . **F** _____

(**Note.** Do **not** include child support payments. See **Pub. 503**, Child and Dependent Care Expenses, for details.)

G **Child Tax Credit** (including additional child tax credit):
- If your total income will be less than $55,000 ($82,000 if married), enter "2" for each eligible child.
- If your total income will be between $55,000 and $84,000 ($82,000 and $119,000 if married), enter "1" for each eligible child plus "1" **additional** if you have four or more eligible children. **G** _____

H Add lines A through G and enter total here. (**Note.** This may be different from the number of exemptions you claim on your tax return.) ▶ **H** _____

For accuracy, complete all worksheets that apply. {
- If you plan to **itemize or claim adjustments to income** and want to reduce your withholding, see the **Deductions and Adjustments Worksheet** on page 2.
- If you have **more than one job** or are **married and you and your spouse both work** and the combined earnings from all jobs exceed $35,000 ($25,000 if married) see the **Two-Earner/Two-Job Worksheet** on page 2 to avoid having too little tax withheld.
- If **neither** of the above situations applies, **stop here** and enter the number from line H on line 5 of Form W-4 below.

- - - - - - - - - - - - - - - - - Cut here and give Form W-4 to your employer. Keep the top part for your records. - - - - - - - - - - - - - - - - - -

Form **W-4**

Department of the Treasury
Internal Revenue Service

Employee's Withholding Allowance Certificate

▶ Whether you are entitled to claim a certain number of allowances or exemption from withholding is subject to review by the IRS. Your employer may be required to send a copy of this form to the IRS.

OMB No. 1545-0074

2006

1 Type or print your first name and middle initial.	Last name		2 Your social security number

Home address (number and street or rural route)	3 ☐ Single ☐ Married ☐ Married, but withhold at higher Single rate. **Note.** If married, but legally separated, or spouse is a nonresident alien, check the "Single" box.
City or town, state, and ZIP code	4 **If your last name differs from that shown on your social security card, check here. You must call 1-800-772-1213 for a new card.** ▶ ☐

5 Total number of allowances you are claiming (from line **H** above **or** from the applicable worksheet on page 2) **5** _____

6 Additional amount, if any, you want withheld from each paycheck . . . . **6** $ _____

7 I claim exemption from withholding for 2006, and I certify that I meet **both** of the following conditions for exemption.
- Last year I had a right to a refund of **all** federal income tax withheld because I had **no** tax liability **and**
- This year I expect a refund of **all** federal income tax withheld because I expect to have **no** tax liability.

If you meet both conditions, write "Exempt" here . . . . ▶ **7**

Under penalties of perjury, I declare that I have examined this certificate and to the best of my knowledge and belief, it is true, correct, and complete.

Employee's signature
(Form is not valid unless you sign it.) ▶

Date ▶

8 Employer's name and address (Employer: Complete lines 8 and 10 only if sending to the IRS.)	9 Office code (optional)	10 Employer identification number (EIN)

For Privacy Act and Paperwork Reduction Act Notice, see page 2.   Cat. No. 10220Q   Form **W-4** (2006)

Form W-4 (2006)   Page **2**

Deductions and Adjustments Worksheet

Note. Use this worksheet *only* if you plan to itemize deductions, claim certain credits, or claim adjustments to income on your 2006 tax return.

1   Enter an estimate of your 2006 itemized deductions. These include qualifying home mortgage interest, charitable contributions, state and local taxes, medical expenses in excess of 7.5% of your income, and miscellaneous deductions. (For 2006, you may have to reduce your itemized deductions if your income is over $150,500 ($75,250 if married filing separately). See *Worksheet 3* in Pub. 919 for details.) . . .   **1** $ _____

2   Enter: { $10,300 if married filing jointly or qualifying widow(er)
            $ 7,550 if head of household
            $ 5,150 if single or married filing separately }   . . . .   **2** $ _____

3   **Subtract** line 2 from line 1. If line 2 is greater than line 1, enter "-0-" . . . .   **3** $ _____

4   Enter an estimate of your 2006 adjustments to income, including alimony, deductible IRA contributions, and student loan interest   **4** $ _____

5   **Add** lines 3 and 4 and enter the total. (Include any amount for credits from *Worksheet 7* in Pub. 919) .   **5** $ _____

6   Enter an estimate of your 2006 nonwage income (such as dividends or interest) . . . .   **6** $ _____

7   **Subtract** line 6 from line 5. Enter the result, but not less than "-0-" . . . .   **7** $ _____

8   **Divide** the amount on line 7 by $3,300 and enter the result here. Drop any fraction . . . .   **8**   _____

9   Enter the number from the **Personal Allowances Worksheet,** line H, page 1 . . . .   **9**   _____

10 **Add** lines 8 and 9 and enter the total here. If you plan to use the **Two-Earner/Two-Job Worksheet,** also enter this total on line 1 below. Otherwise, **stop here** and enter this total on Form W-4, line 5, page 1 .   **10**   _____

Two-Earner/Two-Job Worksheet (See *Two earners/two jobs* on page 1.)

Note. Use this worksheet *only* if the instructions under line H on page 1 direct you here.

1   Enter the number from line H, page 1 (or from line 10 above if you used the **Deductions and Adjustments Worksheet**)   **1**   _____

2   Find the number in **Table 1** below that applies to the **LOWEST** paying job and enter it here . . . .   **2**   _____

3   If line 1 is **more than or equal to** line 2, subtract line 2 from line 1. Enter the result here (if zero, enter "-0-") and on Form W-4, line 5, page 1. **Do not** use the rest of this worksheet . . . .   **3**   _____

Note. If line 1 is *less than* line 2, enter "-0-" on Form W-4, line 5, page 1. Complete lines 4–9 below to calculate the additional withholding amount necessary to avoid a year-end tax bill.

4   Enter the number from line 2 of this worksheet . . . .   **4**   _____

5   Enter the number from line 1 of this worksheet . . . .   **5**   _____

6   **Subtract** line 5 from line 4 . . . .   **6**   _____

7   Find the amount in **Table 2** below that applies to the **HIGHEST** paying job and enter it here . . . .   **7** $ _____

8   **Multiply** line 7 by line 6 and enter the result here. This is the additional annual withholding needed . .   **8** $ _____

9   Divide line 8 by the number of pay periods remaining in 2006. For example, divide by 26 if you are paid every two weeks and you complete this form in December 2005. Enter the result here and on Form W-4, line 6, page 1. This is the additional amount to be withheld from each paycheck . . . .   **9** $ _____

Table 1: Two-Earner/Two-Job Worksheet

Married Filing Jointly						All Others	
If wages from **HIGHEST** paying job are—	AND, wages from **LOWEST** paying job are—	Enter on line 2 above	If wages from **HIGHEST** paying job are—	AND, wages from **LOWEST** paying job are—	Enter on line 2 above	If wages from **LOWEST** paying job are—	Enter on line 2 above
$0 - $42,000	$0 - $4,500	0	$42,001 and over	32,001 - 38,000	6	$0 - $6,000	0
	4,501 - 9,000	1		38,001 - 46,000	7	6,001 - 12,000	1
	9,001 - 18,000	2		46,001 - 55,000	8	12,001 - 19,000	2
	18,001 and over	3		55,001 - 60,000	9	19,001 - 26,000	3
				60,001 - 65,000	10	26,001 - 35,000	4
$42,001 and over	$0 - $4,500	0		65,001 - 75,000	11	35,001 - 50,000	5
	4,501 - 9,000	1		75,001 - 95,000	12	50,001 - 65,000	6
	9,001 - 18,000	2		95,001 - 105,000	13	65,001 - 80,000	7
	18,001 - 22,000	3		105,001 - 120,000	14	80,001 - 90,000	8
	22,001 - 26,000	4		120,001 and over	15	90,001 - 120,000	9
	26,001 - 32,000	5				120,001 and over	10

Table 2: Two-Earner/Two-Job Worksheet

Married Filing Jointly		All Others	
If wages from **HIGHEST** paying job are—	Enter on line 7 above	If wages from **HIGHEST** paying job are—	Enter on line 7 above
$0 - $60,000	$500	$0 - $30,000	$500
60,001 - 115,000	830	30,001 - 75,000	830
115,001 - 165,000	920	75,001 - 145,000	920
165,001 - 290,000	1,090	145,001 - 330,000	1,090
290,001 and over	1,160	330,001 and over	1,160

 Printed on recycled paper

BOE-663-D (FRONT) REV. 6 (11-02)
REGULATIONS ORDER

STATE OF CALIFORNIA
BOARD OF EQUALIZATION

Please enter the quantity of each publication you wish to order and send your completed order form to the State Board of Equalization, Supply Unit, 3920 West Capitol Avenue, West Sacramento, CA 95691 or FAX your order to (916) 372-6078.

NAME OF BUSINESS	FOR OFFICE USE ONLY	REQUEST ☐ New ☐ One Time ☐ Replacement
ATTENTION	RECEIVED BY	IS FOR ☐ Distribution Change
MAILING ADDRESS	DATE REQUEST RECEIVED	
CITY STATE ZIP	SHIPPED BY	
TELEPHONE NUMBER ( )	DATE MATERIAL SHIPPED	

SALES AND USE TAX REGULATIONS *(No Charge)*

QTY.	NO.	TITLE
	1500.	Foreword

SERVICE ENTERPRISES

QTY.	NO.	TITLE
	1501.	Service Enterprises Generally
	1501.1.	Research and Development Contracts
	1502.	Computers, Programs, and Data Processing
	1502.1.	Word Processing
	1503.	Hospitals, Institutions and Homes for the Care of Persons
	1504.	Mailing Lists and Services
	1505.	Morticians
	1506.	Miscellaneous Service Enterprises
	1507.	Technology Transfer Agreements

CONTRACTORS AND SUBCONTRACTORS

QTY.	NO.	TITLE
	1521.	Construction Contractors
	1521.4.	Factory-Built Housing

MANUFACTURERS, PRODUCERS, PROCESSORS

QTY.	NO.	TITLE
	1524.	Manufacturers of Personal Property
	1525.	Property Used in Manufacturing
	1525.1.	Manufacturing Aids
	1525.2.	Manufacturing Equipment
	1525.3.	Manufacturing Equipment — Leases of Tangible Personal Property
	1525.5.	Manufacturing By-Products and Joint-Products
	1525.7.	Rural Investment Exemption
	1526.	Producing, Fabricating and Processing Property Furnished By Consumers – General Rules
	1527.	Sound Recording
	1528.	Photographers, Photostat Producers, Photo Finishers and X-Ray Laboratories
	1529.	Motion Pictures
	1530.	Foundries
	1531.	Fur Dressers and Dyers
	1532.	Teleproduction or Other Postproduction Service Equipment
	1533.	Liquefied Petroleum Gas
	1533.1.	Farm Equipment and Machinery
	1533.2.	Diesel Fuel Used in Farming Activities or Food Processing
	1534.	Timber Harvesting Equipment and Machinery
	1535.	Racehorse Breeding Stock

GRAPHIC ARTS AND RELATED ENTERPRISES

QTY.	NO.	TITLE
	1540.	Advertising Agencies, Commercial Artists and Designers
	1541.	Printing and Related Arts
	1541.5.	Printed Sales Messages
	1543.	Publishers

INSTALLERS, REPAIRERS, RECONDITIONERS

QTY.	NO.	TITLE
	1546.	Installing, Repairing, Reconditioning in General
	1548.	Retreading and Recapping Tires
	1549.	Fur Repairers, Alterers and Remodelers
	1550.	Reupholsterers
	1551.	Repainting and Refinishing
	1553.	Miscellaneous Repair Operations

SPECIFIC BUSINESSES ENGAGED IN RETAILING

QTY.	NO.	TITLE
	1565.	Auctioneers
	1566.	Automobile Dealers and Salesmen
	1567.	Banks and Insurance Companies
	1568.	Beer, Wine, and Liquor Dealers
	1569.	Consignees and Lienors of Tangible Personal Property for Sale
	1570.	Charitable Organizations
	1571.	Florists
	1572.	Memorial Dealers
	1573.	Court Ordered Sales, Foreclosures and Repossessions
	1574.	Vending Machine Operators

SPECIFIC KINDS OF PROPERTY AND EXEMPTIONS GENERALLY

QTY.	NO.	TITLE
	1583.	Modular Systems Furniture
	1584.	Membership Fees
	1585.	Cellular Telephones, Pagers, and other Wireless Telecommunication Devices
	1586.	Works of Art and Museum Pieces for Public Display
	1587.	Animal Life, Feed, Drugs and Medicines
	1588.	Seeds, Plants and Fertilizer
	1589.	Containers and Labels
	1590.	Newspapers and Periodicals
	1591.	Medicines and Medical Supplies, Devices and Appliances
	1591.1	Medical Devices, Appliances and Supplies
	1591.2	Wheelchairs, Crutches, Canes, and Walkers

BOE-663-D (BACK) REV. 6 (11-02)

BOE-400-SPA REV. 1 (FRONT) (7-05)
APPLICATION FOR SELLER'S PERMIT

STATE OF CALIFORNIA
BOARD OF EQUALIZATION

1. PERMIT TYPE: *(check one)* ☐ **Regular** ☐ **Temporary**

FOR BOARD USE ONLY

2. TYPE OF OWNERSHIP *(check one)*   * Must provide partnership agreement

☐ Sole Owner   ☐ Husband/Wife Co-ownership
☐ Corporation   ☐ Limited Liability Company (LLC)
☐ General Partnership   ☐ Unincorporated Business Trust
☐ Limited Partnership (LP) *   ☐ Limited Liability Partnership (LLP) *
(Registered to practice law, accounting or architecture)
☐ Registered Domestic Partnership
☐ Other *(describe)* _____

TAX	IND	OFFICE	PERMIT NUMBER
S			

NAICS CODE	BUS CODE	A.C.C.	REPORTING BASIS	TAX AREA CODE

PROCESSED BY	PERMIT ISSUE DATE ___ / ___ / ___

RETURN TYPE
☐ (1) 401-A ☐ (2) 401-EZ
VERIFICATION
☐ DL ☐ PA ☐ Other

3. NAME OF SOLE OWNER, CORPORATION, LLC, PARTNERSHIP, OR TRUST

4. STATE OF INCORPORATION OR ORGANIZATION

5. BUSINESS TRADE NAME/"DOING BUSINESS AS" [DBA] *(if any)*

6. DATE YOU WILL BEGIN BUSINESS ACTIVITIES *(month, day, and year)*

7. CORPORATE, LLC, LLP OR LP NUMBER FROM CALIFORNIA SECRETARY OF STATE

8. FEDERAL EMPLOYER IDENTIFICATION NUMBER (FEIN)

CHECK ONE ☐ Owner/Co-Owners ☐ Partners ☐ Registered Domestic Partners ☐ Corp. Officers ☐ LLC Officers/Managers/Members ☐ Trustees/Beneficiaries

Use additional sheets to include information for more than three individuals.

9. FULL NAME *(first, middle, last)*

10. TITLE

11. SOCIAL SECURITY NUMBER *(corporate officers excluded)*

12. DRIVER LICENSE NUMBER *(attach copy)*

13. HOME ADDRESS *(street, city, state, zip code)*

14. HOME TELEPHONE NUMBER ( )

15. NAME OF A PERSONAL REFERENCE NOT LIVING WITH YOU   16. ADDRESS *(street, city, state, zip code)*

17. REFERENCE TELEPHONE NUMBER ( )

18. FULL NAME OF ADDITIONAL PARTNER, OFFICER, OR MEMBER *(first, middle, last)*

19. TITLE

20. SOCIAL SECURITY NUMBER *(corporate officers excluded)*

21. DRIVER LICENSE NUMBER *(attach copy)*

22. HOME ADDRESS *(street, city, state, zip code)*

23. HOME TELEPHONE NUMBER ( )

24. NAME OF A PERSONAL REFERENCE NOT LIVING WITH YOU   25. ADDRESS *(street, city, state, zip code)*

26. REFERENCE TELEPHONE NUMBER ( )

27. FULL NAME OF ADDITIONAL PARTNER, OFFICER, OR MEMBER *(first, middle, last)*

28. TITLE

29. SOCIAL SECURITY NUMBER *(corporate officers excluded)*

30. DRIVER LICENSE NUMBER *(attach copy)*

31. HOME ADDRESS *(street, city, state, zip code)*

32. HOME TELEPHONE NUMBER ( )

33. NAME OF A PERSONAL REFERENCE NOT LIVING WITH YOU   34. ADDRESS *(street, city, state, zip code)*

35. REFERENCE TELEPHONE NUMBER ( )

36. TYPE OF BUSINESS *(check one that best describes your business)*
☐ Retail ☐ Wholesale ☐ Mfg. ☐ Repair ☐ Service ☐ Construction Contractor ☐ Leasing

37. NUMBER OF SELLING LOCATIONS *(if 2 or more, see Item No. 66)*

38. WHAT ITEMS WILL YOU SELL?

39. CHECK ONE
☐ Full Time ☐ Part Time

40. BUSINESS ADDRESS *(street, city, state, zip code) [do not list P.O. Box or mailing service]*

41. BUSINESS TELEPHONE NUMBER ( )

42. MAILING ADDRESS *(street, city, state, zip code) [if different from business address]*

43. BUSINESS FAX NUMBER ( )

44. BUSINESS WEBSITE ADDRESS
www.

45. BUSINESS EMAIL ADDRESS

46. DO YOU MAKE INTERNET SALES?
☐ Yes ☐ No

47. NAME OF BUSINESS LANDLORD

48. LANDLORD ADDRESS *(street, city, state, zip code)*

49. LANDLORD TELEPHONE NUMBER ( )

50. PROJECTED MONTHLY GROSS SALES
$

51. PROJECTED MONTHLY TAXABLE SALES
$

52. ALCOHOLIC BEVERAGE CONTROL LICENSE NUMBER *(if applicable)*
___ ___ - ___ ___ ___ ___ ___

53. SELLING NEW TIRES?
☐ Yes ☐ No

54. SELLING COVERED ELECTRONIC DEVICES?
☐ Yes ☐ No

55. SELLING TOBACCO AT RETAIL?
☐ Yes ☐ No

(continued on reverse)

— tear at perforation —

BOE-400-SPA REV. 1 (BACK) (7-05)

56. NAME OF PERSON MAINTAINING YOUR RECORDS	57. ADDRESS *(street, city, state, zip code)*	58. TELEPHONE NUMBER
59. NAME OF BANK OR OTHER FINANCIAL INSTITUTION *(note whether business or personal)*		60. BANK BRANCH LOCATION
61. NAME OF MERCHANT CREDIT CARD PROCESSOR *(if you accept credit cards)*		62. MERCHANT CARD ACCOUNT NUMBER
63. NAMES OF MAJOR CALIFORNIA-BASED SUPPLIERS	64. ADDRESSES *(street, city, state, zip code)*	65. PRODUCTS PURCHASED

ADDITIONAL SELLING LOCATIONS (List All Other Selling Locations)

66. PHYSICAL LOCATION OR STREET ADDRESS *(attach separate list, if required)*

OWNERSHIP AND ORGANIZATIONAL CHANGES (Do Not Complete for Temporary Permits)

67. ARE YOU BUYING AN EXISTING BUSINESS?

☐ Yes ☐ No   If yes, complete items 70 through 74.

68. ARE YOU CHANGING FROM ONE TYPE OF BUSINESS ORGANIZATION TO ANOTHER (FOR EXAMPLE, FROM A SOLE OWNER TO A CORPORATION OR FROM A PARTNERSHIP TO A LIMITED LIABILITY COMPANY, ETC.)?

☐ Yes ☐ No   If yes, complete items 70 and 71.

69. OTHER OWNERSHIP CHANGES *(please describe)*:

70. FORMER OWNER'S NAME	71. SELLER'S PERMIT NUMBER
72. PURCHASE PRICE $	73. VALUE OF FIXTURES & EQUIPMENT $

74. IF AN ESCROW COMPANY IS REQUESTING A TAX CLEARANCE ON YOUR BEHALF, PLEASE LIST THEIR NAME, ADDRESS, TELEPHONE NUMBER, AND THE ESCROW NUMBER

TEMPORARY PERMIT EVENT INFORMATION

75. PERIOD OF SALES FROM: ___/___/___ THROUGH: ___/___/___	76. ESTIMATED EVENT SALES $	77. SPACE RENTAL COST *(if any)* $	78. ADMISSION CHARGED? ☐ Yes ☐ No
79. ORGANIZER OR PROMOTER OF EVENT *(if any)*	80. ADDRESS *(street, city, state, zip code)*	81. TELEPHONE NUMBER ( )	

82. ADDRESS OF EVENT *(If more than one, use line 66, above. Attach separate list, if required.)*

CERTIFICATION

All Corporate Officers, LLC Managing Members, Partners, or Owners must sign below.
I am duly authorized to sign the application and certify that the statements made are correct to the best of my knowledge and belief.
I also represent and acknowledge that the applicant will be engaged in or conduct business as a seller of tangible personal property.

NAME *(typed or printed)*	SIGNATURE	DATE
NAME *(typed or printed)*	SIGNATURE	DATE
NAME *(typed or printed)*	SIGNATURE	DATE

FOR BOARD USE ONLY

SECURITY REVIEW	FORMS	PUBLICATIONS
☐ BOE-598 ($ ____) *or* ☐ BOE-1009	☐ BOE-8 ☐ BOE-400-Y	☐ PUB 73 ☐ PUB DE 44
REQUIRED BY APPROVED BY	☐ BOE-162 ☐ BOE-519	
	☐ BOE-467 ☐ BOE-1241-D	
	REGULATIONS	RETURNS
	☐ REG. 1668 ☐ REG. 1698	
	☐ REG. 1700 ☐ _____	

FIELD OFFICES
CALL FOR ADDRESSES

City	Area Code	Number
Bakersfield	661	395-2880
Culver City	310	342-1000
El Centro	760	352-3431
Eureka*	707	445-6500
Fresno	559	248-4219
Kearny Mesa	858	636-3191
Laguna Hills	949	461-5711
Long Beach	562	901-2483
Norwalk	562	466-1694
Oakland	510	622-4100
Rancho Mirage	760	346-8096
Redding	530	224-4729
Riverside	951	680-6400
Sacramento	916	227-6700
Salinas	831	443-3003
San Diego	619	525-4526
San Francisco	415	356-6600
San Jose	408	277-1231
San Marcos	760	510-5850
Santa Ana	714	558-4059
Santa Rosa	707	576-2100
Suisun City	707	428-2041
Van Nuys	818	904-2300
Ventura	805	677-2700
West Covina	626	480-7200

Business Located
Out-of-State
916-227-6600

*Office closed June 30, 2005. For dates and times of services in the Eureka area, please visit our website at *www.boe.ca.gov* or call the Information Center at 800-400-7115.

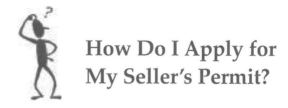

How Do I Apply for My Seller's Permit?

Step 1: Complete Your Application

Complete the application on page 5. If your business is an ongoing operation, check permit type "Regular." If your business will operate at the location(s) for 90 days or less, check "Temporary." Please provide **all** the information requested on the application. If you do not, this will delay the issuance of your permit. Refer to the "Tips" on page 4. If you need assistance, please call your local Board office or the Information Center at 800-400-7115.

Note: If your business is located outside California, you also need to complete form BOE-403-B, *Registration Information for Out-of-State Account.* Visit our website at *www.boe.ca.gov,* call the Out-of-State Office at 916-227-6600, or the Information Center at 800-400-7115, to request a copy by mail or by fax (select the automated fax-back option).

For information regarding whether or not your out-of-state corporation qualifies to transact business in the State of California, you may visit the Secretary of State's website at *www.ss.ca.gov.* For information regarding the minimum franchise tax for corporations, please visit the California Taxes Information Center's website at *www.taxes.ca.gov.*

Step 2: Send Your Application for Processing

Send or take your application to the district office nearest your place of business. If you plan to apply in person, contact the local office to find out when they are open. Note: A permit is required before you begin making sales. Advise the Board if you have an urgent need for a permit.

Step 3: After Your Application Is Approved

If your application is complete, you should receive your permit in about two weeks. Based on the information in your application, the Board will provide you with regulations, forms, and other publications that may help you with your business. Or, you may choose to view and download information from our website at *www.boe.ca.gov.* You will also be informed as to when to file tax returns: monthly, quarterly, fiscal or calendar yearly. You will also start receiving tax returns for reporting and paying the taxes due on your sales and purchases. If you do not receive a return, download one from our website, or call the district office nearest you. You may also be eligible to e-file your return, visit our website for details.

Post your permit at your place of business in a location easily seen by your customers.

Tips for Filling Out Your Application

Item 1: Permit Type

Check whether you are applying for a **regular** or **temporary** permit. You may apply for a temporary permit if you intend to make sales for a period of 90 days or less. Otherwise, you must apply for a regular permit.

Items 2–8: Business Identification Information

Check your type of ownership and provide all of the information requested. Partnerships should provide a copy of their written partnership agreement, if one exists. If it is filed with us at the time you apply for a permit and it specifies that all business assets are held in the name of the partnership, we will attempt to collect any delinquent tax liability from the partnership's assets before we attempt to collect from the partners' personal assets. The "Registered Domestic Partnership" ownership box should only be checked if both persons are registered as domestic partners with the Office of the Secretary of State.

Items 9–35: Ownership Information

Indicate whether those listed are owners, partners, etc., and enter their driver license or California Identification Card number and, except in the case of corporate officers, their social security number. Also, provide a reference for each person, who does not live with that person. This information will be kept in strict confidence. If mailing your application, you must provide a photocopy of your driver license or California Identification Card.

Items 36–49, 66: Type of Business, Selling Locations, and Landlord Information

Check whether the business is a retailer, wholesaler, etc., and whether the business is full time or part time. Describe the types of items you will sell. Avoid using broad descriptions, such as "general merchandise." Instead, list specific examples such as sports equipment or garden supplies. Indicate the number of selling locations, the address, telephone number, website and email address of the business, as well as the landlord's name, address, and telephone number. If there are multiple selling locations, additional addresses can be listed on the reverse side (Item 66). Tax returns and other materials will be sent to the business address unless a different mailing address is specified (Item 42).

Items 50–51: Projected Monthly Sales

Indicate your projected monthly gross and taxable sales. If unsure, provide an estimate. Your projection helps to determine how often you will need to file a return. If your actual sales vary, we may adjust your filing frequency.

Items 52–55: Related Program Information

Provide your Alcoholic Beverage Control license number, if applicable. Indicate if you will be selling new tires, covered electronic devices, or tobacco products. We will contact you to determine if you need to register for any of these other programs.

Items 56–65: Related Party Information

Identify the person maintaining your records, your bank, and if you accept credit cards, your merchant card account. Also, identify major California-based suppliers and the products that you purchase from them.

Items 67–74: Ownership and Organizational Changes

If you are purchasing a business, or changing from one type of business organization to another, provide the previous owner's name and seller's permit number. If you are purchasing a business, you should request a tax clearance in advance to assure that you won't have to pay any taxes owed by the previous owner.

Items 75–82: Temporary Permit Event Information

Applicants for a temporary permit must complete each item in this section.

Certification

Each owner, co-owner, partner, or corporate officer must sign the application.

Where Can I Get Help?

No doubt you will have questions about how the Sales and Use Tax Law applies to your business operations. For assistance, you may take advantage of the resources listed below.

INTERNET
www.boe.ca.gov

You can log onto our website for additional information. For example, you can find out what the tax rate is in a particular county, or you can download numerous publications — such as laws, regulations, pamphlets, and policy manuals — that will help you understand how the law applies to your business. You can also verify sellers' permit numbers online, read about upcoming Taxpayers' Bill of Rights hearings, and obtain information on Board field office addresses and telephone numbers.

Another good resource — especially for starting businesses — is the California Tax Information Center at *www.taxes.ca.gov.*

CLASSES

You may enroll in a basic sales and use tax class offered by some local Board offices. You should call ahead to find out when your local office conducts classes for beginning sellers.

WRITTEN TAX ADVICE

It is best to get tax advice from the Board in writing. You may be relieved of tax, penalty, or interest charges if we determine you did not correctly report tax because you reasonably relied on our written advice regarding a transaction.

For this relief to apply, your request for advice must be in writing, identify the taxpayer to whom the advice applies, and fully describe the facts and circumstances of the transaction.

Send your request for written advice to: State Board of Equalization; Audit and Information Section, MIC:44; PO Box 942879, Sacramento, CA 94279-0044.

INFORMATION CENTER
800-400-7115

FOR TDD ASSISTANCE

From TDD phones: 800-735-2929
From voice phones: 800-735-2922

Customer service representatives are available from 8 a.m. through 5 p.m., Monday-Friday, excluding state holidays.

Faxback Service. To order fax copies of selected forms and notices, call 800-400-7115 and choose the faxback option. You can call at any time for this service.

Translator Services. We can provide bilingual services for persons who need assistance in a language other than English.

TAXPAYERS' RIGHTS
ADVOCATE OFFICE

If you would like to know more about your rights as a taxpayer or if you are unable to resolve an issue with the Board, please contact the Taxpayers' Rights Advocate office for help at 916-324-2798 (or toll-free, 888-324-2798). Their fax number is 916-323-3319.

If you prefer, you can write to: State Board of Equalization; Taxpayers' Rights Advocate, MIC:70; PO Box 942879; Sacramento, CA 94279-0070.

To obtain a copy of publication 70, *The California Taxpayers' Bill of Rights*, you may visit our website or call our Information Center.

FIELD OFFICES

See page 3.

This page intentionally blank.

IRS Form 8300 (Rev. December 2004)

OMB No. 1545-0892
Department of the Treasury
Internal Revenue Service

Report of Cash Payments Over $10,000 Received in a Trade or Business

► See instructions for definition of cash.

► Use this form for transactions occurring after December 31, 2004. Do not use prior versions after this date.
For Privacy Act and Paperwork Reduction Act Notice, see page 5.

FinCEN Form 8300 (Rev. December 2004)

OMB No. 1506-0018
Department of the Treasury
Financial Crimes
Enforcement Network

1 Check appropriate box(es) if: **a** ☐ Amends prior report;   **b** ☐ Suspicious transaction.

Part I   Identity of Individual From Whom the Cash Was Received

2 If more than one individual is involved, check here and see instructions . . . . ► ☐

3 Last name | **4** First name | **5** M.I. | **6** Taxpayer identification number

7 Address (number, street, and apt. or suite no.) | **8** Date of birth . ► (see instructions) | M M D D Y Y Y Y

9 City | **10** State | **11** ZIP code | **12** Country (if not U.S.) | **13** Occupation, profession, or business

14 Identifying document (ID) | **a Describe ID** ► | **b Issued by** ►
c Number ►

Part II   Person on Whose Behalf This Transaction Was Conducted

15 If this transaction was conducted on behalf of more than one person, check here and see instructions . . . . . ► ☐

16 Individual's last name or Organization's name | **17** First name | **18** M.I. | **19** Taxpayer identification number

20 Doing business as (DBA) name (see instructions) | Employer identification number

21 Address (number, street, and apt. or suite no.) | **22** Occupation, profession, or business

23 City | **24** State | **25** ZIP code | **26** Country (if not U.S.)

27 Alien identification (ID) | **a Describe ID** ► | **b Issued by** ►
c Number ►

Part III   Description of Transaction and Method of Payment

28 Date cash received   M M D D Y Y Y Y | **29** Total cash received $ _____ .00 | **30** If cash was received in more than one payment, check here . . . ► ☐ | **31** Total price if different from item 29 $ _____ .00

32 Amount of cash received (in U.S. dollar equivalent) (must equal item 29) (see instructions):

a U.S. currency $ _____ .00   (Amount in $100 bills or higher $ _____ .00)
b Foreign currency $ _____ .00   (Country ► _____)
c Cashier's check(s) $ _____ .00   ⎫ Issuer's name(s) and serial number(s) of the monetary instrument(s) ►
d Money order(s) $ _____ .00   ⎬
e Bank draft(s) $ _____ .00   ⎭
f Traveler's check(s) $ _____ .00

33 Type of transaction

a ☐ Personal property purchased   **f** ☐ Debt obligations paid
b ☐ Real property purchased   **g** ☐ Exchange of cash
c ☐ Personal services provided   **h** ☐ Escrow or trust funds
d ☐ Business services provided   **i** ☐ Bail received by court clerks
e ☐ Intangible property purchased **j** ☐ Other (specify in item 34) ►

34 Specific description of property or service shown in 33. Give serial or registration number, address, docket number, etc. ►

Part IV   Business That Received Cash

35 Name of business that received cash | **36** Employer identification number

37 Address (number, street, and apt. or suite no.) | Social security number

38 City | **39** State | **40** ZIP code | **41** Nature of your business

42 Under penalties of perjury, I declare that to the best of my knowledge the information I have furnished above is true, correct, and complete.

Signature ► _____ Authorized official   Title ► _____

43 Date of signature   M M D D Y Y Y Y | **44** Type or print name of contact person | **45** Contact telephone number   ( )

IRS Form 8300 (Rev. 12-2004)   Cat. No. 62133S   **FinCEN Form 8300** (Rev. 12-2004)

Multiple Parties
(Complete applicable parts below if box 2 or 15 on page 1 is checked)

Part I   Continued—Complete if box 2 on page 1 is checked

3 Last name	4 First name	5 M.I.	6 Taxpayer identification number

7 Address (number, street, and apt. or suite no.)	8 Date of birth ▶ (see instructions) M M D D Y Y Y Y

9 City	10 State	11 ZIP code	12 Country (if not U.S.)	13 Occupation, profession, or business

14 Identifying document (ID)	a **Describe ID** ▶	b **Issued by** ▶ ....
	c **Number** ▶	

3 Last name	4 First name	5 M.I.	6 Taxpayer identification number

7 Address (number, street, and apt. or suite no.)	8 Date of birth ▶ (see instructions) M M D D Y Y Y Y

9 City	10 State	11 ZIP code	12 Country (if not U.S.)	13 Occupation, profession, or business

14 Identifying document (ID)	a **Describe ID** ▶	b **Issued by** ▶ ....
	c **Number** ▶	

Part II   Continued—Complete if box 15 on page 1 is checked

16 Individual's last name or Organization's name	17 First name	18 M.I.	19 Taxpayer identification number

20 Doing business as (DBA) name (see instructions)	Employer identification number

21 Address (number, street, and apt. or suite no.)	22 Occupation, profession, or business

23 City	24 State	25 ZIP code	26 Country (if not U.S.)

27 Alien identification (ID)	a **Describe ID** ▶	b **Issued by** ▶ ....
	c **Number** ▶	

16 Individual's last name or Organization's name	17 First name	18 M.I.	19 Taxpayer identification number

20 Doing business as (DBA) name (see instructions)	Employer identification number

21 Address (number, street, and apt. or suite no.)	22 Occupation, profession, or business

23 City	24 State	25 ZIP code	26 Country (if not U.S.)

27 Alien identification (ID)	a **Describe ID** ▶	b **Issued by** ▶ ....
	c **Number** ▶	

Comments – Please use the lines provided below to comment on or clarify any information you entered on any line in Parts I, II, III, and IV

Section references are to the Internal Revenue Code unless otherwise noted.

Important Reminders

● Section 6050I (26 United States Code (U.S.C.) 6050I) and 31 U.S.C. 5331 require that certain information be reported to the IRS and the Financial Crimes Enforcement Network (FinCEN). This information must be reported on IRS/FinCEN Form 8300.

● Item 33 box i is to be checked only by clerks of the court; box d is to be checked by bail bondsmen. See the instructions on page 5.

● For purposes of section 6050I and 31 U.S.C. 5331, the word "cash" and "currency" have the same meaning. See *Cash* under *Definitions* on page 4.

General Instructions

Who must file. Each person engaged in a trade or business who, in the course of that trade or business, receives more than $10,000 in cash in one transaction or in two or more related transactions, must file Form 8300. Any transactions conducted between a payer (or its agent) and the recipient in a 24-hour period are related transactions. Transactions are considered related even if they occur over a period of more than 24 hours if the recipient knows, or has reason to know, that each transaction is one of a series of connected transactions.

Keep a copy of each Form 8300 for 5 years from the date you file it.

Clerks of Federal or State courts must file Form 8300 if more than $10,000 in cash is received as bail for an individual(s) charged with certain criminal offenses. For these purposes, a clerk includes the clerk's office or any other office, department, division, branch, or unit of the court that is authorized to receive bail. If a person receives bail on behalf of a clerk, the clerk is treated as receiving the bail. See the instructions for Item 33 on page 5.

If multiple payments are made in cash to satisfy bail and the initial payment does not exceed $10,000, the initial payment and subsequent payments must be aggregated and the information return must be filed by the 15th day after receipt of the payment that causes the aggregate amount to exceed $10,000 in cash. In such cases, the reporting requirement can be satisfied either by sending a single written statement with an aggregate amount listed or by furnishing a copy of each Form 8300 relating to that payer. Payments made to satisfy separate bail requirements are not required to be aggregated. See Treasury Regulations section 1.6050I-2.

Casinos must file Form 8300 for nongaming activities (restaurants, shops, etc.).

Voluntary use of Form 8300. Form 8300 may be filed voluntarily for any suspicious transaction (see *Definitions*) for use by the IRS, even if the total amount does not exceed $10,000.

Exceptions. Cash is not required to be reported if it is received:

● By a financial institution required to file Form 104, Currency Transaction Report.

● By a casino required to file (or exempt from filing) Form 103, Currency Transaction Report by Casinos, if the cash is received as part of its gaming business.

● By an agent who receives the cash from a principal, if the agent uses all of the cash within 15 days in a second transaction that is reportable on Form 8300 or on Form 104, and discloses all the information necessary to complete Part II of Form 8300 or Form 104 to the recipient of the cash in the second transaction.

● In a transaction occurring entirely outside the United States. See Publication 1544, Reporting Cash Payments Over $10,000 (Received in a Trade or Business), regarding transactions occurring in Puerto Rico, the Virgin Islands, and territories and possessions of the United States.

● In a transaction that is not in the course of a person's trade or business.

When to file. File Form 8300 by the 15th day after the date the cash was received. If that date falls on a Saturday, Sunday, or legal holiday, file the form on the next business day.

Where to file. File the form with the Internal Revenue Service, Detroit Computing Center, P.O. Box 32621, Detroit, MI 48232.

Statement to be provided. You must give a written or electronic statement to each person named on a required Form 8300 on or before January 31 of the year following the calendar year in which the cash is received. The statement must show the name, telephone number, and address of the information contact for the business, the aggregate amount of reportable cash received, and that the information was furnished to the IRS. Keep a copy of the statement for your records.

Multiple payments. If you receive more than one cash payment for a single transaction or for related transactions, you must report the multiple payments any time you receive a total amount that exceeds $10,000 within any 12-month period. Submit the report within 15 days of the date you receive the payment that

causes the total amount to exceed $10,000. If more than one report is required within 15 days, you may file a combined report. File the combined report no later than the date the earliest report, if filed separately, would have to be filed.

Taxpayer identification number (TIN). You must furnish the correct TIN of the person or persons from whom you receive the cash and, if applicable, the person or persons on whose behalf the transaction is being conducted. You may be subject to penalties for an incorrect or missing TIN.

The TIN for an individual (including a sole proprietorship) is the individual's social security number (SSN). For certain resident aliens who are not eligible to get an SSN and nonresident aliens who are required to file tax returns, it is an IRS Individual Taxpayer Identification Number (ITIN). For other persons, including corporations, partnerships, and estates, it is the employer identification number (EIN).

If you have requested but are not able to get a TIN for one or more of the parties to a transaction within 15 days following the transaction, file the report and attach a statement explaining why the TIN is not included.

Exception: *You are not required to provide the TIN of a person who is a nonresident alien individual or a foreign organization if that person does not have income effectively connected with the conduct of a U.S. trade or business and does not have an office or place of business, or fiscal or paying agent, in the United States. See* Publication 1544 *for more information.*

Penalties. You may be subject to penalties if you fail to file a correct and complete Form 8300 on time and you cannot show that the failure was due to reasonable cause. You may also be subject to penalties if you fail to furnish timely a correct and complete statement to each person named in a required report. A minimum penalty of $25,000 may be imposed if the failure is due to an intentional or willful disregard of the cash reporting requirements.

Penalties may also be imposed for causing, or attempting to cause, a trade or business to fail to file a required report; for causing, or attempting to cause, a trade or business to file a required report containing a material omission or misstatement of fact; or for structuring, or attempting to structure, transactions to avoid the reporting requirements. These violations may also be subject to criminal prosecution which, upon conviction, may result in imprisonment of up to 5 years or fines of up to $250,000 for individuals and $500,000 for corporations or both.

Definitions

Cash. The term "cash" means the following:

● U.S. and foreign coin and currency received in any transaction.

● A cashier's check, money order, bank draft, or traveler's check having a face amount of $10,000 or less that is received in a designated reporting transaction (defined below), or that is received in any transaction in which the recipient knows that the instrument is being used in an attempt to avoid the reporting of the transaction under either section 6050I or 31 U.S.C. 5331.

Note. Cash does not include a check drawn on the payer's own account, such as a personal check, regardless of the amount.

Designated reporting transaction. A retail sale (or the receipt of funds by a broker or other intermediary in connection with a retail sale) of a consumer durable, a collectible, or a travel or entertainment activity.

Retail sale. Any sale (whether or not the sale is for resale or for any other purpose) made in the course of a trade or business if that trade or business principally consists of making sales to ultimate consumers.

Consumer durable. An item of tangible personal property of a type that, under ordinary usage, can reasonably be expected to remain useful for at least 1 year, and that has a sales price of more than $10,000.

Collectible. Any work of art, rug, antique, metal, gem, stamp, coin, etc.

Travel or entertainment activity. An item of travel or entertainment that pertains to a single trip or event if the combined sales price of the item and all other items relating to the same trip or event that are sold in the same transaction (or related transactions) exceeds $10,000.

Exceptions. A cashier's check, money order, bank draft, or traveler's check is not considered received in a designated reporting transaction if it constitutes the proceeds of a bank loan or if it is received as a payment on certain promissory notes, installment sales contracts, or down payment plans. See Publication 1544 for more information.

Person. An individual, corporation, partnership, trust, estate, association, or company.

Recipient. The person receiving the cash. Each branch or other unit of a person's trade or business is considered a separate recipient unless the branch receiving the cash (or a central office linking the branches), knows or has reason to know the identity of payers making cash payments to other branches.

Transaction. Includes the purchase of property or services, the payment of debt, the exchange of a negotiable instrument for cash, and the receipt of cash to be held in escrow or trust. A single transaction may not be broken into multiple transactions to avoid reporting.

Suspicious transaction. A transaction in which it appears that a person is attempting to cause Form 8300 not to be filed, or to file a false or incomplete form. The term also includes any transaction in which there is an indication of possible illegal activity.

Specific Instructions

You must complete all parts. However, you may skip Part II if the individual named in Part I is conducting the transaction on his or her behalf only. For voluntary reporting of suspicious transactions, see Item 1 below.

Item 1. If you are amending a prior report, check box 1a. Complete the appropriate items with the correct or amended information only. Complete all of Part IV. Staple a copy of the original report to the amended report.

To voluntarily report a suspicious transaction (see *Definitions*), check box 1b. You may also telephone your local IRS Criminal Investigation Division or call 1-800-800-2877.

Part I

Item 2. If two or more individuals conducted the transaction you are reporting, check the box and complete Part I for any one of the individuals. Provide the same information for the other individual(s) on the back of the form. If more than three individuals are involved, provide the same information on additional sheets of paper and attach them to this form.

Item 6. Enter the taxpayer identification number (TIN) of the individual named. See *Taxpayer identification number (TIN)* on page 3 for more information.

Item 8. Enter eight numerals for the date of birth of the individual named. For example, if the individual's birth date is July 6, 1960, enter 07 06 1960.

Item 13. Fully describe the nature of the occupation, profession, or business (for example, "plumber," "attorney," or "automobile dealer"). Do not use general or nondescriptive terms such as "businessman" or "self-employed."

Item 14. You must verify the name and address of the named individual(s). Verification must be made by examination of a document normally accepted as a means of identification when cashing checks (for example, a driver's license, passport, alien registration card, or other official

document). In item 14a, enter the type of document examined. In item 14b, identify the issuer of the document. In item 14c, enter the document's number. For example, if the individual has a Utah driver's license, enter "driver's license" in item 14a, "Utah" in item 14b, and the number appearing on the license in item 14c.

Note. You must complete all three items (a, b, and c) in this line to make sure that Form 8300 will be processed correctly.

Part II

Item 15. If the transaction is being conducted on behalf of more than one person (including husband and wife or parent and child), check the box and complete Part II for any one of the persons. Provide the same information for the other person(s) on the back of the form. If more than three persons are involved, provide the same information on additional sheets of paper and attach them to this form.

Items 16 through 19. If the person on whose behalf the transaction is being conducted is an individual, complete items 16, 17, and 18. Enter his or her TIN in item 19. If the individual is a sole proprietor and has an employer identification number (EIN), you must enter both the SSN and EIN in item 19. If the person is an organization, put its name as shown on required tax filings in item 16 and its EIN in item 19.

Item 20. If a sole proprietor or organization named in items 16 through 18 is doing business under a name other than that entered in item 16 (e.g., a "trade" or "doing business as (DBA)" name), enter it here.

Item 27. If the person is not required to furnish a TIN, complete this item. See *Taxpayer Identification Number (TIN)* on page 3. Enter a description of the type of official document issued to that person in item 27a (for example, "passport"), the country that issued the document in item 27b, and the document's number in item 27c.

Note. You must complete all three items (a, b, and c) in this line to make sure that Form 8300 will be processed correctly.

Part III

Item 28. Enter the date you received the cash. If you received the cash in more than one payment, enter the date you received the payment that caused the combined amount to exceed $10,000. See *Multiple payments* under *General Instructions* for more information.

Item 30. Check this box if the amount shown in item 29 was received in more than one payment (for example, as installment payments or payments on related transactions).

Item 31. Enter the total price of the property, services, amount of cash exchanged, etc. (for example, the total cost of a vehicle purchased, cost of catering service, exchange of currency) if different from the amount shown in item 29.

Item 32. Enter the dollar amount of each form of cash received. Show foreign currency amounts in U.S. dollar equivalent at a fair market rate of exchange available to the public. The sum of the amounts must equal item 29. For cashier's check, money order, bank draft, or traveler's check, provide the name of the issuer and the serial number of each instrument. Names of all issuers and all serial numbers involved must be provided. If necessary, provide this information on additional sheets of paper and attach them to this form.

Item 33. Check the appropriate box(es) that describe the transaction. If the transaction is not specified in boxes a–i, check box j and briefly describe the transaction (for example, "car lease," "boat lease," "house lease," or "aircraft rental"). If the transaction relates to the receipt of bail by a court clerk, check box i, "Bail received by court clerks." This box is only for use by court clerks. If the transaction relates to cash received by a bail bondsman, check box **d,** "Business services provided."

Part IV

Item 36. If you are a sole proprietorship, you must enter your SSN. If your business also has an EIN, you must provide the EIN as well. All other business entities must enter an EIN.

Item 41. Fully describe the nature of your business, for example, "attorney" or "jewelry dealer." Do not use general or nondescriptive terms such as "business" or "store."

Item 42. This form must be signed by an individual who has been authorized to do so for the business that received the cash.

Comments

Use this section to comment on or clarify anything you may have entered on any line in Parts I, II, III, and IV. For example, if you checked box b (Suspicious transaction) in line 1 above Part I, you may want to explain why you think that the cash transaction you are reporting on Form 8300 may be suspicious.

Privacy Act and Paperwork Reduction Act Notice. Except as otherwise noted, the information solicited on this form is required by the Internal Revenue Service (IRS) and the Financial Crimes Enforcement Network (FinCEN) in order to carry out the laws and regulations of the United States Department of the Treasury. Trades or businesses, except for clerks of criminal courts, are required to provide the information to the IRS and FinCEN under both section 6050I and 31 U.S.C. 5331. Clerks of criminal courts are required to provide the information to the IRS under section 6050I. Section 6109 and 31 U.S.C. 5331 require that you provide your social security number in order to adequately identify you and process your return and other papers. The principal purpose for collecting the information on this form is to maintain reports or records which have a high degree of usefulness in criminal, tax, or regulatory investigations or proceedings, or in the conduct of intelligence or counterintelligence activities, by directing the Federal Government's attention to unusual or questionable transactions.

You are not required to provide information as to whether the reported transaction is deemed suspicious. Failure to provide all other requested information, or providing fraudulent information, may result in criminal prosecution and other penalties under Title 26 and Title 31 of the United States Code.

Generally, tax returns and return information are confidential, as stated in section 6103. However, section 6103 allows or requires the IRS to disclose or give the information requested on this form to others as described in the Code. For example, we may disclose your tax information to the Department of Justice, to enforce the tax laws, both civil and criminal, and to cities, states, the District of Columbia, to carry out their tax laws. We may disclose this information to other persons as necessary to obtain information which we cannot get in any other way. We may disclose this information to Federal, state, and local child support agencies; and to other Federal agencies for the purposes of determining entitlement for benefits or the eligibility for and the repayment of loans. We may also provide the records to appropriate state, local, and foreign criminal law enforcement and regulatory personnel in the performance of their official duties. We may also disclose this information to other countries under a tax treaty, or to Federal and state agencies to enforce Federal nontax criminal laws and to combat terrorism.

The IRS authority to disclose information to combat terrorism expired on December 31, 2003. Legislation is pending that would reinstate this authority. "In addition, FinCEN may provide the information to those officials if they are conducting intelligence or counter-intelligence activities to protect against international terrorism."

You are not required to provide the information requested on a form that is subject to the Paperwork Reduction Act unless the form displays a valid OMB control number. Books or records relating to a form or its instructions must be retained as long as their contents may become material in the administration of any law under Title 26 or Title 31.

The time needed to complete this form will vary depending on individual circumstances. The estimated average time is 21 minutes. If you have comments concerning the accuracy of this time estimate or suggestions for making this form simpler, you can write to the Tax Products Coordinating Committee, Western Area Distribution Center, Rancho Cordova, CA 95743-0001. Do not send this form to this office. Instead, see *Where To File* on page 3.

This page intentionally blank.

Form **8850** (Rev. January 2006) Department of the Treasury Internal Revenue Service	**Pre-Screening Notice and Certification Request for the Work Opportunity and Welfare-to-Work Credits** ▶ See separate instructions.

OMB No. 1545-1500

Job applicant: Fill in the lines below and check any boxes that apply. Complete only this side.

Your name _____ Social security number ▶ _____

Street address where you live _____

City or town, state, and ZIP code _____

Telephone number (___) ___ - _____

If you are under age 25, enter your date of birth (month, day, year) ___ / ___ / ___

Work Opportunity Credit

1 ☐ Check here if you are a Hurricane Katrina employee. Enter the address of your main home on August 28, 2005, and the state and county or parish in which it was located.

_____

2 ☐ Check here if you received a conditional certification from the state employment security agency (SESA) or a participating local agency for the work opportunity credit.

3 ☐ Check here if **any** of the following statements apply to you.
   - I am a member of a family that has received assistance from Temporary Assistance for Needy Families (TANF) for any 9 months during the last 18 months.
   - I am a veteran and a member of a family that received food stamps for at least a 3-month period within the last 15 months.
   - I was referred here by a rehabilitation agency approved by the state, an employment network under the Ticket to Work program, or the Department of Veterans Affairs.
   - I am at least age 18 but **not** age 25 or older and I am a member of a family that:
     a Received food stamps for the last 6 months **or**
     b Received food stamps for at least 3 of the last 5 months, **but** is no longer eligible to receive them.
   - Within the past year, I was convicted of a felony or released from prison for a felony **and** during the last 6 months I was a member of a low-income family.
   - I received supplemental security income (SSI) benefits for any month ending within the last 60 days.

Welfare-to-Work Credit

4 ☐ Check here if you received a conditional certification from the SESA or a participating local agency for the welfare-to-work credit.

5 ☐ Check here if you are a member of a family that:
   - Received TANF payments for at least the last 18 months, **or**
   - Received TANF payments for any 18 months beginning after August 5, 1997, **and** the earliest 18-month period beginning after August 5, 1997, ended within the last 2 years, **or**
   - Stopped being eligible for TANF payments within the last 2 years because federal or state law limited the maximum time those payments could be made.

All Applicants

Under penalties of perjury, I declare that I gave the above information to the employer on or before the day I was offered a job, and it is, to the best of my knowledge, true, correct, and complete.

Job applicant's signature ▶ _____ **Date** ___ / ___ / ___

For Privacy Act and Paperwork Reduction Act Notice, see page 2. Cat. No. 22851L Form **8850** (Rev. 01-06)

For Employer's Use Only

Employer's name _____ Telephone no. (___) ___ - _____ EIN ▶ _____

Street address _____

City or town, state, and ZIP code _____

Person to contact, if different from above _____ Telephone no. (___) ___ - _____

Street address _____

City or town, state, and ZIP code _____

If, based on the individual's age and home address, he or she is a member of group 4 or 6 (as described under Members of Targeted Groups in the separate instructions), enter that group number (4 or 6) . . . . ▶ ____

Date applicant: Gave information ___/___/___   Was offered job ___/___/___   Was hired ___/___/___   Started job ___/___/___

Complete Only If Box 1 on Page 1 is Checked

State and county or parish of job _____

☐ Check if the individual was not my employee on August 28, 2005 and this is the first time the employee has been hired by me since August 28, 2005.

Under penalties of perjury, I declare that the applicant completed this form on or before the day a job was offered to the applicant and that the information I have furnished is, to the best of my knowledge, true, correct, and complete. Based on the information the job applicant furnished on page 1, I believe the individual is a member of a targeted group or a long-term family assistance recipient. I hereby request a certification that the individual is a member of a targeted group or a long-term family assistance recipient.

Employer's signature ▶ _____   Title _____   Date ___/___/___

Privacy Act and Paperwork Reduction Act Notice

Section references are to the Internal Revenue Code.

Section 51(d)(12) permits a prospective employer to request the applicant to complete this form and give it to the prospective employer. The information will be used by the employer to complete the employer's federal tax return. Completion of this form is voluntary and may assist members of targeted groups and long-term family assistance recipients in securing employment. Routine uses of this form include giving it to the state employment security agency (SESA), which will contact appropriate sources to confirm that the applicant is a member of a targeted group or a long-term family assistance recipient. This form may also be given to the Internal Revenue Service

for administration of the Internal Revenue laws, to the Department of Justice for civil and criminal litigation, to the Department of Labor for oversight of the certifications performed by the SESA, and to cities, states, and the District of Columbia for use in administering their tax laws. We may also disclose this information to other countries under a tax treaty, to federal and state agencies to enforce federal nontax criminal laws, or to federal law enforcement and intelligence agencies to combat terrorism.

You are not required to provide the information requested on a form that is subject to the Paperwork Reduction Act unless the form displays a valid OMB control number. Books or records relating to a form or its instructions must be retained as long as their contents may become material in the administration of any Internal Revenue law. Generally, tax returns and return information are confidential, as required by section 6103.

The time needed to complete and file this form will vary depending on individual circumstances. The estimated average time is:

Recordkeeping . . . .5 hrs., 30 min.
Learning about the law or the form . . . . 24 min.
Preparing and sending this form to the SESA . . . . 30 min.

If you have comments concerning the accuracy of these time estimates or suggestions for making this form simpler, we would be happy to hear from you. You can write to the Internal Revenue Service, Tax Products Coordinating Committee, SE:W:CAR:MP:T:T:SP, 1111 Constitution Ave. NW, IR-6406, Washington, DC 20224.

Do not send this form to this address. Instead, see *When and Where To File* in the separate instructions.

Instructions for Form 8850

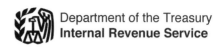

Department of the Treasury
Internal Revenue Service

(Rev. January 2006)

Pre-Screening Notice and Certification Request for the Work Opportunity and Welfare-to-Work Credits

Section references are to the Internal Revenue Code unless otherwise noted.

General Instructions

What's New

• The work opportunity credit and the welfare-to-work credit are now allowed for qualified individuals who begin work for you before January 1, 2006.

 These credits may be extended with respect to employees who began work for you after December 31, 2005. See What's Hot in Tax Forms, Pubs, and Other Tax Products at www.irs.gov/ formspubs to find out if the credits have been extended.

• The Katrina Emergency Relief Act of 2005 added a new targeted group, Hurricane Katrina employee, identified as group 9.

Purpose of Form

Employers use Form 8850 to pre-screen and to make a written request to a state employment security agency (SESA) (unless the employee checks only the Hurricane Katrina employee box) to certify an individual as:

• A member of a targeted group for purposes of qualifying for the work opportunity credit or

• A long-term family assistance recipient for purposes of qualifying for the welfare-to-work credit.

Submitting Form 8850 to the SESA (unless the employee checks only the Hurricane Katrina employee box) is but one step in the process of qualifying for the work opportunity credit or the welfare-to-work credit. The SESA must certify the job applicant is a member of a targeted group or is a long-term family assistance recipient. After starting work, the employee must meet the minimum number-of-hours-worked requirement for the work opportunity credit or the minimum number-of-hours, number-of-days requirement for the welfare-to-work credit. The employer may elect to take the applicable credit by filing Form 5884, Work Opportunity Credit, or Form 8861, Welfare-to-Work Credit.

 The certification requirements described above do not apply to Hurricane Katrina employees. For an employer of a Hurricane Katrina employee, this form is used to accept reasonable evidence that the worker is a Hurricane Katrina employee. It is the employer's responsibility to ascertain that the place where the employee lived on August 28, 2005, (the address on line 1 of the form) is in fact in the core disaster area (see pages 2 and 3 for a list of these

areas). The employer is not required to ask employees to furnish any documentary evidence.

Who Should Complete and Sign the Form

The job applicant gives information to the employer on or before the day a job offer is made. This information is entered on Form 8850. Based on the applicant's information, the employer determines whether or not he or she believes the applicant is a member of a targeted group (as defined under Members of Targeted Groups) or a long-term family assistance recipient (as defined under Welfare-to-Work Job Applicants). If the employer believes the applicant is a member of a targeted group or a long-term family assistance recipient, the employer completes the rest of the form no later than the day the job offer is made. Both the job applicant and the employer must sign Form 8850 no later than the date for submitting the form to the SESA.

Instructions for Employer

When and Where To File

Do not file Form 8850 with the Internal Revenue Service. Instead, if required, file it with the work opportunity tax credit (WOTC) coordinator for your SESA no later than the 21st day after the job applicant begins work for you. Although electronic filing of Form 8850 is permitted, at the time these instructions were published, no state was equipped to receive Form 8850 electronically. See Announcement 2002-44 for details. You can find Announcement 2002-44 on page 809 of Internal Revenue Bulletin 2002-17 at *www.irs.gov/pub/irs-irbs/ irb02-17.pdf.*

To get the name, address, phone and fax numbers, and email address of the WOTC coordinator for your SESA, visit the Department of Labor Employment and Training Administration (ETA) web site at *www.ows.doleta.gov/employ/tax.asp.*

 Never include Form 8850 with a tax return or otherwise send it to the IRS, regardless of the employee's targeted group. Form 8850 should be filed with the state SESA unless the employee checks only the Hurricane Katrina employee box, in which case the employer should keep the Form 8850 for its records.

Cat. No. 24833J

Additional Requirements for Certification

In addition to filing Form 8850, you must complete and send to your state's WOTC coordinator either:
• ETA Form 9062, Conditional Certification Form, if the job applicant received this form from a participating agency (e.g., the Jobs Corps) or
• ETA Form 9061, Individual Characteristics Form, if the job applicant did not receive a conditional certification.

You can get ETA Form 9061 from your local public employment service office or you can download it from the ETA web site at *www.ows.doleta.gov/employ/tax.asp.*

Recordkeeping

Keep copies of Forms 8850, along with any transmittal letters that you submit to your SESA, as long as they may be needed for the administration of the Internal Revenue Code provisions relating to the work opportunity credit and the welfare-to-work credit. Records that support these credits usually must be kept for 3 years from the date any income tax return claiming the credits is due or filed, whichever is later.

 Hurricane Katrina employee. *Form 8850 should not be filed with the state SESA for employees who only check box 1 on Form 8850. Employers should keep Form 8850 for their records. If a prior version of Form 8850 was sent to the state SESA indicating the employee is a Hurricane Katrina employee, the employer and employee should complete this version of Form 8850 for the employer to retain for its records. Do not attach Form 8850 to a tax return.*

Members of Targeted Groups

A job applicant may be certified as a member of a targeted group if he or she is described in one of the following groups.

1. **Qualified IV-A recipient.** A member of a family receiving assistance under a state plan approved under part A of title IV of the Social Security Act relating to Temporary Assistance for Needy Families (TANF). The assistance must be received for any 9 months during the 18-month period that ends on the hiring date.

2. **Qualified veteran.** A veteran who is a member of a family receiving assistance under the Food Stamp program for at least a 3-month period during the 15-month period ending on the hiring date. See section 51(d)(3). To be considered a veteran, the applicant must:
• Have served on active duty (not including training) in the Armed Forces of the United States for more than 180 days or have been discharged or released from active duty for a service-connected disability and
• Not have a period of active duty (not including training) of more than 90 days that ended during the 60-day period ending on the hiring date.

3. **Qualified ex-felon.** An ex-felon who:
• Has been convicted of a felony under any Federal or state law,
• Is hired not more than 1 year after the conviction or release from prison for that felony, and

• Is a member of a family that had income on an annual basis of 70% or less of the Bureau of Labor Statistics lower living standard during the 6 months immediately preceding the earlier of the month the income determination occurs or the month in which the hiring date occurs.

4. **High-risk youth.** An individual who is at least 18 but not yet 25 on the hiring date and lives within an empowerment zone, enterprise community, or renewal community.

5. **Vocational rehabilitation referral.** An individual who has a physical or mental disability resulting in a substantial handicap to employment and who was referred to the employer upon completion of (or while receiving) rehabilitation services by a rehabilitation agency approved by the state, an employment network under the Ticket to Work program, or the Department of Veterans Affairs.

6. **Summer youth employee.** An individual who:
• Performs services for the employer between May 1 and September 15,
• Is age 16 but not yet age 18 on the hiring date (or if later, on May 1),
• Has never worked for the employer before, and
• Lives within an empowerment zone, enterprise community, or renewal community.

7. **Food stamp recipient.** An individual who:
• Is at least age 18 but not yet age 25 on the hiring date, and
• Is a member of a family that —
a. Has received food stamps for the 6-month period ending on the hiring date or
b. Is no longer eligible for such assistance under section 6(o) of the Food Stamp Act of 1977, but the family received food stamps for at least 3 months of the 5-month period ending on the hiring date.

8. **SSI recipient.** An individual who is receiving supplemental security income benefits under title XVI of the Social Security Act (including benefits of the type described in section 1616 of the Social Security Act or section 212 of Public Law 93-66) for any month ending within the 60-day period ending on the hiring date.

9. **Hurricane Katrina employee.** A Hurricane Katrina employee is:
• A person who, on August 28, 2005, had a main home in the core disaster area and, within a two-year period beginning on this date, is hired to perform services principally in the core disaster area; or
• A person who, on August 28, 2005, had a main home in the core disaster area, was displaced from the main home as a result of Hurricane Katrina, and was hired during the period beginning on August 28, 2005, and ending on December 31, 2005, for a job located outside the core disaster area.

Gulf Opportunity (GO) Zone (Core Disaster Area). The GO Zone (also called the core disaster area) covers the portion of the Hurricane Katrina disaster area determined by the Federal Emergency Management Agency (FEMA) to be eligible for either individual only or both individual and public assistance from the Federal

Government. The GO Zone covers the following areas in three states.

a. **Alabama.** The counties of Baldwin, Choctaw, Clarke, Greene, Hale, Marengo, Mobile, Pickens, Sumter, Tuscaloosa, and Washington.

b. **Louisiana.** The parishes of Acadia, Ascension, Assumption, Calcasieu, Cameron, East Baton Rouge, East Feliciana, Iberia, Iberville, Jefferson, Jefferson Davis, Lafayette, Lafourche, Livingston, Orleans, Plaquemines, Pointe Coupee, St. Bernard, St. Charles, St. Helena, St. James, St. John the Baptist, St. Martin, St. Mary, St. Tammany, Tangipahoa, Terrebonne, Vermilion, Washington, West Baton Rouge, and West Feliciana.

c. **Mississippi.** The counties of Adams, Amite, Attala, Choctow, Claiborne, Clarke, Copiah, Covington, Forrest, Franklin, George, Greene, Hancock, Harrison, Hinds, Holmes, Humphreys, Jackson, Jasper, Jefferson, Jefferson Davis, Jones, Kemper, Lamar, Lauderdale, Lawrence, Leake, Lincoln, Lowndes, Madison, Marion, Neshoba, Newton, Noxubee, Oktibbeha, Pearl River, Perry, Pike, Rankin, Scott, Simpson, Smith, Stone, Walthall, Warren, Wayne, Wilkinson, Winston, and Yazoo.

Empowerment zones, enterprise communities, and renewal communities. For details on all empowerment zones, enterprise communities, and renewal communities, you can use the RC/EZ/EC Address Locator at *www.hud.gov/crlocator*. For details about empowerment zones, enterprise communities, and renewal communities, call 1-800-998-9999, or contact your SESA. For more information about empowerment zones, enterprise communities, and renewal communities, see Publication 954, Tax Incentives for Distressed Communities.

 Under section 1400, parts of Washington, DC, are treated as an empowerment zone. For details, use the RC/EZ/EC Address Locator at www.hud.gov/crlocator *or see Notice 98-57, on page 9 of Internal Revenue Bulletin 1998-47 at* www.irs.gov/pub/ irs-irbs/irb98-47.pdf. *Also, there are no areas designated in Puerto Rico, Guam, or any U.S. possession.*

Welfare-to-Work Job Applicants

An individual may be certified as a long-term family assistance recipient if he or she is a member of a family that:

• Has received TANF payments for at least 18 consecutive months ending on the hiring date, or

• Receives TANF payments for any 18 months (whether or not consecutive) beginning after August 5, 1997, and the earliest 18-month period beginning after August 5, 1997, ended within the last 2 years, or

• Stopped being eligible for TANF payments because Federal or state law limits the maximum period such assistance is payable and the individual is hired not more than 2 years after such eligibility ended.

Member of a family

With respect to the qualified IV-A recipient, qualified veteran, food stamp recipient, and long-term family assistance recipient, an individual whose family receives assistance for the requisite period meets the family assistance requirement of the applicable group if the individual is included on the grant (and thus receives assistance) for some portion of the specified period.

This page intentionally blank.

**Employment
Development
Department**
State of California

This form will be the basic record of YOUR ACCOUNT. **DO NOT FILE THIS FORM UNTIL YOU HAVE PAID WAGES THAT EXCEED $100.00.** Please read the **INSTRUCTIONS** on page 2 before completing this form. **PLEASE PRINT OR TYPE..** Return this form to: ➡	EMPLOYMENT DEVELOPMENT DEPARTMENT ACCOUNT SERVICES GROUP MIC 28 PO BOX 826880 SACRAMENTO CA 94280-0001 **(916) 654-7041 FAX (916) 654-9211 www.edd.ca.gov**

REGISTRATION FORM FOR COMMERCIAL EMPLOYERS, PACIFIC MARITIME, AND FISHING BOATS

ACCOUNT NUMBER	DEPT. USE	QUARTER	ON-LINE PROCESS DATE	TAS CODE

Industry specific registration forms are required relative to each type of employer. Please use the appropriate form to register.

Commercial/Pacific Maritime/Fishing Boat	DE 1	Household Workers	DE 1HW
Agricultural	DE 1AG	Non-profit	DE 1NP
Government/Public Schools/Indian Tribes	DE 1GS	Personal Income Tax Only	DE 1P

A. THIS IS A:

☐ New business ☐ Hired employees ☐ Change in form - (Individual to corporation; partnership to corporation; merger; corporation to LLC, etc.)
☐ Change of partner(s) ☐ Purchased on-going business ☐ All ☐ Part ☐ Other _____

IF THE BUSINESS WAS PURCHASED, PROVIDE THE FOLLOWING INFORMATION:

Previous Owner   Business Name   Purchase Price   Date of Transfer   EDD Account Number

B. HAVE YOU EVER REGISTERED A BUSINESS WITH THE DEPARTMENT?
☐ No ☐ Yes

IF YES, ENTER THE FOLLOWING:
ACCT NUMBER   BUSINESS NAME   ADDRESS

C. INDICATE FIRST QUARTER AND YEAR IN WHICH WAGES EXCEED $100. ☐ Jan.-Mar. 20___ ☐ Apr.-June 20___ ☐ July-Sept. 20___ ☐ Oct.-Dec. 20___

D. BUSINESS NAME (DBA)	OWNERSHIP BEGAN OPERATING	FEDERAL I.D. NUMBER
	MONTH: DAY: YEAR:	
E. INDIVIDUAL OWNER	SOCIAL SECURITY NUMBER	DRIVER'S LICENSE #
F. CORPORATION/LLC/LLP/LP NAME	SECRETARY OF STATE CORP/LLC/LLP/LP I.D. NO.	

G. List all partners*, corporate officers, or LLC/LLP members/managers/officers	**TITLE** (partner, officer title, LLC/LLP member/manager)	**SOCIAL SECURITY NUMBER**	**DRIVER'S LICENSE #**

*If entity is a **Limited Partnership**, indicate General Partner with an (*). List additional partners, LLC/LLP members/officers/managers on a separate sheet.

H. MAILING ADDRESS	CITY	STATE	ZIP CODE	PHONE NUMBER ( )
I. BUSINESS ADDRESS (if different from mailing address)	CITY	STATE	ZIP CODE	PHONE NUMBER ( )

J. ORGANIZATION TYPE

☐ (IN) INDIVIDUAL OWNER ☐ (AS) ASSOCIATION ☐ (LQ) LIQUIDATION ☐ (JV) JOINT VENTURE
☐ (HW) HUS/WIFE CO-OWNERSHIP ☐ (LC) LIMITED LIABILITY CO. ☐ (LP) LIMITED PARTNERSHIP ☐ (RC) RECEIVERSHIP
☐ (GP) GENERAL PARTNERSHIP ☐ (PL) LIMITED LIABILITY PARTNERSHIP ☐ (TR) TRUSTEESHIP ☐ (BK) BANKRUPTCY
☐ (CP) CORPORATION   ☐ (EA) ESTATE ADMINISTRATION ☐ (OT) OTHER (Specify) _____

K. EMPLOYER TYPE   ☐ (01) COMMERCIAL   ☐ (22) PACIFIC MARITIME   ☐ (25) FISHING BOAT

L. INDUSTRY ACTIVITY: Identify the industry and specific product or service that represents the greatest portion of your sales receipts or revenue. Check one:

☐ SERVICES ☐ RETAIL ☐ WHOLESALE ☐ MANUFACTURING ☐ OTHER _____

Describe specific product and/or service in detail.

Number of CA Employees _____   Are there multiple locations for this business? ☐ No ☐ Yes

M. CONTACT PERSON FOR BUSINESS   TITLE/COMPANY NAME   ADDRESS   PHONE ( )

N. DECLARATION
These statements are hereby declared to be correct to the best knowledge and belief of the undersigned.

Signature _____ Title _____ Date _____
(Owner, Partner, Officer, Member, Manager, etc.)

O. PAYROLL TAX EDUCATION: Attend a payroll tax seminar that will help you understand how, what, and when to report state payroll taxes. Visit our Web site at **www.edd.ca.gov/taxsem** or call us at (888) 745-3886 for more information.

INSTRUCTIONS FOR REGISTRATION FORM FOR COMMERCIAL/PACIFIC MARITIME/FISHING BOAT EMPLOYERS

An employer is required by law to file a registration form with the Employment Development Department (EDD) within **fifteen (15) calendar days** after paying over $100 in wages for employment in a calendar quarter, or whenever a change in ownership occurs. Please complete all items on the front of this DE 1 and do **one** of the following:

- Mail your completed registration form to EDD, Account Services Group MIC 28, PO Box 826880, Sacramento, CA 94280-0001 **or**
- Fax your completed registration form to EDD at (916) 654-9211 **or**
- Call for telephone registration at (916) 654-8706

There are industry specific registration forms related to each type of employer. Please use the appropriate form to register. A complete list of registration forms is located on the front of this form.

NEED MORE HELP OR INFORMATION?

- Call Account Services Group (ASG) in Sacramento at (916) 654-7041 with questions regarding this form or the registration and account number assignment process.
- Contact the nearest Taxpayer Education and Assistance (TEA) office listed in your local telephone directory under State Government, EDD or call a TEA Customer Service Representative at 1-888-745-3886 with questions about whether your business entity is subject to reporting and paying state payroll taxes. For TTY (nonverbal) access, call 1-800-547-9565.
- Access the EDD Web site at **www.edd.ca.gov**

A. STATUS OF BUSINESS - Check the box that best describes why you are completing this form. If the business was purchased, provide previous owner and business name, purchase price, date ownership was transferred to this ownership and EDD account number.

B. PRIOR REGISTRATION - If any part of the ownership shown in items E, F, or G are operating or have ever operated at another location, check "Yes" and provide account number, business name, and address.

C. WAGES - Check the box for the quarter in which you first paid over $100 in wages.

D. BUSINESS NAME - Enter the name by which your business is known to the public. Enter "None" if no business name is used. Enter the date the new ownership began operating. Enter Federal Employer Identification Number. If not assigned, enter "Applied For".

E. INDIVIDUAL OWNER - Enter the full given name, middle initial, surname, title, social security number, and driver's license number.

F. CORPORATION/LLC/LLP/LP NAME - Enter Corporation/LLC/LLP/LP name exactly as spelled and registered with the Secretary of State. Include the California Corporate/LLC/LLP/LP identification number.

G. LIST ALL PARTNERS, CORPORATE OFFICERS, OR LLC/LLP MEMBERS/MANAGERS/OFFICERS - Enter the name, title, social security number and driver's license of each individual.

H. MAILING ADDRESS - Enter the mailing address where EDD correspondence and forms should be sent. Provide daytime business phone number.

I. BUSINESS ADDRESS - Enter the California address and telephone number where the business is physically conducted. If there is more than one California location, list the business addresses on a separate sheet and attach to this form.

J. ORGANIZATION TYPE - Check the box that best describes the legal form of the ownership shown in items E, F, or G.

K. EMPLOYER TYPE - Check the box that best describes your employer type.

L. INDUSTRY ACTIVITY - Check the box that best describes the industry activity of your business. Describe the particular product or service in detail. This information is used to assign an Industrial Classification Code to your business. If you would like more information on industry coding or the North American Industry Classification System (NAICS), you can visit the Web site:
www.census.gov/epcd/www/naics.html

Enter the number of California employees. Check "Yes" if there are multiple locations under this EDD Account Number.

M. CONTACT PERSON FOR BUSINESS - Enter the name, title/company address, and phone number of the person authorized by the ownership shown in items E, F, or G to provide EDD staff information needed to maintain the accuracy of your employer account.

N. DECLARATION - This declaration should be signed by one of the names shown in item(s) E or G.

O. PAYROLL TAX EDUCATION - EDD provides educational opportunities for taxpayers to learn how to report employees' wages and pay taxes, pointing out the pitfalls that create errors and unnecessary billings. Help is only a telephone call or Web site away.

We will **notify** you of your **EDD Account Number** by mail. To help you understand your tax withholding and filing responsibilities, you will be sent a **California Employer's Guide, DE 44**. Please keep your account status current by notifying ASG of all future changes to the original registration information.

Index

C

J

L

M

S

T

U

V

W

Y

Z

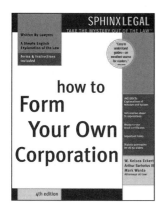

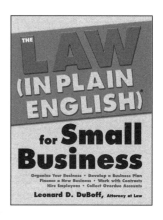

Sphinx® Publishing's State Titles

Up-to-Date for Your State

California Titles

How to File for Divorce in CA (5E)	$26.95
How to Settle & Probate an Estate in CA (2E)	$28.95
How to Start a Business in CA (2E)	$21.95
How to Win in Small Claims Court in CA (2E)	$18.95
Landlords' Legal Guide in CA (2E)	$24.95
Make Your Own CA Will	$18.95
Tenants' Rights in CA (2E)	$24.95

Florida Titles

How to File for Divorce in FL (8E)	$28.95
How to Form a Limited Liability Co. in FL (3E)	$24.95
How to Form a Partnership in FL	$22.95
How to Make a FL Will (7E)	$16.95
How to Win in Small Claims Court in FL (7E)	$18.95
Incorporate in FL (7E)	$29.95
Land Trusts in Florida (6E)	$29.95
Landlords' Rights and Duties in FL (10E)	$24.95
Probate and Settle an Estate in FL (6E)	$29.95
Start a Business in FL (8E)	$29.95

Georgia Titles

How to File for Divorce in GA (5E)	$21.95
How to Start a Business in GA (4E)	$21.95

Illinois Titles

Child Custody, Visitation and Support in IL	$24.95
File for Divorce in IL (4E)	$26.95
How to Make an IL Will (3E)	$16.95
How to Start a Business in IL (4E)	$21.95
Landlords' Legal Guide in IL	$24.95

Maryland, Virginia and the District of Columbia Titles

File for Divorce in MD, VA, and DC (2E)	$29.95
How to Start a Business in MD, VA, or DC	$21.95

Massachusetts Titles

How to Form a Corporation in MA	$24.95
How to Start a Business in MA (4E)	$21.95
Landlords' Legal Guide in MA (2E)	$24.95

Michigan Titles

How to File for Divorce in MI (4E)	$24.95
How to Make a MI Will (3E)	$16.95
How to Start a Business in MI (4E)	$24.95

Minnesota Titles
How to File for Divorce in MN	$21.95
How to Form a Corporation in MN	$24.95
How to Make a MN Will (2E)	$16.95

New Jersey Titles
File for Divorce in NJ	$24.95
How to Start a Business in NJ	$21.95

New York Titles
Child Custody, Visitation and Support in NY	$26.95
File for Divorce in NY	$26.95
How to Form a Corporation in NY (2E)	$21.95
How to Make a NY Will (3E)	$16.95
How to Start a Business in NY (2E)	$18.95
How to Win in Small Claims Court in NY (3E)	$18.95
Tenants' Rights in NY	$21.95

North Carolina and South Carolina Titles
How to File for Divorce in NC (4E)	$26.95
How to Make a NC Will (3E)	$16.95
How to Start a Business in NC or SC	$24.95
Landlords' Rights & Duties in NC	$21.95

Ohio Titles
How to File for Divorce in OH (3E)	$24.95
How to Form a Corporation in OH	$24.95
How to Make an OH Will	$16.95

Pennsylvania Titles
Child Custody, Visitation and Support in PA	$26.95
How to File for Divorce in PA (4E)	$24.95
How to Form a Corporation in PA	$24.95
How to Make a PA Will (2E)	$16.95
How to Start a Business in PA (3E)	$21.95
Landlords' Legal Guide in PA	$24.95

Texas Titles
Child Custody, Visitation and Support in TX	$22.95
File for Divorce in TX (5E)	$27.95
How to Form a Corporation in TX (3E)	$24.95
How to Probate and Settle an Estate in TX (4E)	$26.95
How to Start a Business in TX (4E)	$21.95
How to Win in Small Claims Court in TX (2E)	$16.95
Landlords' Legal Guide in TX	$24.95
Write Your Own TX Will (4E)	$16.95

Washington Titles
File for Divorce in Washington	$24.95

Sphinx® Publishing's National Titles
Valid in All 50 States

LEGAL SURVIVAL IN BUSINESS

The Complete Book of Corporate Forms (2E)	$29.95
The Complete Hiring and Firing Handbook	$19.95
The Complete Limited Liability Kit	$24.95
The Complete Partnership Book	$24.95
The Complete Patent Book	$26.95
The Complete Patent Kit	$39.95
The Entrepreneur's Internet Handbook	$21.95
The Entrepreneur's Legal Guide	$26.95
Financing Your Small Business	$16.95
Fired, Laid-Off or Forced Out	$14.95
Form Your Own Corporation (5E)	$29.95
The Home-Based Business Kit	$14.95
How to Buy a Franchise	$19.95
How to Form a Nonprofit Corporation (3E)	$24.95
How to Register Your Own Copyright (5E)	$24.95
HR for Small Business	$14..95
Incorporate in Delaware from Any State	$26.95
Incorporate in Nevada from Any State	$24.95
The Law (In Plain English)® for Restaurants	$16.95
The Law (In Plain English)® for Small Business	$19.95
The Law (In Plain English)® for Writers	$14.95
Making Music Your Business	$18.95
Minding Her Own Business (4E)	$14.95
Most Valuable Business Legal Forms You'll Ever Need (3E)	$21.95
Profit from Intellectual Property	$28.95
Protect Your Patent	$24.95
The Small Business Owner's Guide to Bankruptcy	$21.95
Start Your Own Law Practice	$16.95
Tax Power for the Self-Employed	$17.95
Tax Smarts for Small Business	$21.95
Your Rights at Work	$14.95

LEGAL SURVIVAL IN COURT

Attorney Responsibilities & Client Rights	$19.95
Crime Victim's Guide to Justice (2E)	$21.95
Legal Research Made Easy (4E)	$24.95
Winning Your Personal Injury Claim (3E)	$24.95

LEGAL SURVIVAL IN REAL ESTATE

The Complete Kit to Selling Your Own Home	$18.95
The Complete Book of Real Estate Contracts	$18.95
Essential Guide to Real Estate Leases	$18.95
Homeowner's Rights	$19.95
How to Buy a Condominium or Townhome (2E)	$19.95
How to Buy a Condominium or Towhnhouse	$14.95
How to Buy Your First Home (2E)	$14.95
How to Make Money on Foreclosures	$16.95
The Mortgage Answer Book	$14.95
Sell Your Own Home Without a Broker	$14.95
The Weekend Landlord	$16.95
The Weekend Real Estate Investor	$14.95
Working with Your Homeowners Association	$19.95

LEGAL SURVIVAL IN SPANISH

Cómo Comprar su Primera Casa	$8.95
Cómo Conseguir Trabajo en los Estados Unidos	$8.95
Cómo Hacer su Propio Testamento	$16.95
Cómo Iniciar su Propio Negocio	$8.95
Cómo Negociar su Crédito	$8.95
Cómo Organizar un Presupuesto	$8.95
Cómo Solicitar su Propio Divorcio	$24.95
Guía de Inmigración a Estados Unidos (4E)	$24.95
Guía de Justicia para Víctimas del Crimen	$21.95
Guía Esencial para los Contratos de Arrendamiento de Bienes Raices	$22.95
Inmigración y Ciudadanía en los EE.UU. Preguntas y Respuestas	$16.95
Inmigración a los EE.UU. Paso a Paso (2E)	$24.95
Manual de Beneficios del Seguro Social	$18.95
El Seguro Social Preguntas y Respuestas	$16.95
¡Visas! ¡Visas! ¡Visas!	$9.95

LEGAL SURVIVAL IN PERSONAL AFFAIRS

101 Complaint Letters That Get Results	$18.95
The 529 College Savings Plan (2E)	$18.95
The 529 College Savings Plan Made Simple	$7.95
The Alternative Minimum Tax	$14.95
The Antique and Art Collector's Legal Guide	$24.95
The Childcare Answer Book	$12.95
Child Support	$18.95
The Complete Book of Insurance	$18.95
The Complete Book of Personal Legal Forms	$24.95
The Complete Credit Repair Kit	$19.95
The Complete Legal Guide to Senior Care	$21.95
The Complete Personal Bankruptcy Guide	$21.95
Credit Smart	$18.95
The Easy Will and Living Will Kit	$16.95
Fathers' Rights	$19.95
File Your Own Divorce (6E)	$24.95
The Frequent Traveler's Guide	$14.95
Gay & Lesbian Rights (2E)	$21.95
Grandparents' Rights (4E)	$24.95
How to Parent with Your Ex	$12.95
How to Write Your Own Living Will (4E)	$18.95
How to Write Your Own Premarital Agreement (3E)	$24.95
The Infertility Answer Book	$16.95
Law 101	$16.95
Law School 101	$16.95
The Living Trust Kit	$21.95
Living Trusts and Other Ways to Avoid Probate (3E)	$24.95
Make Your Own Simple Will (4E)	$26.95
Mastering the MBE	$16.95
Money and Divorce	$14.95
My Wishes	@1.95
Nursing Homes and Assisted Living Facilities	$19.95
Power of Attorney Handbook (6E)	$24.95
Quick Cash	$14.95
Seniors' Rights	$19.95
Sexual Harassment in the Workplace	$18.95
Sexual Harassment:Your Guide to Legal Action	$18.95
Sisters-in-Law	$16.95
The Social Security Benefits Handbook (4E)	$18.95
Social Security Q&A	$12.95
Starting Out or Starting Over	$14.95
Teen Rights (and Responsibilities) (2E)	$14.95
Unmarried Parents' Rights (and Responsibilities) (3E)	$16.95
U.S. Immigration and Citizenship Q&A	$18.95
U.S. Immigration Step by Step (2E)	$24.95
U.S.A. Immigration Guide (5E)	$26.95
What They Don't Teach You in College	$12.95
What to Do—Before "I DO"	$14.95
When Happily Ever After Ends	$14.95
The Wills and Trusts Kit (2E)	$29.95
Win Your Unemployment Compensation Claim (2E)	$21.95
Your Right to Child Custody, Visitation and Support (3E)	$24.95